CONSTITUTIONAL REFORM

Reshaping the British Political System

CONSTITUTIONAL REFORM

RESHAPING THE BRITISH POLITICAL SYSTEM

Third Edition

RODNEY BRAZIER

OXFORD

UNIVERSITY PRESS

OXFORD
UNIVERSITY PRESS

Great Clarendon Street, Oxford OX2 6DP

Oxford University Press is a department of the University of Oxford.
It furthers the University's objective of excellence in research, scholarship,
and education by publishing worldwide in

Oxford New York

Auckland Cape Town Dar es Salaam Hong Kong Karachi
Kuala Lumpur Madrid Melbourne Mexico City Nairobi
New Delhi Shanghai Taipei Toronto

With offices in

Argentina Austria Brazil Chile Czech Republic France Greece
Guatemala Hungary Italy Japan Poland Portugal Singapore
South Korea Switzerland Thailand Turkey Ukraine Vietnam

Oxford is a registered trade mark of Oxford University Press
in the UK and in certain other countries

Published in the United States
by Oxford University Press Inc., New York

First edition 1991
Second edition 1998
Third edition 2008

British Library Cataloguing in Publication Data

Data available

Library of Congress Cataloging in Publication Data

Data available

Typeset by Newgen Imaging Systems (P) Ltd., Chennai, India
Printed in Great Britain
on acid-free paper by
Ashford Colour Press Ltd, Gosport, Hampshire

ISBN 978–0–19–923304–5

3 5 7 9 10 8 6 4 2

Preface

The last edition of this book was published nine months after the new Labour Government had swept to power in 1997. That Government promised an unprecedented amount of constitutional change. More than ten years later it is certainly time to take stock, to assess the Labour Government's reforms, and to suggest where we should go from here. Indeed, constitutional reform was given a great new impetus when Mr Gordon Brown became Prime Minister: his first statement to the House of Commons in that office was designed to restore trust in politics through further possible and very wide-ranging constitutional changes. It must be stressed, however, that this edition—indeed, this book—is not intended to represent a reaction to the policies of any one political party or group. Constitutional history did not begin in 1997, and it is necessary occasionally to put the present constitution into a longer historical perspective. Labour has started the job of constitutional reform, and is to be heartily congratulated on being the first Government to give such priority to the subject. But it has not finished the job, and I will argue that some of its handiwork is unsatisfactory. Mr Brown is to be commended for starting a national debate about the state of the constitution. This new edition represents a significant revision of the earlier text, and some of my earlier ideas have been adapted to reflect the newer constitutional world in which the United Kingdom now lives. I have taken the opportunity to add two new chapters, one on the future of the United Kingdom as a constitutional entity, and the other on the codification of the constitution. I am grateful to the publishers of the *Cambridge Law Journal* and the *Northern Ireland Legal Quarterly* respectively for their generous permission to use parts of articles which first appeared in those publications as the bases for those chapters.

The fundamental purposes of this new edition, therefore, remain the same as for its predecessors. The book examines shortcomings in the British constitution and proposes further reform. Those shortcomings remain widely understood, and accordingly throughout this book it remains my aim to suggest practical improvements rather than rehearsing in detail those things that are wrong with British constitutional law and practice. I have deliberately kept the book relatively short. It aims to ask questions, to set out lines of inquiry and possible answers, to invite the reader to think about a better constitution and how we might achieve it. The Bibliography at the end of this edition has been considerably expanded and should help the reader to do those things. References to statutes and official papers are included in the Bibliography, which is presented under the various chapter headings. If this edition stimulates further thought about the state of the British constitution I would consider it to be a success.

I extend my sincere thanks to Joanna Godfrey at Oxford University Press: she has been a model of cheerful help and support with this new edition. And I repeat my thanks to successive cohorts of students in my classes on Constitutional Reform, who have continued (perhaps unwittingly) to give me additional intellectual stimulation in writing about constitutional development.

R. B.

University of Manchester
10 September 2007

Contents

1   The story so far   1

2   Constitution-making   8

3   The parties and the constitution   26

4   Voting reform   42

5   The second-chamber paradox   64

6   Ministers' powers   77

7   A constitutional guiding light   93

8   Union, dissolution, or federation?   108

9   Defending rights   124

10   Government, law, and the judges   138

11   Codifying the constitution   154

Bibliography   168

Index   177

1

The story so far

Not very much was done to alter the fundamentals of the British constitution during most of the twentieth century. True, the first decade of that period saw a constitutional clash between the two Houses of Parliament which led to major reductions in the powers of the second chamber enshrined in the Parliament Act 1911. Other crises and events[1] caused further constitutional adjustments to be made from time to time, as will be explained in the following chapter. But the essentials of the uncodified British constitution remained largely in place, usually disturbed only when absolutely necessary, despite the massive social and economic changes which took place in the United Kingdom in those hundred years.

From the 1960s, however, it became more fashionable to argue for constitutional reform. As will be noted in Chapter 3, though, these arguments fell largely on deaf ears as far as the two main political parties were concerned. By contrast the Liberal Party, and its successor in title the Liberal Democrats, consistently sought to persuade the nation that a radical new constitutional order was needed. But the party lacked the electoral success necessary to achieve much in practical terms. Yet the Labour Party became a late convert to the cause of constitutional reform in the late 1980s, for reasons which will be rehearsed in Chapter 3, and the party was to have the zeal of the convert when it was able to act on its ideas after winning the 1997 general election.

The first edition of this book was published in 1991, with a second edition following just after Mr Tony Blair had become Prime Minister. I will not bore the reader by setting out here a list of the reforms for which I argued in those editions, or give a checklist noting which of them have since (by coincidence no doubt) been adopted. References to such matters will be made at appropriate points throughout the book. This will be done not just in the context of constitutional history since 1997, because despite the impression sometimes given by Ministers in the present Government, constitutional history did not begin on May Day of that year when Labour swept to power. But just one matter is worth noting at this stage because of its overarching importance. I explained in the first edition why a radical change was needed in the methodology of constitutional change, a topic which had been

---

[1] As Prime Minister, Mr Harold Macmillan famously, and so accurately, explained what makes Government difficult: 'Events, dear boy, events.'

inadequately addressed before then. I floated the idea of creating a standing Royal Commission on the constitution—a Constitutional Commission—which would adopt new methods to help with the development of the British constitution, not least to strive for a more consensual approach to constitutional reform: this idea is elaborated in Chapter 2. While in the main this notion found little favour, it is heartening to note two developments over the past decade which have moved in directions similar to those which might be taken by such a Commission.

First, since 1997 more careful preparations have preceded constitutional legislation than used to be the case.[2] These activities have variously embraced occasional all-party talks, more public consultation (including the use of, albeit geographically-limited, referendums), more reliance on parliamentary committees which have examined constitutional issues—not least the House of Lords Select Committee on the Constitution—and even the creation of a Department for Constitutional Affairs (which, alas, turned out to be short-lived). Such developments contained elements of what might be achieved by an appropriately-constituted Constitutional Commission. Secondly, Mr Gordon Brown is clearly more interested in constitutional change than his predecessor, and appears to want a more consensual approach to it. It is too early in his premiership to know exactly how much he will try to do by consensus, although he has started what he calls a national debate about the future shape of the British constitution. His ideas for possible, particular, changes will be examined at appropriate places in subsequent chapters.

And so today the British constitution is very different from what it was towards the end of the twentieth century, thanks in the main to the Labour Government's massive reform programme. A history of infrequent and, in effect, normally unavoidable constitutional changes ended in 1997, when most of the Labour Party's promised alterations to the constitution were given effect, together with several—though unco-ordinated—methodological innovations.

Diagnoses and prescriptions

As confidence in Victorian England was moving towards its zenith Charles Dickens published *Our Mutual Friend*. In it, Mr Podsnap (enunciating clearly, for he was addressing a foreigner) said: 'We Englishmen are Very Proud of our Constitution, Sir. It was Bestowed Upon Us By Providence. No Other Country is so Favoured as This Country.' Podsnap concluded, regretfully no doubt, that foreign countries were 'a mistake'.[3] Men of affairs, including the great contemporary writers on the

[2] But not always. The history of the Constitutional Reform Act 2005, and the creation of the Ministry of Justice in 2007, remained object lessons in how not to do constitutional reform: see Ch. 10.

[3] C. Dickens, *Our Mutual Friend* (London, 1865), Ch. xi.

constitution, agreed with Podsnap's sentiments—at least in so far as they lauded the advantages of the Victorian constitution. As Empire gave way to Commonwealth, the general view in Britain that the Westminster constitution was near perfect encouraged successive Governments to endow newly independent states with versions of it (although there were remarkable differences, such as, occasionally, a federal structure and, usually, a Bill of Rights). This pride provided a further disincentive to learn anything of a constitutional nature from abroad. But doubts about the British constitution emerged in the 1960s and grew through the following decades.

It is fashionable to ascribe most of the responsibility for these new uncertainties on Mrs Margaret Thatcher.[4] On this view, the subtle balance of powers in the constitution was totally thrown out by her imperious premiership from 1979 to 1990. As Prime Minister she ruthlessly seized and shifted levers of power which her predecessors either left untouched or used with restraint. Those Ministers who were not 'one of us' were sacked, and others more congenial were put in their places; the disbursement of patronage, and the winning of general elections, kept backbenchers to heel; she interfered to an unprecedented extent in Ministers' departmental responsibilities; she reduced the collective authority of the Cabinet, and ruled through Cabinet committees or (more frequently) through hand-picked, informal groups of Ministers; in the Cabinet system, in short, she made herself first above inferiors. She manipulated the press, she cut down the authority of other centres of power, such as local councils, she elbowed aside inconvenient civil liberties, she politicized the senior civil service. As with all good caricatures, there is much truth in that sketch. But even if it were an entirely accurate reflection of Mrs Thatcher's effect on the constitution, that would be a poor basis on which to deconstruct and reconstruct it. Mrs Thatcher was not immortal. Her successor in 1990, Mr John Major, reverted to more traditional forms: Mr Tony Blair in his turn preferred a more presidential style, and Mr Brown thus far has reverted to more traditional Cabinet Government. Indeed, as will be seen later, the present Prime Minister began his premiership in 2007 by promising to reduce prime-ministerial powers. But to construct a new constitutional edifice solely as a response to any one Prime Minister's mode of governance would be misguided. That said, there are wholly undesirable features of the British constitution which pre-dated Mrs Thatcher's accession and which survived her resignation.

When Lord Hailsham coined his chilling phrase 'elective dictatorship',[5] Mrs Thatcher had only just been elected Leader of the Opposition. He was describing a Labour Government, returned by a minority of the electorate, which (he claimed) was able to legislate as it wished on whatever it wished—even to bring about, as Labour had promised, irreversible changes in society—because no external

---

[4] See, e.g. P. McAuslan and J. F. McEldowney (eds.), *Law, Legitimacy and the Constitution* (London: Sweet & Maxwell, 1985); K. Ewing and C. Gearty, *Freedom under Thatcher: Civil Liberties in Modern Britain* (Oxford: Clarendon Press, 1990).

[5] See Lord Hailsham, *The Dilemma of Democracy* (London: Collins, 1978), 9–11.

restraints existed to stop it from doing so. This was dictatorship, tempered only by the requirement of fighting regular general elections, but dictatorship none-theless. When that Labour Government was rejected in 1979 and Lord Hailsham became Mrs Thatcher's Lord Chancellor, we heard no more from him about this awful spectre. Yet the elective dictatorship of the 1970s survived and prospered in the 1980s: indeed, there were examples of changes brought about in that latter decade, such as privatization, which were truly irreversible in a way in which no policy of the previous Labour Government had been irreversible. Party discipline among Conservative Members of Parliament, underpinned by the loyalty to Mrs Thatcher which her remarkable general election victories engendered, meant that Bills were, on the whole, passed at the Government's request, utterly unhindered by any entrenched laws or rights beyond the reach of Parliament. The Conservative administration's opponents often cite a long list of its Acts and actions which they label as authoritarian, undemocratic, and illiberal and which would have been dif-ficult (and in some cases impossible) to pass or to take in any other western democ-racy which enjoys special constitutional guarantees. While reasonable people can hold different views about the necessity or desirability of some of that Government's measures, the ease with which they—and, it must be stressed, those of earlier Governments—have been translated into law or administrative practice is very worrying. Moreover, as will be explained in the following chapter, similar objections can be made to some of the legislative activity of the present Labour Government.

Members of Parliament had abdicated parliamentary sovereignty in favour of elective dictatorship long before Mrs Thatcher became Prime Minister. The House of Commons has allowed the power over the Crown which it had secured in earlier times to be usurped, without a fight, by the Government. Not every administration will take full advantage of elective dictatorship, but that is not the point: the funda-mental objection is that such a dictatorship has come to pass, and the powers which it confers can be exercised at will at any time. Indeed, how much more convincing today—and how much more disturbing—is Walter Bagehot's characterization of the House of Commons as an electoral college which chooses the Government.[6] Today that is its primary function, and it is one which, thanks to party cohesive-ness, is accomplished on election night when one party has secured a majority of seats. In this modern elective dictatorship, once the Commons has been used as an indirect electoral college its members are content, on the whole, to take their orders. Catalogues of reasons have been compiled explaining why this has happened, and certainly things like the growth of the party and whip system, based on inducements and threats, have contributed mightily. Common to all those reasons, however, is one factor: the supine manner in which Members of Parliament have allowed successive Prime Ministers (including, it must be said, Mr Blair) to benefit from elective dictatorship. Nowadays few would dispute that the powers of the Prime

---

[6] See W. Bagehot, *The English Constitution* (first pub., 1867; London: Fontana, 1963), 157–8.

Minister have increased, are increasing, and ought to be diminished. The remedy is in Members' own hands. They can curb prime-ministerial authority with their voices and, if necessary, with their votes—a point which will be developed in later chapters. If they choose not to act in this way, it is little wonder that others canvass constitutional reforms in order to redress the balance of power. It should, again, be noted that Mr Brown has initiated a process which might lead to a reduction in some of the Prime Minister's authority: this will be examined in Chapter 6.

As concerns about the accretion of governmental power have grown, the short-comings of other institutions and the absence of countervailing safeguards became more apparent. The House of Lords cannot be expected to challenge the might of elected dictatorship, for its authority has long been limited by convention and by law. It has proved a significant inconvenience for Labour Governments and an irritant for Conservative Governments, but it lacks both legal power and political authority to do much more. The judges have tried to meet the challenges thrown up by aspects of elective dictatorship, not least through judicial review, but they can only work with the raw materials supplied to them by the law. It is true, of course, that they have been handed another weapon in the form of the Human Rights Act 1998, but its firepower is limited.[7] There is still no higher or special law which the judiciary could enforce in order to strike a balance between, on the one hand, the executive and the legislature, and, on the other, the rights of the citizen. Those rights which the citizen does have can be restricted or abolished by ordinary legislation. The Human Rights Act 1998 does not, in law, restrict parliamentary sovereignty.

All this, and more, has led to demands for constitutional reform. The nostrums which have been suggested include the introduction of proportional representation for elections to the House of Commons, a Bill of Rights, an elected replacement for the House of Lords, devolution of power, and a written constitution. Indeed, as will be seen at appropriate places in this book, Mr Brown as Prime Minister has endorsed a national debate on such matters. Such calls have come from a variety of sources, and the detailed prescriptions will be considered in this book. A number of extra-parliamentary bodies have carried the torch of reform. For example, Charter 88 is an all-party and non-party campaign for major constitutional recon-struction. It demands the adoption of a new constitutional settlement which would incorporate electoral reform, an elected second chamber, and a Bill of Rights, all enshrined in a written constitution.[8] The Institute of Public Policy Research, too, has worked on the case for, and the shape of, a new constitutional settlement. The Constitution Unit has also done very valuable work on constitutional reform, as will be seen in Chapter 3. The Liberal Democrats are continuing the struggle for radical change begun many years ago by the Liberal Party, including proposals for the introduction of proportional representation, an elected upper house, more

---

[7] See Ch. 9.
[8] See now Charter 88, *Unlocking Democracy* (London: Charter 88, 2000).

devolution of power, and a Bill of Rights; the adoption of a written constitution is envisaged in the long term. The Labour Party's constitutional policy underwent a sea-change in opposition, and because the Labour Government has been in charge of the British constitution since 1997, Chapter 3 will include an examination of its policy, and particular reforms will be considered in appropriate chapters in this book. In summary, however, Labour's programme encompassed devolution of power to Scotland, Wales, and the regions of England, the reform of the House of Lords (first removing the hereditary peers, then instituting an elected second chamber), a referendum on the voting system for the House of Commons, freedom of information legislation, the incorporation into domestic law of the European Convention on Human Rights, and possibly a new system for appointing judges. In short, the Labour Government assumed office in May 1997 committed to more constitutional change than any previous administration. In 2007 Mr Brown was to refresh the constitutional debate on behalf of the Labour Government.

The Conservative Party was completely out of step. Mrs Thatcher refused to join in the march towards a constitutional utopia. Her view was that Britain's constitution continued to serve the nation well, and that it allows the citizen to enjoy the greatest degree of liberty that is compatible with the rights of others and with the vital interests of the state. Moreover, Mrs Thatcher declared, her Government would not consider any constitutional reform unless it were widely understood and supported in Parliament and in the country. Mr Major wedded himself to that policy, for soon after becoming Prime Minister he said in answer to a parliamentary question that he had no immediate plans for constitutional reform.[9] He maintained that position throughout his premiership, and indeed made the defence of the status quo a vital plank in his 1992 general election campaign. One of his last speeches as Prime Minister confirmed his stance.[10] The Conservative Party has, however, adjusted its view following its electoral rout by the Labour Party at election after election since 1997. As will be seen in Chapter 3, in some respects (such as House of Lords reform) the Conservatives have become more radical than Labour in their constitutional reform policy.

The bases of reform

In this book, I am going to base my consideration of British constitutional reform on a number of precepts. One has already been mentioned, and will be developed in the next chapter: major constitutional upheaval should be based on the ideal of

---

[9]   182 HC Debs. 1107 (13 Dec. 1990).

[10]   290 HC Debs. 1055–66 (20 Feb. 1997). For his Lord Chancellor's support see 573 HL Debs. 1449–56 (3 July 1996).

consensus, so that as far as possible multi-party agreement should precede it. The state of the constitution is a matter of overarching importance in the country's affairs and should not be the exclusive preserve of the party which happens to be the Government. A second precept is that the traditional notions upon which the constitution of the United Kingdom is predicated are worth continuing (or, as the case may be, restoring) and making more effective. In summary, these are that the United Kingdom is a liberal democracy which enjoys a regularly-elected representative legislature, a Government limited in its authority partly by the rule of law and partly by convention, and an independent judiciary. The value of those notions is, to me, self-evident. A third precept is what I will term constitutional propriety, which is a notion that should condition what Governments do. It is generally accepted that the actors in the British constitution—and principally Ministers—should exercise their undoubted legal powers with restraint. This is what A. V. Dicey termed limited Government: the Government's powers, derived from the law, are (or should be) used in such a way that what it does, and how it does it, respects certain values. Elective dictatorship is inimical to such an idea of constitutional propriety—at least if Governments take full advantage of what they are given by that dictatorship. Of course, there are difficulties with a principle of constitutional propriety. Who is to say what is constitutionally appropriate? Different politicians may well take various views; the Government may claim propriety while the Opposition denies it. Proof of a breach of propriety in such circumstances will be impossible. But a notion of constitutional propriety has some worth. It can provide guidelines for action, even if they are mainly of a negative kind. It would, for example, clearly be wrong for the Government to procure the enactment of legislation subversive of the democratic basis of the constitution, or to enact retrospective criminal laws, or to confiscate property without compensation, or to abolish access to the courts, or to pack the courts with members of the Government party prepared to do Ministers' bidding.[11] It would be helpful if a mechanism could be devised through which politicians could work towards a fuller explanation of limited Government, or constitutional propriety, and a mechanism which could do this as a small part of its purpose will be suggested in the next chapter.

Before any particular constitutional problem is analysed against that background with a view to seeing how it might be resolved, a very important practical question must be addressed. It involves the appropriate methodology of constitutional reform in the United Kingdom, and it will be considered in Chapter 2.

---

[11] Some of those actions would, of course, breach the Human Rights Act 1998; and recommendations for judicial appointments are now in the hands of an independent commission—although the Lord Chancellor retains the final word: see Ch. 10.

had no part in shaping such legislation. Why is that? One reason is that it can only act on a reference from the Lord Chancellor.[11] The Government would have to be persuaded that any such reference would be appropriate, and there are several factors which would make constitutional law references inappropriate. The Law Commission is composed entirely of lawyers. While the Law Commission has had necessarily to tackle issues of social policy in some of its work, the Commissioners would probably claim no particular competence in constitutional affairs, which are to a large degree bound up with politics. Politicians, quite fairly, consider themselves to be the experts on the state of the constitution, having opinions about it which they would say are worth more than those of any law reform body. In any case, the Law Commission is hard-pressed by its current load, and it would not be feasible, even if it were sensible, for the Commission to be given a whole new area of difficult work. As a result, no aspect of constitutional law (as distinct from administrative law) has formed any part of the Law Commission's law reform programmes, and no specific constitutional law reference has been made.

Even without the help of the official law-reform bodies, there is clearly no shortage of mechanisms for bringing about constitutional change in the United Kingdom. What persuades Ministers to seek information or advice about constitutional affairs from outside Government? While precise categorization is impossible, some half-dozen reasons may be discerned which have prompted Governments to go beyond their membership and beyond the civil service for inquiry, analysis, and advice. First, the national gravity of a constitutional problem may require a national solution arrived at by as many of the political parties as possible. The invitation from Asquith to Bonar Law to talk on Privy Counsellor terms about Ulster in 1913 is the best example of that. In the nature of things, such an overture will not often be made from such an acute cause. Secondly, events might take place which require public explanations of what has happened (or what is alleged to have happened) and guidance (and perhaps new rules) for the future. Public disquiet or alarm often produce an irresistible demand for independent investigation and report. Occurrences such as those which led to the Royal Commissions on the Rebellion in Ireland and on Honours, the Donoughmore Committee on Ministers' Powers, the Falkland Islands Review, the Radcliffe Committee on Ministerial Memoirs, the Royal Commission on Standards of Conduct in Public Life, the Scott inquiry into arms to Iraq, the Committee on Standards in Public Life, and the Butler Review of Intelligence on Weapons of Mass Destruction can all be seen as instances of that process.[12] Thirdly, there might be pressure for constitutional change with which Ministers do not particularly sympathize but which might lead to serious loss of political support for the Government if it were to reject

---

[11] Law Commissions Act 1965, s. 3.
[12] See respectively Cd. 8729 (1916); Cmd. 1789 (1922); Cmd. 4060 (1932); Cmnd. 8787 (1983); Cmnd. 6386 (1976); Cmnd. 6526 (1976); HC 115 (1995–6); Cm. 2850 (1995); HC 898 (2003–4).

the case for reform out of hand. Ministers might decide that an official inquiry would be the least of all evils; in setting one up the Government would be seen to be doing something and time would be bought. When the report is received, the Government might take months formulating its response to the recommendations, and may find itself supplied with new reasons why nothing of importance could or should be done. The appointment of the Royal Commission on the Constitution, as a direct response to growing Nationalist feeling in Scotland and Wales, could be viewed in that way. Fourthly, public concern about alleged infringements of the law or the improper use or the inappropriate ambit of state power might produce calls for independent inquiries which a Government finds inexpedient to resist. Thus the Privy Counsellors' inquiry into the interception of communications in 1957, several investigations into the legal response to terrorism in Northern Ireland, and the Franks Committee on section 2 of the Official Secrets Act 1911 could be said to be instances of such a process.[13] Fifthly, technical issues may arise on which Ministers need expert advice before deciding how to proceed: examples might include the Wilson Committee on Public Records,[14] the several inquiries into the permissible scope of civil servants' political activities, and, indeed, into the civil service itself. Most Speaker's Conferences fit into such a category, too. Lastly, the Government itself might decide that a particular constitutional development is timely and commit itself to the principle of reform, and then seek cross-party support for detailed changes. The most notable instances of that would be the Labour Government's commitment in 1968 to reform the composition and powers of the House of Lords, proceeding through the forum of all-party talks, and the present Government's Joint Consultative Cabinet Committee with the Liberal Democrats.[15]

If the Government decides, for any of those reasons, to seek outside help, the method to be used more or less chooses itself. If a given topic has a high political content which would be best considered by the Prime Minister, or a senior Minister, and their counterparts, Privy Counsellor or inter-party talks would be appropriate. Alternatively, if the situation demands a detailed and independent investigation, representatives of the great and the good may be asked to man a departmental committee of inquiry or a Royal Commission. It is, of course, for independent bodies, such as the departmental select committees of the House of Commons, the Constitution Committee of the House of Lords, and the Electoral Commission, to choose their own topics of inquiry.

If such an analysis is broadly correct, one general conclusion is starkly clear. Generally Governments are reactive, not proactive, in deciding whether to set in motion machinery outside the four walls of Government to give advice about constitutional reform. The instances cited in the first five categories just summarized

[13] See respectively Cmnd. 283 (1957); Cmnd. 5185 (1972); Cmnd. 5879 (1975); Cmnd. 7497 (1979); Cmnd. 5104 (1972).
[14] Cmnd. 8204 (1981).
[15] See Ch. 3.

account for practically all of the occasions this century on which Ministers have gone outside Government on constitutional matters. Those categories comprise situations in which the Government reacted to events which had, in effect, left them with little alternative but to set up some form of consultation or inquiry. It is only in the sixth category that it can be said that a Government decided entirely of its own volition to initiate change and to ease its enactment through external consultations—and then only two actual examples fit at all happily into it. Governments are pushed into activating such mechanisms in constitutional affairs. They do not look ahead and use departmental committees, Royal Commissions, inter-party talks and the like in a planned way, in order to see how ministerial initiatives on the constitution might be improved. Rather, those mechanisms are resorted to only when events leave them no other choice. In general, Governments much prefer to announce constitutional changes, more or less in their final form, without any prior public consultation or independent consideration of them. As will be noted in the next chapter, even Mr Brown's wide-ranging review of many parts of the British constitution will not disturb those general conclusions: the promised national conversation will be carried out in a limited way.

The British constitution represents the triumph of gradualism. It has been shaped by people who have had to work the constitutional system, change often being made as a response to events. The constitution has been adapted thus over the years with little reference to constitutional theory. If the constitution is working well enough from a Government's point of view, there is no need to change it, even less to set in hand inquiries into the desirability of any of the reforms which are mooted by others from time to time. If a particular problem arises which cannot be ignored, then an appropriate investigation can be mounted and, if necessary, corrective legislation can be passed. If a select committee of either House makes recommendations on a constitutional matter, they will be considered by Ministers, and a response will be made even if no further ministerial action follows. If the Government itself perceives that a change in law or practice is desirable, action can be taken. In the light of all that, ad hockery may be seen as not such a pejorative term after all.

This approach, it could be argued, has dealt adequately with constitutional problems in the past. Why change that which works? To those who assert that this system has not adequately answered demands for radical changes the reply may be made that the solution is in the proponents' hands. For they must convince the electorate that they should be given power so that their ideas might be put into practice; or, if that is impossible, they must convince one of the two main parties to adopt them. After all, that latter strategy has recently been effective in relation to the Labour Party, for who would have thought even (say) by 1990 that Labour would commit itself to devolution throughout Great Britain, to the incorporation of the European Convention on Human Rights, to a two-stage plan for the reform of the House of Lords, to a referendum on the electoral system, and so on?[16] Moreover,

16 See Ch. 3.

from the point of view of either a Conservative or Labour Government, there would be dangers in moving away from the present manner of going about constitutional reform. If an independent and respected inquiry were to be charged with a systematic review of the constitution, it might recommend solutions which were politically inconvenient for Ministers but resistance to which might be difficult to justify.

In a state of affairs such as this, how might a case for changing the machinery of constitutional reform be expressed? A fundamental point is that the condition of the constitution is qualitatively different in character from any other area of public policy and, as a result, it should not be left entirely to the wishes of the Government of the day. British parliamentary democracy implies, at least in theory, that the Government proposes, the Opposition opposes, and Parliament disposes. In that way national policies are adopted and enacted. But the constitutional rules through which that democracy operates are of transcendent importance. So, for example, the rules by which Governments are chosen and through which their policies are put into effect are of a higher order than any other piece of non-constitutional policy which Governments seek to carry out once in office. Ideally, therefore, the methods of settling those rules and practices should as far as possible be arrived at through a political consensus rather than through ordinary policy-making and legislative processes.

The earlier examination of the reasons why Governments have been moved to set up inquiries revealed a major weakness in the present process of constitutional change, namely, its reactive nature. In the daily grind of parliamentary and political life there seems to be no advantage to Ministers in devoting time and energy to rethinking aspects of the constitution, at least not unless work had been done on it in opposition (as was the case with the present Labour Government). The tradition is to do nothing, unless the Government is forced into action, or wishes itself to implement some particular change. Too little thought is given in Government in a planned, unhurried way to whether any part of the constitution could be made to work more efficiently, and how change to one part would affect other parts. It is difficult to think of any other area of national life which has been so effectively cloistered from official scrutiny. That remains my view despite the creation in 2003 of the Department for Constitutional Affairs, about which more in a moment.

Even when a Government does decide that it must do something (or must give the impression of doing something) about a constitutional problem, the existing methods of information-gathering and analysis are not ideal. Assuming that the constitutional difficulty is to be examined beyond Whitehall, a mechanism has to be established afresh for each new inquiry: there is no body of continuing expertise independent of Government which could be tapped, no corpus of technical knowledge which might have been built up over the years and which would be available as a result. There are significant limitations in the terms of reference and the working methods of some of the traditional types of inquiry. A Speaker's Conference, for example, will be concerned only with the details of electoral law and practice, never nowadays with fundamental electoral questions. A Commons departmental select committee can investigate only the department which it oversees. True, of course, the Constitution Committee of the House of Lords has an apparently open-ended remit allowing it to keep the whole of the British constitution under review, but there is only so much that it can achieve with peers who are mostly part-time legislators, and with limited resources—just one part-time Legal Adviser, for instance. Opportunities for public participation can prove to be limited: some inquiries deliberate in public; departmental committees usually invite public contributions, but not always; none has issued draft proposals for comment before finally deciding on recommendations. If public confidence in the constitution and the means of reviewing it is to be enhanced, greater public involvement than is currently allowed would have to become the norm.

But after such criticisms and comments, it is right to welcome the creation in 2003 of the Department for Constitutional Affairs (DCA). The ancient Lord Chancellor's Department was abolished. Following the passage of the Constitutional Reform Act 2005, the Lord Chancellor (who was also given the title, conferred under the royal prerogative, of Secretary of State for Constitutional Affairs) headed the DCA, and under the Act he or she may be a member of either House, and need not be a lawyer. The Lord Chancellor ceased to sit judicially; the House of Lords has elected its own Lord Speaker (the first of whom happened to be female); the Lord Chancellor's hand in judicial appointments is firmly guided by the Judicial Appointments Commission.[17] This marks, in British terms, a spectacular statutory recognition of the separation of powers doctrine, and ends the embodiment of the Lord Chancellor as the living denial of that doctrine. Almost all constitutional matters were concentrated in one, purpose-built, Government department, with the usual range of junior ministerial representation in each House. It was unambiguously the lead department in constitutional affairs in the United Kingdom. As will be seen in Chapter 10, the Department was merged into a new Ministry of Justice in 2007. I must, however, add my view that the DCA did not constitute, within its four walls, the whole of a perfect apparatus for constitutional reform. I have already mentioned some deficient ways in which we go about reforming the constitution. I want now to consider a better way.

A Constitutional Commission

The question of how a constitution may be improved is one which is common to all developed states. The technical answer about how formal amendments may be made is invariably provided in the text of a constitution,[18] but that does not necessarily

---

[17] See Ch. 10.

[18] For the texts of five national constitutions see S. E. Finer, V. Bogdanor, and B. Rudden, *Comparing Constitutions* (Oxford: Clarendon Press, 1995).

describe any non-legal steps which should be taken before that stage is reached—whether, for example, public opinion, or political parties outside the Government, should be consulted. It is instructive to describe the processes through which the Australian constitution has been reviewed and developed in recent years.[19]

In important respects Australia's constitution is based on that of the United Kingdom, albeit with a federal structure copied to some extent from the United States. Australia has a parliamentary and Cabinet system of Government, and, while she has a written constitution, constitutional conventions have been just as important as in Britain. The Commonwealth of Australia Constitution Act 1900 provides in section 128 that any proposed law which would amend the constitution must be passed by both Houses of the Commonwealth Parliament and be approved by the electors in each State before it may receive the royal assent. Of fifty-four proposals for constitutional amendments made under section 128 since 1901, only a small minority have enjoyed the bipartisan support which in practice is necessary in order to achieve enactment. But what of the pre-amendment stage? Australia resorted to ad hoc investigations into possible constitutional reform, of which the most important were a Royal Commission which reported in 1929, and a Joint Parliamentary Committee which sat from 1956 to 1959. But that ad hoc approach was discarded in two more recent initiatives, namely the Constitutional Convention, which deliberated from 1973 to 1985, and the Constitutional Commission, which was appointed in 1985 and which reported three years later. The purpose of the Constitutional Convention was to provide a forum of delegates from Commonwealth and State Governments and Oppositions—a gathering of politicians—in which the bipartisan support essential for the success of constitutional amendments might be built. That is not, however, how the work of the Convention developed: its main and lasting achievement was to identify and declare conventions of the Australian constitution and in doing so to reduce many of them to writing. This change of course was largely brought about by the impossibility of achieving cross-party agreement in the wake of the dismissal of the Whitlam Government in 1975. Thirty-three conventions were recognized and declared by the Convention in 1983, including those relating to the powers of the Queen of Australia, the appointment and powers of the Governor-General, the composition and functions of the Executive Council, the timing of elections, and the independence of the judiciary. Inevitably, perhaps, some of the statements of conventions seem more helpful than others, but the consensus achieved was impressive, with only a small number of the thirty-three conventions being adopted by votes cast on party lines.

---

[19] See, e.g. C. Sampford, ' "Recognize and Declare": An Australian Experiment in Codifying Conventions', (1987) 7 *Oxford Journal of Legal Studies* 369. Useful comparative commentary on reviews of the Irish and German constitutions is given in J. Morison, 'The Report of the Constitution Review Group in the Republic of Ireland', and G. Gornig and S. Reckewerth, 'The Revision of the German Basic Law', [1977] *Public Law* 55 and 137.

The Commonwealth Government subsequently announced the setting up of the Australian Constitutional Commission. Its sweeping terms of reference were to inquire into, and in 1988 to report on, the revision of the Australian constitution. The Commission was required to seek the views of the public, business, trade unions, financial institutions, and other interested groups and individuals, and was to hold public hearings for the purpose. The Commission circulated draft proposals widely for comment. Its six members were the Chairman, Sir Maurice Byers, QC (a former Commonwealth Solicitor-General), two politicians, a judge of the Federal Court of Australia, and two academics. In its fundamental review the Commission was helped by five advisory committees, each of which consisted of prominent Australians (including judicial, political, and academic figures), each under the chairmanship of an eminent lawyer or former or serving judge. The committees were directed to involve the public in their work, so that their proposals might be as generally acceptable as possible.

The Constitutional Commission's recommendations were, with some minor reservations, unanimous—itself a major achievement. The Commissioners tried to preserve the framework and principles of the 1900 Act, but they found 'some significant problems' which their recommendations were designed to remove. The report is a massive, two-volume, 1,195-page analysis in which the summary of recommendations alone runs to thirty-two pages.[20] The Constitutional Commission hoped that its report would contribute to an informed, continuing debate on constitutional issues and would provide the foundation for further proposed alterations to be put to referendums in the future. The fact that the membership of the Australian Constitutional Commission—unlike that of the Constitutional Convention—was not dominated by politicians may have brought it significant public respect. That the clutch of the Commission's proposals which was submitted to a national referendum was subsequently rejected is perplexing,[21] but that only detracts in part from the merits of the whole exercise. Systematic and wide consultation of public opinion, including the publication of draft proposals for comment, provided a model of how policies relating to a constitution should be formulated. But the very wide terms of reference which the Commission enjoyed probably would not find favour with the Conservative or Labour Parties for any equivalent machinery in Britain.

In the light of the defects in the existing methods of reviewing the British constitution, and of the Australian experience, I want to suggest a new way of doing things to the United Kingdom constitution.

What is needed, I believe, is a permanent advisory Constitutional Commission with the status of a standing Royal Commission. In essence, it might have two tasks.

[20] *Final Report of the Constitutional Commission* (Canberra: Australian Government Printing Service, 1988).

[21] For possible explanations see H. P. Lee, 'Reforming the Australian Constitution' [1988] *Public Law* 535.

One would be to consider and report on any constitutional provisions which, in its opinion, were in need of clarification or reformulation. For ease of reference, that might be labelled its declaratory role. The other task—its reforming role—would be to consider any aspect of the United Kingdom constitution referred to it by a Minister, probably the Lord Chancellor, and to report on whether and how it might be reformed. It must be stressed from the start that the Government would have a large degree of control over the Commission's work through the requirement that the Commission could only exercise its reforming function following a ministerial reference. If the Commission were able to gain the confidence of the Government, however, Ministers might feel encouraged to increase the number and scope of such references. If (as would be essential) such a Constitutional Commission were to have the support at least of the Conservative and Labour Parties, they would have to have a say in its composition. Discussions through the usual channels might produce agreement on membership. Politicians are among the principal actors in the constitution: it would be essential that the Commission had some politician members and perhaps senior back-benchers in the House of Commons would form the nucleus of the Commission. Equally, the Commission ought to include representatives of the law, industry, universities, and other walks of life. The chair would have to be taken by a respected and impartial public figure; all the Commissioners would have part-time appointments. The Commission should have access to official advice from Government departments, especially what is now the Ministry of Justice, and could seek other evidence; it would need adequate resources, certainly enough to enable it to pay for research. Public consultation, as exemplified by the Australian Constitutional Commission, would be very important, and it would be a welcome development if the Australian example of publishing draft proposals for comment were to be followed. Progress through expert committees, as in the Australian Constitutional Commission, would be an efficient way forward, especially because any other method of working would demand too great a commitment from part-time Commissioners. The Commission's final reports could be laid before Parliament and published as White Papers.

The declaratory role of the Constitutional Commission should not be too threatening to the main political parties, for it would be limited to consideration of existing rules and practices which are unclear or which would be better for being expressed authoritatively: constitutional conventions would be the obvious and main area of work. Parts of the British constitution remain unclear, and disagreement exists between the political parties (and others) about some of its requirements. Examples include the appropriate chain of events which should occur after the return of a hung Parliament; the nature and extent of the Sovereign's powers to dissolve Parliament, to dismiss a Government, and to refuse assent to legislation; and the requirements of some aspects of the doctrine of ministerial responsibility to Parliament. Progress might be made by agreeing on and giving definition to the shadowy parts of the constitution which the Commission thought to be both important and yet unclear.

If such formulations were not possible, the Commission could suggest what the relevant practice might be for the future. That work would echo the progress made in Australia by the Constitutional Convention. The Constitutional Commission's final reports ought to receive considerable respect from, among others, those who daily work the constitution. In that way, reports issued as part of the Commission's declaratory role in times of political tranquillity could prove of value in times of constitutional crisis.

If the Commission proved its worth in its declaratory work, and in carrying out any references which the Government might ask it to undertake in the place of ad hoc inquiries, rather bolder references might follow. The political parties might feel able to agree on references concerning fundamental constitutional reform for the United Kingdom. In a forum such as a Constitutional Commission protagonists and antagonists could argue their cases rationally, without the party-political rhetoric which frequently clouds such matters—deliberations worthy of the subjects might take place. Aspects of administrative law, too, might be appropriate for references to the Commission. Other work for it will be suggested in later chapters.

A Constitutional Commission of this type would be a typically British answer to a very British problem. It would be non-statutory, all-party, and advisory. But beyond that it would be a single body which could act as a clearing-house for constitutional ideas, and, being permanent, it should establish a body of expertise (supplemented, of course, by officials in the Ministry of Justice) which no succession of ad hoc mechanisms could possibly rival. Public opinion would be canvassed to an unprecedented extent. The creation of a Constitutional Commission would put in place a means of taking a planned look at the constitutional system. Naturally, such a Commission might be seen by the Conservative Party as a challenge to its constitutional conservatism. And any Government which set up a Constitutional Commission would certainly want to proceed with caution. But perhaps the two main parties would be wise to give at least private consideration to the idea, because support for it (or something like it) might be the price demanded one day by a smaller party (or parties) for coalition, or a party pact, in the event of the return of a hung Parliament. It should be remembered that Mr Edward Heath as Prime Minister and Leader of the Conservative Party felt able to offer the Liberal Party a Speaker's Conference on proportional representation in February 1974 as part of his suggested coalition deal. Advance planning for a repeat of such an event might be prudent. And, indeed, a Commission along those lines would build on the recent constitutional co-operation between Labour and the Liberal Democrats.[22] But the main political parties will have reservations about and raise objections to the principle of such a Commission; two of these objections need to be addressed now.

One (which would certainly be endorsed by the Treasury) is that a Constitutional Commission would require additional human and financial resources, not least

[22] See Ch. 3.

to pay for research: by contrast, the existing system is cheap. The main answer to that is that the shaping of the best structure for the country's constitution is vital, and has as legitimate a claim on public spending as anything else. Why should the development of the country's constitution, of all aspects of national life, be conducted on the cheap? All other areas of law can be calmly considered by authoritative and impartial bodies to ensure sensible development. Most aspects of English law have a Rolls-Royce service from the Law Commission, but the constitution usually has to falter before the Government is reluctantly persuaded to despatch the equivalent of the Automobile Association to patch it up. This is completely unsatisfactory. Another objection from the two main political parties might be that the existence of such a Constitutional Commission would slow down the implementation of constitutional changes which they might wish to introduce. This can be explained through the following hypothesis. Suppose that such a Commission had been in existence when the Labour Party came to power in 1997. It might have considered itself bound to refer its clutch of constitutional policies to the Commission for its consideration. There would then have been a significant delay before the Commission could report on them, and the Labour Government might not have been prepared to countenance such a delay. Now while things could happen in that fashion, there would be another way of proceeding. References made by the Government to the Constitutional Commission would often be preceded by discussions through the usual channels; Labour, in opposition, could have asked the Government to refer the principal constitutional issues raised in its policy review to the Commission. It might become an accepted practice that, the Commission's other commitments permitting, Opposition requests for references would be acquiesced in by the Government of the day—without, of course, any implication that the Government agreed in any way with the proposals so referred. After consideration, the Commission might approve some of those ideas and reject others. But its role would be *advisory*, and nothing would stop any party putting whatever it wished into its general election manifesto, or prevent it, once it became the Government, from implementing its policies whether or not they had been reviewed by the Commission and regardless of any view expressed on them by the Commission.

There would be a separate matter for a Constitutional Commission to consider, which could be important in a strategy for constitutional reform. Parliament is the supreme legislative body in the United Kingdom: the electorate has no formal or legal part to play in the process of enacting legislation. The only power which voters possess is that of changing the composition of the House of Commons at a general election. There is no tradition of formal consultation of the voters about legislation by the Government, other than on a dissolution of Parliament. Instead, Members of Parliament are returned to represent their constituents and are expected to get on with that task. There are two difficulties inherent in such a theory of representation which are relevant here. One manifests itself when each major political party has Members of Parliament who have different views on a given issue, so that the electorate's opinion on that issue cannot be taken by means of a general election. For that reason, the view of the electorate about whether the United Kingdom should join the European Community could not have been ascertained at a general election. In any case, an appeal to the electors faces the near impossibility of conducting a general election on one issue. Voters will—irritatingly for the political parties, who might think that they had posed one clear question—inevitably take other factors into account. Then who can say what answer voters had given to the main question? The 1910 general elections were conducted, in the main, on the issue of the House of Lords; the February 1974 poll took place against the background at least of the question, 'Who governs Britain?'; but those were wholly exceptional cases. The other difficulty with this theory of representation surfaces when there is a clear majority in the country on a particular issue, but an equally clear majority of the House of Commons in the opposite direction. Capital punishment is the paradigm case.

The obvious mechanism which could be used to resolve such difficulties is the referendum.[23] When a referendum is proposed, however, Members of Parliament often invoke the shade of Edmund Burke. Are not Members of Parliament, they ask, representatives of their constituents? Must they not decide questions in the House of Commons as best they can, of course taking into account their constituents' opinions as one factor (but only one factor) in making up their minds how to speak and vote? If referendums became the norm, would not Members be reduced to voting according to instructions—and then where would their independence be? (It would be impertinent to remark that Members often vote now according to the instructions of their Whips, but let that pass.) Even so, Governments and Parliaments have been prepared to embrace the use of referendums in constitutional affairs since 1973, both where the political parties were split internally (as with the European Community referendum in 1975), and where there was a very important issue to be decided (as with the Northern Ireland border polls, the devolution referendums in 1979 and in 1997, and elected city mayors). Those referendums were, of course, advisory only: they did not commit the Government in any formal sense to act on the results, nor could they have bound Parliament to do so. Is there not a case, based on those precedents, for further constitutional questions being submitted to advisory referendums? Referendums are widely used around the world. In Australia and Ireland, for example, they are a compulsory prerequisite for constitutional change; Switzerland uses them as a routine part of the machinery of Government; some states in the United States (such as California) regularly employ the referendum as a means of testing the opinions of electors. Voters in the

---

[23] See generally V. Bogdanor, *The People and the Party System* (Cambridge: Cambridge University Press, 1981); Electoral Reform Society and the Constitution Unit, *Report of the Commission on the Conduct of Referendums* (London: Constitution Unit, 1996); Constitution Unit, *Delivering Constitutional Reform* (London: Constitution Unit, 1996), 65–90; 5th Report of the Committee on Standards in Public Life, *The Funding of Political Parties*, Cm. 4057 (1998), Ch. 12; Political Parties, Elections and Referendums Act 2000, Part VII.

United Kingdom, as elsewhere, are much better educated than they were in Burke's day, and on the whole they are able to decide issues as intelligently as their elected representatives, provided they have been given adequate and comprehensible information. Concern would be expressed, no doubt mainly by Members of Parliament, that such an initiative would open the floodgates to referendums on all kinds of other matters. It would have to be emphasized, in trying to assuage such concern, that referendums would be restricted to questions about the British constitution, wholly in line with the historical precedents. Questions relating to the fundamental structure of the constitution are of a higher order of importance than those in other areas of national policy, and that in itself is a reason for resorting to unusual methods to resolve them: no argument arises for employing the referendum in any other policy field.

There are, to be sure, other questions which must be satisfactorily answered about referendums before they could be used with confidence more generally to guide constitutional development in the United Kingdom. First, would such referendums be advisory or decisive? On the face of it the doctrine of parliamentary sovereignty would render that a rather odd question, for Parliament is supreme and a referendum could only be advisory. But we must be careful, because it would be a brave (or foolhardy) Government which, having posed a referendum question were then to reject the answer on the ground that, in the view of Ministers, it was the wrong answer. Parliamentary sovereignty might prove an inadequate defence in such political circumstances, and politicians would have to be prepared, in effect, to accept a reduction in their freedom of action as a price to pay for more referendums.

Secondly, assuming that in principle there were to be more referendums, how would certain practical issues be resolved? For instance, would the voters' views be taken before the relevant legislation had been passed and on the basis of a Government's proposals, or afterwards (with acceptance at the referendum being the key to activating the legislation)? There are precedents in both directions, with the former road having been taken over the present Labour Government's devolution plans, and the latter over the 1978 proposals for Scottish and Welsh Assemblies. Again, would a simple majority be enough to resolve the question, or would a minimum threshold be required to underline the legitimacy of a given vote? The two sets of devolution referendums again provide contradictory precedents. Thirdly, would constitutional referendums be held under ad hoc statutes passed for each plebiscite (as now), or under a standing Referendums Act which could be used as required? The reason why the Political Parties, Elections and Referendums Act 2000, Part VII, sets out detailed rules to ensure fairness in the conduct of referendums, but is silent about the circumstances in which such polls are to be held, is surely so that Governments have enhanced control over whether there should be any given referendum at all: for Ministers can always fall back on the difficulties of enacting fresh primary legislation in a given case. Finally, how can the state ensure that voters honestly answer the question set in a referendum, and prevent them from giving whichever answer the Government does not want, so as to give an unpopular Government a bloody nose? It cannot.

Of overriding importance in a referendum process would be that voters received timely, understandable, and helpful information from both sides of the question. Without that any referendum would be worthless.

The Liberal Democrats have always accepted the case for the general use of referendums to provide essential popular authority for major constitutional changes.[24] The Labour Government, too, has recognized the need to obtain the electorate's explicit consent for several (although not all) of its constitutional plans. The Government has already instituted referendums in Scotland and Wales on the Scottish Parliament and the Welsh Assembly, and in Northern Ireland on the Good Friday Agreement; a referendum was held in London to obtain approval for a Mayor and a Greater London Assembly; referendums have also been promised on the electoral system for the House of Commons, on possible English regional assemblies,[25] and on whether the euro should replace the pound sterling. (But Labour held no referendums on, for example, the Human Rights Bill or on reform of the House of Lords.) Even the Conservative Party supported the Good Friday Agreement referendum; if the party were ever to recommend adoption of the Euro, or any further extension of the powers of the European Union, it is committed first to hold a referendum. That neither main party accepted the usefulness of referendums when this book was first published but now both do is naturally a matter of satisfaction.

A noble enterprise?

Constitutional reform has been the Cinderella of public policy-making in the United Kingdom. It has been generally ignored by the main political parties when preparing their election manifestos—although strikingly not in 1997, and to a much more limited extent at subsequent general elections. Governments have only reluctantly embarked on reviews of constitutional matters, and then have relied on a variety of ad hoc investigations which have been unable to bring any accumulated expertise to bear. Throughout the long history of the British constitution there has been no systematic and authoritative reconsideration of it. Even those who press for radical change seem to have given no thought to appropriate methodology. Institutions such as the Ministry of Justice, the Constitution Committee of the House of Lords, and the Constitutional Affairs Committee and the Public Administration Select Committee of the House of Commons all have important

---

[24] See Liberal Democrats, *For the People, By the People* (London: Liberal Democrat Policy Paper No. 83, 2007).

[25] Which we are unlikely to experience: see Ch. 8.

parts to play. But the degree of public participation in the making of constitutional rules is depressingly low, and yet the formulation of those rules—deciding how the country should be governed—should be a noble enterprise in which citizens have a right to take an important part. It is regrettable that the Green Paper issued by the Government shortly after Mr Brown became Prime Minister, *The Governance of Britain*,[26] which promised a rebalancing of powers from the executive to the legislature, and from both to 'the people', envisaged rather nebulous consultations about the ideas set out in it, including 'citizens' juries', and no referendums. There was no mention of institutional constructs along the lines proposed in this chapter. Indeed, the Secretary of State for Justice and the Lord Chancellor stated that he was opposed to the use, for example, of a constitutional convention or assembly in the national debate advocated in the Green Paper.[27]

Accordingly, the Constitutional Commission which is proposed would draw on the Australian experience, adopting features which would be of advantage and adapting it so as to reassure nervous politicians. There is much useful work to be done. Where the constitution is unclear, it might bring clarity. When a constitutional problem arises, it could provide analysis and advice. As political confidence in the Commission grew, it might consider the great constitutional issues of the day. The Constitutional Commission could be a means through which the British constitution might be brought out of the last century, where much of it still lies, to meet the challenges of the twenty-first.

[26] Cm. 7170 (2007); see further in particular Chs. 3 and 6.

[27] *The Times*, 12 July 2007. The Prime Minister envisaged legislation on the Green Paper being introduced in the 2007–2008 session of Parliament.

3

The parties and the constitution

Anyone can argue for any change to the British constitution. But in the main only politicians in Government can carry it out. It is therefore instructive to examine the attitude of the main political parties towards constitutional change. This is the purpose of this chapter, although detailed analysis of their policies on particular aspects of constitutional reform will be carried out in later chapters.

The Labour Government which swept to power on May Day 1997 did so committed to make many and vital reforms to the British constitution. Its first Queen's Speech confirmed that Parliament would be asked in the 1997–8 session to approve several changes, including devolution to Scotland and Wales, and the incorporation into domestic law of the European Convention on Human Rights.[1] But even as recently as the early 1980s the Labour Party was still maintaining its historical stance as a constitutionally conservative party, albeit with some notable exceptions (such as a wish to do something about the House of Lords).

New policies for old Labour

During the last Conservative Government (especially under Mrs Margaret Thatcher) elective dictatorship was revealed at its most awesome. That Government was able to implement its radical policies free, in the main, from significant constitutional checks and balances. It was in that context that the Labour Party—appalled by the substance of Thatcherite policies—undertook a root-and-branch review of all its policies during the 1980s. If it had no other reason to do this, then its defeat at Mrs Thatcher's hands in three consecutive general elections would have provided an irresistible motive. That review came to its conclusion in 1989 when the party adopted a comprehensive statement of policy entitled *Meet the Challenge: Make the Change*.[2]

---

[1] On Labour's plans and first years see R. Blackburn and R. Plant (eds.), *Constitutional Reform: The Labour Government's Agenda* (London: Longman, 1999).

[2] (London: Labour Party, 1989).

It was during that review process that the Labour Party abandoned its cautious approach to constitutional reform. With the exception of the false starts in trying to devolve power to Scotland and Wales in the 1970s, and of almost reforming the House of Lords in the 1960s, Labour had been almost as constitutionally conservative as the Conservative Party. Indeed, it could be said that down to the 1980s (and with a few significant exceptions) there was almost, in effect, a bipartisan approach to constitutional policy. But what eighty years of political experience had failed to persuade Labour to do ten years of Thatcherism brought about—Labour's conversion to the view that something had to be done about the constitution. The 1989 policy statement committed Labour to the challenging aims of putting individual rights back to the centre of the stage, of providing a major extension of those rights, and of extending democracy. But Labour was not then prepared to overcome its historical antipathy towards a Bill of Rights: the party still thought that because such a Bill would give the judges too much power it had no place in the plans of a party of the left; and in any case Labour believed that such a Bill could not be entrenched, so that its usefulness in preventing a determined Government from further infringing liberty was undermined. Instead Labour decided that, in Government, it would sponsor a series of new statutes (on, for example, freedom of information and data protection), statutes which would have been known collectively as a Charter of Rights. But no change was envisaged to the electoral system for the House of Commons: first-past-the-post would stay. Devolution, however, was maintained as official policy, with a commitment to establish a Scottish Assembly or Parliament which would enjoy legislative powers including the ability to vary tax rates in Scotland. Devolution to Wales was mentioned in the policy paper far more tentatively. That circumspect approach was, of course, adopted in the light of the decisive rejection of devolution by the Welsh electorate in the 1979 referendum. On Northern Ireland, the party thought that the long-term goal should be a united Ireland achieved by consensual and peaceful means, although (understandably) no details of how that might be brought about were given in the paper. England would have been given about ten regional authorities to which power would be devolved from Westminster. The administration of justice would have undergone major changes, especially through the creation of a Ministry of Legal Administration to replace the Lord Chancellor's Department, and to take over all of the Lord Chancellor's functions save the purely judicial one of sitting as a judge; the new Minister would have been an MP, not a peer. A judicial appointments commission would have been set up to recommend judicial appointments to the Minister, thus taking the main responsibility for such important and sensitive matters away from politicians.

Meet the Challenge: Make the Change represented the fullest commitment ever to constitutional reform by either of the two main British political parties. Labour had positioned itself on the ground which is traditionally occupied by the third party in British politics, but with the obvious practical difference that the Labour Party would be able, one day, to pass them into law. With the accession to power in 1990 of an apparently less confrontational and less ideologically driven Conservative Prime Minister, Mr John Major, it would have been understandable if the momentum had gone out of Labour's push for constitutional change. But far from that happening Labour's constitutional plans survived the party's metamorphosis into new Labour during the 1990s, and moreover some of those policies (contrary to what was to be the new Labour trend) were to be given a more radical edge. Labour in the 1990s was, for instance, to embrace for the first time the need to incorporate the European Convention on Human Rights into English law, and was to offer a referendum on voting reform. The party could claim that, however much other old Labour (and voter-unfriendly) policies were abandoned or trimmed in the 1990s, its constitutional reform programme emerged, on the whole, unscathed[3] and, indeed, in some respects in a more challenging prospectus.

Stunned by its fourth drubbing at the polls in 1992, the Labour Party produced a revised statement of its constitutional policy under the title *A New Agenda for Democracy*,[4] which was approved by the annual conference in 1993. That paper concentrated on a number of key areas, in particular, a Bill of Rights, Lords reform, devolution and local and regional Government, reform of the judiciary, and freedom of information.[5] Given that the party's Plant Commission was in the process of conducting a detailed review of the voting system for the Commons, there was no mention of that subject in the paper;[6] after the Plant Report was published the then Labour leader, Mr John Smith, was to commit Labour to hold a referendum on the subject, a promise repeated in his turn by Mr Tony Blair. Of most significance in *A New Agenda for Democracy* was a new and full-hearted acceptance of the need for a Bill of Rights: out went the timid Charter of Rights, and in came a proposal to incorporate the European Convention on Human Rights into domestic law. This would be followed by work on a home-grown Bill of Rights to modernize the then 40-year-old European Convention, which would embrace such matters as freedom of information, data protection, and the rights of disabled people. Of more immediate impact than that longer-term aspiration was a decision contained in *A New Agenda for Democracy* on the future of the House of Lords. Now there was to be a two-stage plan, the first being the exclusion of hereditary peers from the House, followed in the second stage by the setting up of a democratically-elected second chamber. The party's commitments to devolve power to Scotland, to Wales (now with a clear promise to introduce a Welsh Assembly), to Northern Ireland, and to the English regions were all confirmed, along with promises to enact legislation

---

[3] But the idea of replacing the Lord Chancellor's Department with a Ministry of Legal Administration went the way of other old Labour policies.

[4] (London: Labour Party, 1993).

[5] Some other matters were mentioned briefly, including the need to reform prerogative powers (especially as they are used in foreign affairs and defence).

[6] See Ch. 4.

on freedom of information, and on the reform of the judiciary. Tucked away at the end of *A New Agenda for Democracy* was another, and surprising, development. Neither the Conservatives nor Labour had up to then accepted that there might be a case for the introduction of a written constitution for the United Kingdom. But the 1993 paper concluded by saying that, while Labour's constitutional reforms would not of themselves amount to a formal written constitution, they would represent, once enacted, a significant step in that direction; and the paper explicitly left open the question of whether at a later stage progress should be made towards formal codification.[7]

Some influences on new Labour

Constitutional reform policies are not formulated by the political parties in ignorance of work being done by others to reshape the constitution. While the Labour Party was developing such policies a number of organizations were formulating proposals for change, aimed in large measure at restraining the power of central Government.[8] Charter 88, the Institute for Public Policy Research, Liberty, and the Democratic Audit (to take just four examples) had all been working on aspects of constitutional reform.[9] Two important newcomers entered the deliberative process in the 1990s, each bringing a distinctive perspective to the debate on constitutional reform. The independent and non-partisan (though centre-left-leaning) Constitution Unit started work in 1995, geared not to the assessment of the merits or otherwise of particular constitutional reforms, but to an examination of the nuts and bolts of *how* such changes could and should be implemented.[10] Although the Labour Party had written an ambitious shopping-list of reforms for the constitution during the late 1980s and the early 1990s, it had given little or no thought to the question of how the various measures could be enacted, or how each one would relate to the others. Nor had Labour described its legislative priorities for constitutional Bills; and it had given no indication of the speed with which existing

---

   7 That account was a very simplified version of what would be necessary, for it ignored all the other areas which would have to be addressed by a written constitution but which Labour's reforms would not touch. See Ch. 11 for a detailed consideration of a possible codified constitution.

   8 See D. Oliver, 'Constitutional Reform Moves Up the Agenda' [1995] *Public Law* 193.

   9 The Institute for Public Policy Research had embraced the whole field of reform by publishing *The Constitution of the United Kingdom* in 1991, subsequently republished as *A Written Constitution for the United Kingdom* (London: Mansell, 1993). This set out the text of a comprehensive (and reformed) British constitution.

   10 The Unit's terms of reference include instructions to examine the steps necessary to produce a coherent and acceptable programme of constitutional reform, with particular reference to timing and sequence, the parliamentary and consultative processes to be followed, resource implications, and the constraints on any legislative timetable.

parliamentary procedures would permit an ambitious programme to be carried out (even less, whether that programme could be achieved along with proper, detailed parliamentary examination of the relevant Bills); nor had the party explained what kinds of public consultation would be necessary or desirable.[11] It was to fill such lacunae that the Constitution Unit was set up. It produced a series of excellent reports, including in particular one which analysed in detail questions of methodology.[12] Those who are concerned with the reform of the British constitution owe a debt to the Constitution Unit for setting out so clearly the practical considerations which attach to constitutional reform but which are usually, albeit understandably, lost in the arguments about particular institutional reforms.

The Constitution Unit was established after the Scottish Constitutional Convention had been at work for six years. The significance of that Convention[13] lies not only in the detailed and comprehensive work which it carried out on devolution policy but also in my view in its very existence. For the Convention represented the first attempt ever in the United Kingdom to develop constitutional policy through debate in a cross-party, and non-party, group. In doing so the Convention sought to draw in different political parties, and representatives of industry, commerce, the trade unions, the churches, and others, so as to raise the level of the discussion above mere party-political exchange. The boycott of the Convention by the Conservative and Scottish National Parties limited its all-party potential, but representatives of the Labour and Liberal Democrat Parties did take a full part in the task of establishing how a Scottish Parliament could work. There are no exact precedents for such an approach.[14] The Convention worked towards as broad an agreement as possible in Scotland and the United Kingdom as a whole on a plan for a Scottish Parliament, and eventually published a detailed final report which, despite the Convention's disparate membership, was a unanimous one.[15] This highly unusual mechanism showed that cross-party (albeit not all-party) agreement on constitutional matters can be achieved.

In 1996 there was to be a development which was more important nationally than the Scottish Constitutional Convention, and which was to continue that important cross-party approach to constitutional reform.

---

[11] Save for commitments to a number of referendums.

[12] *Delivering Constitutional Reform* (London: Constitution Unit, 1996).

[13] See J. McFadden, 'The Scottish Constitutional Convention' [1995] *Public Law* 215.

[14] See Ch. 2.

[15] See *Scotland's Parliament: Scotland's Right* (Edinburgh: Scottish Constitutional Convention, 1995).

The Labour–Liberal Democrat constitutional programme

Labour's embrace of constitutional reform in the 1980s and 1990s moved it nearer to the Liberal Democrats. True to their radical origins the Liberal Democrats had maintained an unwavering commitment to massive constitutional reform, with the aspiration of crowning it all by the creation of a federal United Kingdom governed through a written constitution which would be adopted by the people at a referendum.[16] Given that Labour and the Liberal Democrats by the early 1990s had separately adopted a largely common constitutional agenda (with important differences), a logical—though unprecedented—step would have been to reach a formal agreement between them on a constitutional programme. In the summer of 1996, when the return of a hung Parliament at the forthcoming general election was still a possibility, the leaders of the two parties agreed on an investigation whether such an accord could be achieved. The setting-up of the two-party Joint Consultative Committee on Constitutional Reform was the result. Its conclusions were of crucial importance because they were to form the basis of a new Labour Government's constitutional policies.

The Joint Consultative Committee's terms of reference required it to consider each party's then current constitutional reform proposals, to examine whether there might be enough common ground to enable the two parties to reach agreement on a legislative programme on such reform, to consider the means by which such a programme might best be implemented, and to report. The committee consisted of parliamentary representatives of each party, together with others sympathetic to the two parties, including a Queen's Counsel and a Professor of Constitutional Law. The committee published a unanimous report (the 'Joint Report').[17]

The Joint Report confirmed the Labour and Liberal Democrat belief that the United Kingdom was one of the most centralized countries in Europe. It noted that demands for greater decentralization had grown in the constituent parts of the United Kingdom, and especially in Scotland and Wales. The two parties accordingly proposed to meet those demands and at the same time (as they insisted) to strengthen the union of the whole kingdom by creating—within the first session of the new Parliament—a Scottish Parliament and a Welsh Assembly. The Scottish Parliament would assume legislative competence over all those matters which were then the responsibility of the Scottish Office, including health, housing, education,

---

16 Liberal Democrats, *For the People, By the People* (London: Liberal Democrat Policy Paper No. 83, 2007), Chs. 2, 6. That document is a comprehensive statement of Liberal Democrat constitutional reform policy, and is required reading for constitutional reformers.

17 *Report of the Joint Consultative Committee on Constitutional Reform* (London: Labour Party and the Liberal Democrats, 1997).

local Government, and law and order. The Parliament would be elected by the additional member system. Resources would be found annually for Scotland by the Westminster Parliament, but the Scottish Parliament might have the power to vary the basic rate of income tax by three pence in the pound upwards or downwards. A Labour Government would hold a pre-legislative referendum in Scotland on the basis of proposals to be published in a White Paper. Two questions would be posed in that referendum, one asking for support for the general scheme, the other for the tax-varying plan. If there were a positive vote at the referendum legislation would follow, and clearly parliamentary opposition to it would be harder to sustain in the light of a positive referendum vote in Scotland. As far as Wales was concerned, the Joint Committee committed a new Government to establish an Assembly elected by the additional member system (at the urging of the Liberal Democrats, acquiesced in by the Welsh Labour Party). It would take over Welsh Office functions, control quangos, and provide a forum for the development of policy. It would have no powers to enact primary legislation or to raise revenue. This would be a much more modest affair than the Scottish counterpart. A referendum would be held in Wales on the basis of a White Paper. The Joint Report made no reference to Northern Ireland; it did make some modest suggestions for regional assemblies in England.[18]

The Joint Report recalled that a debate about the appropriate system for electing MPs to Westminster had gone on throughout the twentieth century, and said that the question ought now to be concluded by the people. The Labour Party, however, had no policy on whether the voting system should be changed, although Tony Blair was personally not persuaded of the desirability of change (while some of his senior colleagues, like Robin Cook, were committed to proportional representation). On the other hand the Liberal Democrats, like the Liberal Party before them, were and remain wedded to proportional representation (PR), one obvious reason being that their hopes of translating their share of the vote at parliamentary elections more closely into seats won could only come about under PR. Despite that difference of view between the two parties, they agreed in the Joint Report to advocate the additional member system for the new assemblies in Scotland and Wales, and they also agreed that a national referendum should be held on the voting system for the House of Commons early in the new Parliament. A commission would be set up to agree which PR system should be placed before the voters in the referendum as the only alternative to first-past-the-post: voters would be allowed to vote only for the status quo or for the specified alternative: all other PR—and indeed all other—systems[19] would be left out of account. This proposal can be criticized on

---

[18] Indirectly elected regional chambers would be set up first, followed (where there was local demand) by referendums on directly elected assemblies. The assemblies would bring some democratic accountability to the existing Government Offices for the regions, and to many quangos. For the devolution story see Ch. 8.

[19] Such as the alternative vote, and the second-ballot system: see further Ch. 4.

the ground that it would deny a choice to proponents of other systems, such as the alternative vote and the second-ballot system, as well as to the proponents of other PR systems. A multi-choice referendum ballot paper would accurately reflect the electorate's wishes, but that consequence was to be sacrificed so as to maximize the pro-PR vote.[20]

Despite the dispiriting auguries of failed attempts to reform the House of Lords, Labour and the Liberal Democrats agreed in the Joint Report that the hereditary principle was indefensible as the basis for providing a large part of a House of Parliament, and accepted the need for legislation to be passed to remove hereditary peers from the House of Lords. The Joint Report acknowledged that some heredi-tary peers, including some of the cross-benchers, who had contributed to the work of the House should receive life peerages to enable them to remain members. Labour and the Liberal Democrats agreed that, following the removal of the hereditaries, no one party should enjoy a majority in the House of Lords; they also proposed that, over the course of the new Parliament, the party balance of the remaining life peers should be altered through new creations more accurately to reflect the proportion of votes obtained by each party at the general election. All that would constitute the first stage of Lords reform. In the second, a joint committee of both Houses would consider the structure and functions of a new second chamber which was both democratic and representative. How long this second stage would take, how likely it might be that a cross-party agreement on a new chamber could be achieved, and whether the final solution would prove acceptable to the House of Commons was unclear. Lords reform was to prove more difficult than the authors of the Joint Report implied, because although stage 1 was to be completed within two years of Labour coming to power in 1997, stage 2 had not been enacted as the tenth anniver-sary of that victory came and went.[21]

When the United Kingdom took a major part in drafting the European Convention on Human Rights after the Second World War it was assumed that the resulting international treaty would be incorporated into English law. As with most international treaties it could not become part of English law unless a statute were passed for that purpose. The Convention was ratified by the United Kingdom in 1951, but incorporation did not happen, despite attempts over the years by backbench MPs and peers to do so: no Government before 1997 had accepted the undesirability of the status quo, even though under the then current law British citi-zens who wished to enforce their rights under the Convention had first to exhaust their remedies in English law in British courts and then, if they were still not satis-fied, go to Strasbourg to seek redress from the machinery of the Convention. That was a lengthy process, taking as much as seven years in some cases. The Liberal Democrats had long advocated the drafting and adoption of a new British Bill of

---

[20] See further Ch. 4.
[21] See further Ch. 5.

Rights, and would pause first before doing so only to incorporate the European Convention. Historically the Labour Party had not accepted either proposal, very largely as a result of its distrust of the judiciary whom it had seen as reactionary and hostile to left-wing principles.[22] But the Labour Party changed its mind on this issue in the early 1990s, partly because it believed that the judiciary had tried to safeguard individual rights during the long period of the Conservative Government, partly because Labour no longer thought that Parliament alone could be relied on to be the main guarantor of liberty, and partly because the Labour Party itself had moved from the left to the centre ground. The Labour Party accepted—and repeated its view in the Joint Report—that legislation should be introduced to incorporate the European Convention into English law. The Labour–Liberal Democrat Joint Report acknowledged that the sovereignty of the British Parliament would not be affected by this step—in other words, no attempt would be made to entrench the Convention against easy amendment or repeal. It is widely (though not universally) thought that it would be impossible in the British constitutional system to effect such entrenchment.[23] Rather than attempt to do so, therefore, the two parties proposed that Ministers should be required to make clear to Parliament whether any provision of a subsequent Bill was, or appeared to be, inconsistent with the Convention. If it was, then Parliament could judge whether to accept the Bill. The Joint Report was vague about whether a new, home-grown Bill of Rights would be introduced. It did state that the Convention would need to be updated over time as a model for modern constitutional protection of human rights. In any event incorporation was wholeheartedly to be welcomed: it would cut out the delay, expense, and inconvenience of going to Strasbourg, and would not rule out the adoption of a new and modernized Bill of Rights one day.[24]

Greater freedom of information was also envisaged in the joint Labour–Liberal Democrat agreement. The parties believed (as they put it in their document) that open and accountable Government and freedom of information are essential to democracy, but that the workings of Government were hidden behind a veil of secrecy. In order to correct that situation a Freedom of Information Act would be introduced to give the public access to information about the workings of Government and to allow individuals to see information held about them by Government agencies.[25]

Two general observations may be made about the parties' overall joint constitutional programme. First, whatever the merits and demerits of each of the proposals, at least they emerged from more than merely the internal policy processes of one political party: the joint agreement on these proposals shows that constitutional

---

[22] Ironically, Ministers in the 1997 Labour Government were to criticize judges occasionally in effect for displaying the opposite tendencies towards some of that Government's legislation.

[23] See further Ch. 8.

[24] See further Ch. 9.

[25] See now the Freedom of Information Act 2000.

reform in the United Kingdom can be advanced across the party-political divide. But the joint committee's work involved no public involvement in the policy-making process. Admittedly, the joint committee was set up within six months of the latest date by which a general election had to take place, and most of that time was needed to hammer out agreement. But ideally constitutional reform should be brought about through wide public debate and the involvement of as many political parties as possible, because the constitution of any country is the concern of all its citizens, all of whom should be able if they wish to take part, however indirectly, in its development. The state of a national constitution is of a higher order of importance than any other area of public policy. It is profoundly to be hoped that the Labour–Liberal Democrat co-operation, and indeed the precedent of the Scottish Constitutional Convention, will come to be seen one day as the first steps towards the creation of a more inclusive, more permanent, and wider-ranging public review process dedicated to constitutional reform in the United Kingdom. Secondly, the Joint Report would admit the electorate into the reform process through a national referendum on the voting system, and through local referendums on Scottish, Welsh, and English devolution. Apart from those opportunities for citizens to have a direct say, their approval for the rest of the constitutional package was to be taken as implicit in the election of the Labour Government at the general election in 1997 in which other issues were always bound to predominate. There was, for example, no plan in the Joint Report to consult the people explicitly on the issue of reform of the House of Lords. Nor would any special legislative procedures or parliamentary majorities be required to implement the proposed changes, processes which would constitute an attempt to mark out constitutional legislation as being something special and apart from other law-making. Indeed, the committee published nothing on that part of its terms of reference which required it to consider the means by which a reform programme might best be implemented.[26] All of that is a matter for regret.

We were to learn subsequently that this co-operation on constitutional matters between the two parties took place as the then Leader of the Opposition, Mr Tony Blair, and the then leader of the Liberal Democrats, Mr Paddy Ashdown, were privately preparing the ground for a Labour–Liberal Democrat coalition Government. Mr Ashdown understood that such a coalition would be formed even if the Labour Party were to win the 1997 general election outright (which, of course, it did). The preparatory talks took place over several years, but no coalition was offered by the new Labour Prime Minister.[27] Constitutional policy was, however, to be developed under the new Government through the Joint Consultative Committee of the Cabinet from 1997 to 2001.[28]

---

[26] On referendums generally, see Ch. 2.

[27] P. Ashdown, *The Ashdown Diaries* (London: Allen Lane, 2000), vol. 1, 247 et seq; (2001), vol. 2, 1–24.

[28] See below.

New Labour in power

Labour's huge 179-seat majority at the 1997 general election gave the party the constitutional authority to seek the enactment of its programme, based on its manifesto.[29] The manifesto pledges on constitutional reform generally followed *A New Agenda for Democracy* and the Joint Report. Thus there were commitments on Lords reform, a Freedom of Information Act, devolution to Scotland, Wales, and the English regions, incorporation of the European Convention on Human Rights, and the continuation of the Conservative Government's peacemaking process in Northern Ireland. No mention was made, however, of setting up a judicial appointments commission,[30] or of any review of prerogative powers (both of which had been trailed in *A New Agenda for Democracy*). The first Queen's Speech contained legislative proposals for the eighteen-month-long 1997–8 session, and showed the new Government's constitutional priorities for its first parliamentary session. Legislation would provide for referendums in Scotland and Wales on the Government's devolution plans, followed if approved by substantive devolution legislation. There was to be a Bill to incorporate into United Kingdom law the European Convention on Human Rights. The Human Rights Act 1998 was the result.[31] A Bill would provide for a referendum on a directly elected strategic authority for London and a directly elected London mayor. The Greater London Authority Act 1999 was the substantive outcome.[32] The Government would consider how the funding of the political parties should be reformed. Full legislation on that had to wait for the enactment of the Political Parties, Elections and Referendums Act 2000. In Northern Ireland, the Government would continue to seek reconciliation and a political settlement. The historic Good Friday Agreement 1998 and the Northern Ireland Act 1998 marked, and gave effect to, that settlement.[33] And a White Paper would be published detailing plans for a Freedom of Information Bill, which was enacted in 2000.

To demonstrate its commitment to devolution, the Labour Government introduced the Referendums (Scotland and Wales) Bill into the House of Commons as its very first Bill. Under the resulting Act the people of Scotland and Wales were able to vote at referendums on the Government's proposals for a Scottish Parliament and for a Welsh Assembly, and the Government's plans were endorsed and implemented.[34]

In view of its Queen's Speech commitments to constitutional change in Scotland and Wales, to incorporate the European Convention, and to design freedom of

---

[29] *New Labour: Because Britain Deserves Better* (London: Labour Party, 1997).
[30] But one was to be established later: see Ch. 10.
[31] See Ch. 9.
[32] See Ch. 8.
[33] Ibid.
[34] Ibid.

information legislation, the Cabinet decided that it could not legislate on House of Lords reform in the 1997–8 session (even though that session would last six months longer than usual).[35] But it kept its options open for such legislation to be introduced in the following session, and in deciding on its timing the Government would no doubt take account of peers' treatment of Labour's legislation, especially on devolution. Ministers were keen to point out that Lords reform was in the Government's programme, but denied (not very convincingly) that they were wielding Lords reform as a sword of Damocles over peers' heads. The sword duly fell (to use a not very accurate figure of speech) when the House of Lords Act 1999 was passed. Labour's almost one-hundred year wish to kick the hereditary peers out of the second chamber thereby came true—although not entirely.[36]

The new Prime Minister allocated responsibility for the constitutional reform programme to the relevant departmental Ministers, that programme being overseen by a Cabinet committee chaired by him, and subsequently by the Lord Chancellor. Much more radically he announced the creation of a standing Joint Consultative Cabinet Committee, again chaired by him, on which Liberal Democrat parliamentarians would have five seats.[37] The main purpose of the Committee was to take forward the two parties' joint constitutional programme, but other matters of common concern were not ruled out from discussion. This carrying over from opposition to Government of bipartisan co-operation was to be applauded. It was an initiative which possessed some of the important qualities indicated in the previous chapter which should be enjoyed by the machinery of British constitutional reform.[38] The Joint Committee was wound up, however, in 2001 when a new Liberal Democrat leader, Mr Charles Kennedy, decided that it had outlived its usefulness and because he wanted to distance his party from the Labour Government.

After its second general election victory in 2001 and on the occasion of a Cabinet reshuffle in 2003 the Prime Minister suddenly announced further major constitutional reform. It had not been foreshadowed in his party's manifestos, nor in any public consultation, nor had it been discussed with the senior judiciary, nor any other political party. The office of Lord Chancellor was to be abolished, to be replaced by a Secretary of State for Constitutional Affairs at a new Department for Constitutional Affairs (DCA). A Judicial Appointments Commission was to be established to make recommendations for appointments to judgeships. And a new Supreme Court was to replace the Appellate Committee of the House of Lords. To achieve all this took rather longer than the press release from No. 10 Downing Street seemed to assume that it would. Lord Falconer was immediately appointed Lord Chancellor and Secretary of State for Constitutional Affairs, and the DCA replaced

---

[35] See Ch. 5.

[36] See Ch. 5.

[37] See 299 HC Debs. *113* (written answers 29 July 1997).

[38] For the Liberal Democrats' subsequent statement of constitutional policy see *For the People, By the People* (London: Liberal Democrat Policy Paper No. 83, 2007).

the ancient Lord Chancellor's Department, both being achieved under the royal prerogative. The rest had to await the enactment of what became the Constitutional Reform Act 2005.[39] Whatever the merits of these changes—and there are many—doing constitutional reform in a Cabinet reshuffle and announcing it in a press release on an unsuspecting world is no way to do constitutional reform, as Mr Blair was honest enough to acknowledge some time after the event. The error was to be repeated in his last Cabinet reshuffle in 2007 when Mr Blair merged the DCA and parts of the Home Office into a new Ministry of Justice.[40]

Mr Gordon Brown and his new Lord Chancellor, Mr Jack Straw, brought fresh enthusiasm to constitutional reform within a week of the new Government taking office. The Green Paper *The Governance of Britain* [41] outlined a raft of proposals, most of which would be subject to consultation. The details will be examined in later chapters, in particular in Chapter 6 on Ministers' powers. In brief, however, the document envisaged the transfer of many executive powers (in form, royal prerogative powers) to Parliament, including the authority to deploy the armed forces overseas, the ratification of treaties, and the dissolution of Parliament. The Prime Minister's powers to make many appointments would be modified, and Parliament would gain a role in some of them. House of Lords reform would continue through all-party talks. A long-promised review of the voting systems used in the United Kingdom outside the Westminster Parliament would be published by the end of 2007, with a view to possible change to the way in which MPs are elected. In the longer term there might be a new, British Bill of Rights, and a codified UK Constitution. Legislation to implement some of these changes was promised for the 2007–2008 parliamentary session. This was all an exciting prospect, my only personal regret being that there was no evidence of any consideration about the appropriate methodology of constitutional change.

Cynical observers will dismiss Labour's transition from conservatism in constitutional affairs to being a party which champions major alterations to the British constitution as a political reaction to Thatcherism and four general election defeats. Of course that political reality has played its part, but only a part. The Labour Party had seven years after Margaret Thatcher's demise to trim constitutional policies which would be inconvenient for a Labour Government and to move itself nearer to Conservative attitudes to the constitution. But it did not do so, and to the contrary developed several policies in ways that would make life even more awkward for Labour Ministers, such as enacting the Human Rights Act, and transferring power to the nations and regions of the United Kingdom. And Labour did all this despite the political adage that there are no votes in constitutional reform.

---

[39] See Ch. 10.
[40] Ibid.
[41] Cm. 7170 (2007).

For those who believe that constitutional reform should wherever possible proceed by consensus, or at least by cross-party co-operation, the last few years have been encouraging. Whether through the unofficial and broadly based Scottish Constitutional Convention, or through the two-party Joint Consultative Committee, or through the Joint Consultative Cabinet Committee, or (as will be seen) a Royal Commission on the Reform of the House of Lords, the process of constitutional change has been broadened out beyond single-party initiatives. The use of referendums as a means of legitimizing constitutional change is now accepted—although not for every important constitutional development. Organizations such as the Constitution Unit have shown the value of careful and concentrated work on the mechanics of particular constitutional developments. All of that has come about in the last fifteen years or so.

The Labour Government's huge parliamentary majority, a cohesive parliamentary party, and an Opposition that was still adjusting to its ignominious rejection by the electorate, at what was to prove to be three consecutive general election defeats, all meant that the Government's legislative programme passed quite easily through the House of Commons. The House of Lords was in a relatively weak position to delay matters, given the Government's clear manifesto authority for its constitutional changes—which included a death sentence for the existing House.

The Conservative reaction

True to its name, the Conservative Party historically fought to maintain the principal features of the British constitution. The Duke of Wellington, Prime Minister from 1828 to 1830, typified the old Tory approach by regarding the constitution as an instrument of perfection, to be preserved at all costs. Sir Robert Peel, a successor at No. 10 Downing Street and perhaps the creator of the modern Conservative Party, was to modify that stance to the extent of accepting, in his famous Tamworth election manifesto of 1834, the 'correction of proved abuses', and that the Reform Act of 1832 (which greatly extended the franchise) was in practice irrevocable. Peel's approach was to prove to be the essence of the Conservative Party's attitude to constitutional change to the present day. The burden of proof was to remain squarely on the proponents of change to prove the existence of some constitutional defect or other, and that if, and only if, that burden were discharged might a Conservative Government act to correct it. Thus the Conservatives were to oppose, for example, home rule for Ireland, and House of Lords reform,[42] although they

---

[42] Mr Macmillan's Government, however, was to bring about major and beneficial changes to that House under the Life Peerages Act 1958 and the Peerage Act 1963.

were to preside over limited extensions of the vote to the previously disenfranchised. The Conservatives accepted the seventeenth-century dictum that 'when it is not necessary to change, it is not necessary to change'.[43]

Broadly, that philosophical stance was to endure. To the Conservative Party it was clear enough that the British constitution worked well, and that no convincing case had been made to change it in any significant way. Indeed, Mr John Major as Prime Minister opposed new Labour's entire constitutional reform programme at the 1997 general election,[44] arguing especially strongly that devolution would lead inexorably to the break-up of the union between England and Scotland to the detriment of all.[45] But as general election defeat followed general election defeat for the Conservatives, and as Conservative leader followed Conservative leader—five leaders holding that post from 1997 to the present day[46]—the party had to react to the political fact that the voters, at general elections and at the devolution referendums, had endorsed, among other areas of Labour's programme, radical changes to the old British constitution. The main difference was to be an acceptance, however grudging, that the clock could not be put back on many of Labour's constitutional laws. In particular it appeared that the Scottish Parliament would be safe under a future Conservative administration, buttressed as it had been by the referendum result, and that there was no chance that the hereditary peers could be restored to the House of Lords. But support for first-past-the-post to elect MPs remained, and remains, unshakeable. And in certain respects the Conservatives tried to outflank the Labour Government. Astonishingly, for example, shortly after the Labour Government had achieved stage one of its Lords reform, the party under Mr William Hague committed themselves to a largely-elected second chamber (what would the Iron Duke have made of that?).[47] In other respects, though, Labour's settlement was not guaranteed continuance under a Conservative Government. Mr Michael Howard promised a fresh referendum in Wales on the future of the Welsh Assembly, and suggested an apparently simple and perfectly rational answer to the West Lothian question: 'English votes for English laws'—that is, only MPs from English constituencies should vote on laws applying only to England.

What, then, is current Conservative constitutional policy? Uniquely among the main political parties—and with some exaggeration—it can be said that party policy is what the Conservative leader says it is. Mr David Cameron was elected leader in 2005. He set in train a complete review of all party policies. To help with the development of constitutional policy he appointed a Democracy Task Force,

---

[43] Viscount Falkland in *A Discussion on Infallibility* (1660).

[44] For the Conservatives' case in its 1997 election manifesto see Blackburn and Plant, op. cit., 481–5.

[45] That argument still deserves serious examination: see Ch. 8.

[46] Mr John Major (1990–1997), Mr William Hague (1997–2001), Mr Iain Duncan Smith (2001–2003), Mr Michael Howard (2003–2005), and Mr David Cameron (2005–).

[47] W. Hague, 'A Conservative View of Constitutional Change' (London: Conservative Party, 2000).

chaired by Mr Kenneth Clarke. We will have to wait and see the extent to which its recommendations become official Conservative Party policy. But Mr Cameron has made one specific commitment. He has argued for a new, British Bill of Rights, making it clear that the Human Rights Act 1998 is not necessarily safe from amendment or repeal.[48]

[48] D. Cameron, 'Balancing Freedom and Security: A Modern British Bill of Rights' (London: Conservative Party, 2006). The Task Force has published two reports to date, but they are not yet official party policy. They are: Conservative Party, *An End to Sofa Government* (London: Conservative Party, 2007), and *Power to the People* (London: Conservative Party, 2007) (both available at the party's website).

4

Voting reform

It is difficult to exaggerate the constitutional importance of the voting system which returns Members of Parliament. The Prime Minister has immense political power and patronage, and is able to use them because the party system normally gives the Government, dominated by the Prime Minister, a reliable majority in the House of Commons.[1] Most constitutional reform depends for its implementation on the Government: no significant constitutional change will take place without the blessing of the Prime Minister and Ministers. And so the voting system through which a Government is installed is of critical importance to the British constitution in general and to its reform in particular.[2]

The House of Commons has many functions, but two of them are (or should be) of overriding importance. They are to provide the Government with its political legitimacy, and to represent the electorate. The House of Commons fails in both those purposes.

The failings of democracy

The reverence which politicians accord some ancient constitutional notions does not always spring from sentiment. The Queen in Parliament is very much a case in point. Legal sovereignty must reside somewhere in every political system. It is well settled that legal sovereignty in the United Kingdom is located in the Queen in Parliament, and that (to the satisfaction of subscribers to orthodox learning at any rate) there is little which the Queen in Parliament cannot do.[3] In strict law, of course, the Queen in Parliament is the Queen, the Lords, and the Commons

---

[1] See Ch. 6.

[2] On voting reform generally see especially *Report of the Independent Commission on the Voting System*, Cm. 4090 (1998) (the Jenkins Report); Sir William Wade, *Constitutional Fundamentals* (London: Stevens & Sons, 1980), Ch. 2; D. Oliver, *Constitutional Reform in the United Kingdom* (Oxford: Oxford University Press, 2003), 131–47; M. Dummett, *Principles of Electoral Reform* (Oxford: Oxford University Press, 1997).

[3] Even the Queen in Parliament cannot legislate inconsistently with European Community law: *R v. Secretary of State for Transport, ex p. Factortame (No. 2)* [1991] AC 603. There are many awkward questions about the omnipotence of the Queen in Parliament which will not be gone into here.

coming together to enact legislation. This assembling is notional rather than real, and indeed the whole concept now has about it an air of unreality. For the political power of two component parts of the trinity—the Queen herself and the House of Lords—has been subordinated by convention and by law to the wishes of the House of Commons; in its turn, the House of Commons has permitted its political authority to be exercised by the Government; and as a result the Queen in Parliament in effect means the Government, or the Prime Minister. Legal sovereignty is in practice exercised by—or at least at the request of—Ministers. Small wonder that Governments (and Oppositions wishing to be Governments) revere the idea of the Queen in Parliament, or parliamentary sovereignty, and can become agitated about threats to sovereignty from, for example, the European Union. Legal sovereignty gives them immense political power, largely unchecked by any other authority. (It is true that Mr Gordon Brown has promised to restrict some of the Prime Minister's powers in favour of Parliament: this will be evaluated in Chapter 6.)

But what of citizens? On the optimistic assumption that they have tacitly acquiesced in this constitutional development, what do they get in return for allowing Ministers untrammelled legislative power to interfere in their lives? In Diceyan terms, citizens as electors are left with political sovereignty.[4] As long as Ministers, as the effective legal sovereign, allow regular general elections, the electorate retains the power to alter the composition of the House of Commons and so to confirm or reject the Government of the day. The political sovereign chooses the Government through the indirect method of selecting an electoral college, known more familiarly as the House of Commons. In theory, the college meets to choose a Government, and indeed could pick a different Government at any time. In practice, the electoral college has achieved its purpose as soon as the results on general-election night give one party at least one-half of the Commons seats plus one. From that moment, the Prime Minister or his or her successor is endowed with the political authority to take full charge of the nation's affairs, and in due course to implement the winning party's policies through legislation and otherwise. But this seemingly simple legitimating process conceals difficult questions. The most notorious is, of course, whether it may be said at all convincingly that a Government which achieves a majority of seats is legitimate if it obtains only a minority of electors' votes—which was the result of every general election in the twentieth century bar four.[5] Politicians from the main parties none the less—and not surprisingly—maintain that the party make-up of the House of Commons is everything: a Government which has a majority of Members of Parliament behind it has all the political legitimacy that is required. The Members sitting on the Government benches provide the outward and visible sign of that legitimacy. That way of looking at things has,

---

[4] A. V. Dicey, *Introduction to the Study of the Law of the Constitution* (London: Macmillan, 10th edn., 1962 by E. C. S. Wade), 70–76.

[5] Those of 1900, 1918, 1931, and 1935.

moreover, the approval of a constitutional convention which holds that the person who leads the majority party in the House of Commons is entitled to be appointed Prime Minister by the Queen. It is simply not done, in the British constitution, to look behind the election returns to check the arithmetic of how those Members were elected.

And so the citizen's exercise of ephemeral political sovereignty is complete on marking a cross on a ballot-paper every four or five years. That is not a very active citizenship, but is rather the consequence of a lopsided bargain to which electors are assumed to have assented and which politicians stoutly defend. This imbalance would not matter so much if the Government paid close heed to citizens' wishes. To what extent, however, do the Government and the House of Commons take into account voters' views between elections? Put another way, how well does the Commons discharge its representative function?

If anyone should know in what sense Members of Parliament are representative,[6] it is Members themselves. They would almost certainly refer the inquisitive voter to Edmund Burke, perhaps even citing the famous passage from his 1774 *Speech to the Electors of Bristol*: 'Your representative owes you, not his industry only, but his judgement; and he betrays, instead of serving you, if he sacrifices it to your opinion.' That firmly puts the voter in his or her place: in ruling out any suggestion that constituents might order their Member how to act or vote, a relationship is established in which the Member of Parliament can behave condescendingly to his or her constituents. For although citizens may address their opinions to their Member of Parliament on local and national issues, it must be clearly understood that the Member may reject those opinions out of hand. Naturally, Members of Parliament will say in their defence that they treat their constituents with disdain only at their peril, for the clock starts to tick towards the next polling day as soon as a general election is over. If a Member is dismissive of his or her constituents' opinions and needs, then they can contemptuously reject the MP at the next election. But how many Members have actually been unseated by their constituents in such circumstances?[7] Does the theory that unrepresentative Members are penalized by the loss of their seats actually translate into practice? *Governments* are rejected at elections; Oppositions are voted into power; but that is a very different process. Burke's view of the relationship between Members and their electors has itself become grossly misleading. Members of Parliament can certainly form judgements on issues before them free from pressures from their constituents, but another force—that of party—has subverted their independence. This is especially the case in the House of Commons itself, through the whip system, but the power of

---

[6] For a concise and very useful historical account of theories of representation, see C. Harlow, 'Power from the People? Representation and Constitutional Theory' in P. McAuslan and J. F. McEldowney (eds.), *Law, Legitimacy and the Constitution* (London: Sweet & Maxwell, 1985).

[7] Mr Neil Hamilton's loss of his seat to an Independent in the 1997 general election is certainly one example. Mr Hamilton had attracted heavy criticism for improper financial behaviour while an MP.

party in the constituencies is also very strong, particularly in the selection of parliamentary candidates. While Burke's theory freed Members from any threat of being mandated by their constituents, it provided a political vacuum which the political parties have been delighted to fill.

During the life of a Parliament, the Member owes a duty to represent (in whatever fashion is appropriate) all his or her constituents, rather than just those who voted for him or her. This must be so, for otherwise millions of voters would enjoy no parliamentary representation at all given that in many constituencies more people vote for losing candidates than vote for the returned Member. (Indeed, in safe seats, many electors regularly vote for parties which have no chance of winning, and for their pains are described as wasting their votes.) That MPs represent all their constituents is a fine and accepted theory, but what does it actually imply as far as accountability is concerned? If a Member fails to represent his or her constituents properly, or if he or she misbehaves in a way which incurs their wrath but which (to their minds) produces an inadequate response from the House of Commons itself, they can do nothing to reject the miscreant as their Member until the next general election. The MP might be deselected as the party's candidate, but this amounts only to the prospective loss of the seat, and in any case is an action dependent on his or her own party alone. Should Members have a five-year lease with absolutely no risk of earlier foreclosure? And what of those happy holders of indefinite leases, sitting Members in safe seats? There the selection of a Member is settled by the party holding the seat in whatever way seems appropriate to them. This may be by a constituency-party meeting where only those interested enough or able to turn up have a say, or it may be by a postal ballot of party members. The electorate is, in effect, presented with the party's candidate, on a take it or leave it basis. The candidate will not have the support of electors who vote for other parties: he or she may not (depending on the form of selection procedure) even have the support of most voters in the constituency who are in his or her party. In what sense does he or she start his or her parliamentary career truly representative of his or her constituents?

It has become fashionable, if not actually obligatory, for those reflecting on the British constitution to damn the first-past-the-post electoral system[8] out of hand.[9] It is identified as a root cause of much that has gone wrong in the United Kingdom, and which, in constitutional matters, has produced unrepresentative Members of Parliament and the growth of party power to the detriment of the individual. Anyone who is not a Conservative or Labour supporter who writes of its merits risks being portrayed in a Bateman-type cartoon with the description, 'The person who spoke well of the British voting system.' Risking such a fate, I want to indicate some of the advantages of that method of voting.

---

[8] Wade (note 2 above) 9–10, criticizes the use of that term and argues that it is more accurate to speak of a relative majority system. He is quite right, but for the sake of familiarity I will stick with the old phrase.

[9] On that system see the Jenkins Report (note 2 above), Ch. 3.

The British voting system is simple. Voters are entirely familiar with the easy task of marking one cross against one name on a ballot paper, and then later that day or the next learning the name of the victorious candidate who secured more votes in the constituency than any other person. There is no question of election officials distributing and redistributing votes according to any mathematical (and possibly complicated) formula. The party that gets a majority of Commons seats wins the election. It would be hard to devise a more straightforward method of election involving a secret ballot in 646 constituencies, each having as many candidates as wished to stand. The first-past-the-post system is also decisive. After a general election British voters expect to know the name of the next Prime Minister quickly, and if there is to be a change of Government, they expect to see television pictures of furniture vans outside Number 10 Downing Street on the day after the election as a physical sign of the transfer of power which they have brought about. No question arises—at least, not usually—of politicians conducting negotiations to make practical political sense of what the electors have decreed through the ballot boxes. In that way the first-past-the-post system *is* democratic: it is as a direct result of their ballots that voters produce a parliamentary majority for one party, which then forms the Government. There is no post-election fudging of the voters' decision. This simple and decisive process produces stable Governments, in the sense of one-party majority administrations. Save for the February 1974 result, every general election since 1931 has produced a parliamentary majority for one party. Given the cohesion of party, such a Government is normally assured of being able to conduct its business until the Prime Minister decides to submit the Government to the electorate.

Implicit in all that is the assumption that general elections are primarily about power, rather than representation. Voters are mainly concerned with conferring political power, rather than achieving an exact correlation between numbers of votes cast for any party and the number of seats which it achieves in the House of Commons. By and large people vote for or against the Government. Perhaps more accurately, they vote to keep the Prime Minister in office, or to throw him or her out. The personalities of the party leaders are vitally important in British general elections, which have become presidential in character, and consequently it may be said that it is important that a general election unambiguously gives power to one prime ministerial candidate. It may be that the price to be paid for that in a first-past-the-post system is that the number of seats won will not precisely match the votes given for all parliamentary candidates. Before a radically different—and no doubt more representative—voting system were adopted, it would be of paramount importance to know whether the goal of fair representation in seats won for votes cast was to be equated with, or made superior to, the goal of clearly conferring power on one party.

A final attribute of the existing system is the rooting of each Member of Parliament in his or her local soil. While the relationship between a Member and his or her constituents may sometimes be far from ideal, considerable benefits must flow from it because no one suggests that Members should cease to represent a defined geographical area. Not even the most zealous champions of proportional representation want the perfect proportionality which is secured in, for example, the Netherlands and Israel. There, electors vote for names from each party's national list of candidates, and legislators are returned in strict proportion to votes cast for the parties. These legislators represent everyone and no one and everywhere and nowhere. Conscientious British Members of Parliament keep in touch with their constituents, through surgeries and otherwise, on parochial, national, and world matters, and most people seem to think that this is highly desirable.

Full credit should be given to these advantages before it is decided to sacrifice the current method of voting on the altar of electoral reform. But there are, of course, disagreeable aspects of the first-past-the-post voting system, which in essence are unfairness, and the imbalance in favour of the elective function and against the representative function.

The one-word indictment of the first-past-the-post method is unfairness. It is unfair to smaller parties, unfair to electors who do not vote for the winning candidate, and even unfair to the Conservative and Labour Parties. The first-past-the-post system is ideally suited to a society which is predominantly and accurately represented in its legislature by only two parties, one in and the other out of Government: for that reason it exists happily in the United States of America. But it is notorious that the United Kingdom is not such a society. Smaller parties achieve substantial political support, as evidenced through the number of votes cast for them, but they secure derisory numbers of Members of Parliament. The greatest unfairness to the smaller parties occurred at the 1983 general election, at which the Liberal–SDP Alliance secured over 25 per cent of the electorate's vote—almost eight million crosses—but only 4 per cent (twenty-three) of the seats in the House of Commons. Labour, on the other hand, with some 27 per cent of the vote, was rewarded with 32 per cent (209) of the seats, while the Conservatives won with 42 per cent of the vote and 61 per cent (397) of the seats. At the 2005 general election Labour secured 35 per cent of the votes cast but 55 per cent of the seats; the Conservatives received only 32 per cent of the popular vote and 30 per cent of the seats; the Liberal Democrats obtained 22 per cent of the national vote but only 9 per cent of the seats. The Labour Government was thus confirmed in power with a 66-seat majority, but on a 61 per cent turnout of voters. Put another way, only some 22 per cent of the whole electorate voted Labour.[10] A scheme which is capable of producing such results does violence to the concept of fair play as the British understand it. For the Conservative and Labour duopoly to be broken under the present voting system, there would have to be a political convulsion in which one of those two parties was replaced by a third party—as the Liberals were replaced by

---

[10] The turnout at the 2001 general election had slumped to 59 per cent, the lowest since 1918.

Labour early in the twentieth century—or a change to proportional representation for elections to the House of Commons.

Unfairness is wrought, too, on those voters who do not vote for winning candidates. This is not a small, disaffected minority that cannot take its defeat: it is usually a *majority* of those who vote at general elections. While those in this losing majority have the satisfaction of exercising their right to vote, the practical reward for doing so is non-existent. Voters who do not support the winning candidate in the 450 or so Commons seats which are safe for one party might just as well stay at home, for all that happens to their votes is that they are merely recorded in election statistics. In those seats, the constituency party chooses—democratically or otherwise—the person who is later ritually affirmed as the local Member at the general election. A voting system which permits millions of voters to ask themselves whether it is worth bothering to vote is subversive of democracy.

Those who reap largess from this electoral system do not deserve much sympathy when it discriminates against them. But the first-past-the-post method does operate unfairly against the Conservative and Labour Parties in parts of the United Kingdom, and the phenomenon of the safe seat is, again, the cause. So, for instance, the Labour Party's parliamentary representation has been largely eliminated in south-west England; at the 1997 general election the Conservatives' limited representation in Scotland and Wales was reduced to no representation at all, a situation which improved only marginally at the succeeding two polls. The two main parties in those parts of the country must be as disillusioned as are (say) the Liberal Democrats throughout the United Kingdom.

Inextricably linked in the voting system with unfairness is the supremacy of decisiveness over representativeness. The first-past-the-post system has developed into a mighty engine which can be relied on to produce a Government from one of the two principal parties. But in that development the purpose of gathering a House of Commons which is broadly representative of the electorate has rather faded. This would possibly not be as important as it is if the elective function worked on the basis of a majority of voters conferring a parliamentary majority on the winning party. Patently, however, it does not do so. Mr Tony Blair's landslide parliamentary majority of 179 seats in 1997 was achieved with only 44 per cent of the votes cast; his second victory in 2001 produced a 167-seat majority on just over 42 per cent of votes cast. Mrs Thatcher's 144-seat landslide majority in 1983, and her huge 102-seat majority in 1987, were achieved even though on both occasions some 57 per cent of votes were given to other parties. Almost 60 per cent of voting citizens voted *against* those Governments. To make matters worse, the Labour Government continued in office in 2005 knowing that 65 per cent of votes cast at the election had gone to non-Labour candidates. This is by no means a recent phenomenon. Attlee's 146-seat majority in 1945 was won on under 48 per cent of the vote, and indeed no winning party has been supported by half or more of those going to the polls since the general election of 1935. An additional cause for concern is low turnouts of voters. Are the virtues of the British electoral system—simplicity, decisiveness, its ability to produce stable Governments, and so on—so self-evident as to justify such distortions of the electoral will? Is it really necessary to have a voting system predicated either on the representative function, or (as in Britain) on the elective function?

In all this—and in more than this—the political parties have become over-mighty. President Kennedy began his Inaugural Address by declaring, 'We observe today not a victory of party but a celebration of freedom.' What may be observed in British democracy, by contrast, is indeed the victory of party—over a person's ability to be elected and re-elected to the House of Commons, and over how he or she behaves there. To stand a chance of being elected a Member of Parliament, one of the two main parties, or in some places the Liberal Democrats, must enfold the candidate in its colours. It is rare in England for an Independent candidate to be elected,[11] even at a by-election. In Scotland and Wales, Nationalists are often returned; Northern Ireland has its own pattern of politics, although Unionists have thus far made up most of the province's representation. But those differences in Scotland, Wales, and Northern Ireland do not touch the majority of House of Commons seats located in England, where the grip of the main parties is very tight. To be re-elected, the Member must be reselected in his or her constituency. Clearly, a Member should not be returned to Westminster for life: it should be possible for the party on whose ticket he or she was returned to remove its imprimatur. Equally clearly, though, this party process of reselection reduces the Member's independence. The Labour Party pioneered the regular reselection process: every Labour Member must undergo reselection in his or her constituency once in every Parliament, and several Labour Members have thereby indirectly lost their seats when their constituency parties denied them their backing. The Conservative Party is more circumspect over reselection, but deselection does occasionally happen. In 1990, for example, Sir Anthony Meyer's constituency party deselected him as the Conservative candidate—but then he had, after all, caused an election the previous autumn for the leadership of the Conservative Party by standing against the Prime Minister, Mrs Thatcher.[12] The Conservative machinery for selection and reselection varies from constituency to constituency but, like Labour, physical presence at the relevant meeting is often required. The Liberal Democrats choose their candidates

---

[11] Mr Martin Bell was returned as an Independent at the 1997 general election (see note 7 above); Dr Richard Taylor was elected as an Independent in 2001 and 2005 as part of a campaign to save a local hospital; he was joined at the latter election by Mr Dai Davies (Independent Labour) and Mr George Galloway (Respect).

[12] Another Conservative Member, Mr John Browne, was also deselected in 1990: his Winchester constituency party did so after the House of Commons had suspended him for twenty sitting days for not registering certain of his interests. After the rejection of Mrs Thatcher as Conservative leader, several Conservative Members who had supported her rivals faced deselection attempts.

by secret ballot at constituency party meetings, each member having one vote, and provide easily obtained postal votes for those who will not be there.

The power of party is offensive to democracy if it causes a Member wishing to be confirmed as a party's candidate to defer to his or her constituency-party activists to such a degree that the MP represents them rather than his or her constituents. Indeed, the less democratic the nomination exercise, the more likely it is that the Member will not be accountable even to the broad mass of people belonging to his or her party in the constituency. The views of supporters of that party who do not wish to be active in such things as selection and reselection may count for very little. If the Member is a realist he or she will understand that great respect must be accorded to those who actually have the ability to make the reselection; and yet that important power is wholly unrecognized and unregulated by law.

Once returned to the House of Commons the Member's party expects loyalty. This is not entirely unfair or improper, for it is the price of the party's label which secured the MP's election. But the question is whether the balance of a Member's obligations has tilted too far in favour of the requirements of party. The nonsense that a whip—even a three-line whip—is no more than a summons to attend the House, and that, once there, the Member is completely free to speak and vote as he or she thinks fit, was still being put about, by the Parliamentary Private Secretary to the Prime Minister, in 1986.[13] No one can honestly believe that. Failure to vote with the party on a three-line whip without permission invites a party reaction. This will range (depending on the circumstances and whether the offence is repeated) from a quiet word from a Whip and appeals to future loyalty, to a ticking-off or a formal reprimand (perhaps from the Chief Whip), to any one of a number of threats. The armoury of intimidation includes the menaces that the Member will never get ministerial office, or go on overseas trips sponsored by the party, or be nominated by the party for Commons committee memberships, or that he or she might be deprived of the party's whip in the House, or that he or she might be reported to his or her constituency which might wish to consider this behaviour when reselection comes round again. Such threats might seem like blackmail to a member of the public who might also query how a Member of Parliament could be anything like a free agent in the House in the face of such strictures. Does the Member not enjoy the parliamentary privilege of freedom of speech? How can speech be free in the face of such party threats? The answer to the inquiring citizen is that the whip system is part of the conventionally established machinery of political organization in the House, and has been ruled not to infringe a Member's parliamentary privileges in any way. The political parties are only too aware of the utility of such a system, and would fight in the last ditch to keep it.

Members of Parliament do, of course, defy the orders of their party from time to time. Supporters of the Government do so occasionally even when the consequence

---

[13]   In a letter quoted to the House of Commons: 95 HC Debs. 595 (14 Apr. 1986).

will be that the Government will lose a division. To do that takes courage. Sometimes Members' consciences will permit them to do no other. Yet the Government goes rolling on, annoyed, embarrassed, but still in office, bolstered if necessary by a vote of confidence in the administration.[14] Occasional losses of votes on legislation do not really count for much, in the sense that they do not threaten the Government's life and in any case only account for a tiny proportion of the total number of divisions in the House of Commons.

Within their own hands Members of Parliament hold the remedies for many constitutional ills, particularly those which result from the overweening power of party. Professor Ganz has put in this way:

They have the vote and if they used it more frequently in accordance with their judgement rather than the party whip, the power of the Government would be markedly curtailed ... But it would be simplistic to underestimate the pressures of party loyalty and the party whips. The most potent antidote to the latter would be a system of voting in secret in the House of Commons instead of walking through the division lobbies.[15]

But then, as she points out, no Government is going to introduce secret voting in the House of Commons. If less deference to the dictates of party and greater reliance on personal judgement and constituency feeling are desirable—as I am sure they are—Members need some additional reason for greater resistance to the Whips' entreaties. A new mechanism which would help them do so will be suggested a little later.

Towards a new democracy

I want to turn now to possible reforms in British parliamentary democracy. Let us start at the beginning with a Member of Parliament's selection as a party candidate. The political parties quite rightly have the power to decide who should stand for election to the Commons in their names. But given that that decision effectively elects the Member in the majority of constituencies, it must be right that the method of selection should receive the close attention of the law to ensure that it is democratic, fair, and properly conducted. The only way to make sure that those attributes were achieved would be to introduce primary elections.[16] The central aim of such elections ought to be that the choice of a party's candidate in any constituency should be broadly representative of party opinion in that constituency.

[14] Defeats on votes of confidence are very rare and have related to very special circumstances. Mr John Major's Government had to put down a number of motions of confidence in its final years, all of which it managed to carry.

[15] G. Ganz, *Understanding Public Law* (London: Sweet & Maxwell, 2nd edn., 1994), 27.

[16] This is not a new idea: see e.g. Wade, *Constitutional Fundamentals*, 23–4.

The selection should not be left to a committee or to a particular meeting (both of which contain the danger of choice by faction), or to a body in which any section of the party has a disproportionate say in the outcome. There is no substitute for a secret ballot conducted by post in which every registered and paid-up member of the constituency party has an equal vote.[17] Without such an election a parliamentary candidature should be void. Postal votes are now widely available for parliamentary elections; the inadequacies of meetings where votes were taken about trade union matters have been recognized and countered by legislation providing for postal ballots.[18] The whole drift of democratic development has been towards votes being cast secretly and by methods which ensure that everyone has the opportunity to vote.

Primary elections to choose parliamentary candidates are not unknown in the British political parties. The Liberal Democrats require that they be used; Labour has a selection procedure; some Conservative constituency associations conduct postal ballots of their members. The parties should not, therefore, be taken aback when it is suggested that such commendable procedures should be made universal and fully democratic. Reselection, too, should be general, regular, and democratic. Putting candidates through primary elections would be an exercise of limited value if the lucky winners in safe seats were then rewarded with leases for life. So a fresh primary election would be required in each constituency once in every Parliament if anyone wished to challenge the existing candidate.

As with most suggestions for change, practical considerations will no doubt be cited as reasons for holding back. None seems weighty. The cost of primary elections might not be insignificant, and certainly the question of how public money might be provided would be a proper consideration.[19] Exemptions from the requirement of primary elections would need to be made, for example, for candidates who wished to stand independently of party, or who were representatives of small, or non-national, parties. Candidates standing for, say, the Green Party, should accordingly not be required to undergo primary elections supervised by law.

In my view, however, democratic primaries and reselections are not enough, for too much power would still reside in the hands of the political parties. People who were not supporters of the Member's party would obviously have no say in the primaries, and even those who were registered party members would only be able to call the Member to account at a fixed time in each Parliament. This would not

---

[17] I will not go into the question of what method of voting would be appropriate. The Electoral Commission has recommended changes to the law and practice of postal voting to safeguard its integrity: *Postal Voting Statement* (London: Electoral Commision, 2005).

[18] The 1997 Labour Government acknowledged the soundness of that legislation.

[19] This is linked to the wider, and controversial, question of the funding of political parties. See the Political Parties, Elections and Referendums Act 2000, and the Electoral Administration Act 2006, Part 7; Oliver (note 2 above) 148–55; Electoral Commission, *The Funding of Political Parties* (London: Electoral Commission, 2004).

cover the case in which a Member of Parliament was seriously unrepresentative of general constituency opinion, or whose personal behaviour fell below standards acceptable to his or her constituents. What is needed is some additional device to ensure that a Member pays heed to constituents' views (rather than just to party opinion) and which provides an alternative defence against the blandishments of the Whips. Rousseau believed that the grant of sovereignty by the people to the sovereign power was conditional and could be recalled by the people at any time.[20] It is the notion of recall that is attractive, not in the sense of the people as a body taking back the powers of Government and legislature, but as a recognition of the conditionality of the trust which electors in each constituency put in their Member of Parliament. Constituents should be given a recall power so that if a given proportion of voters in a constituency wanted to force their Member to fight a by-election, they could vote to do so, and if the necessary vote were achieved, his or her seat would be vacated. The recall ballot would be conducted by the Returning Officer and enshrined in statute. Naturally, there would have to be a high threshold to activate the recall, so that frivolous or spiteful attempts to unseat a Member would be frustrated—a simple majority of those voting in the recall ballot would not be sufficient. That threshold would need to be arrived at through a combination of a prescribed minimum turnout and a prescribed minimum vote in favour of recall.

What sort of conduct might attract the operation of the recall power? First, a Member might have misused membership of the House, for example to further his or her personal financial interests in a manner offensive to his or her constituents. They might consider that the action taken against that MP by the House (or, indeed, lack of action) was inadequate. Secondly, a Member might not represent the opinions of his or her constituents on some important local or national issue, for example on local matters on which the Member failed adequately to reflect constituency feeling, perhaps because he or she put his loyalty to the Government line, or his or her co-operation with the Whips, above the duty to represent his or her electors' views. Environmental questions could be especially in point: the routing of major new roads or railway lines, the siting of power-stations or other unwelcome buildings, and the like, might all cause a clash between departmental or commercial wishes and the happiness of constituents, and it would, perhaps, be no bad thing if a Member were to place his or her constituents' happiness above other claims. Issues of national policy, too, can divide Member from voter, but it would be important to argue that issues of private conscience, such as abortion or hunting, should be exempt from the threat of recall as they are exempt from the discipline of the Whips. Thirdly, the use of a recall power might be particularly apt when a Member changed his or her party but declined to resign the seat and fight an immediate by-election. It is not unreasonable to expect a Member who crosses the

---

[20] See J.-J. Rousseau, *Social Contract* (London: Dent, ed. by G. D. H. Cole, 1973), xxvii.

floor of the House, or who joins a new party, to resubmit himself or herself quickly to the electors who had returned the MP in different colours.[21]

Good constituency Members of Parliament would have little to fear either from primaries or from recall. The recall power might be little used, or at least might be little used successfully, but it would serve its purpose by existing as a permanent reminder that those who have entrusted a person to represent them in the House of Commons do not place that trust unconditionally. A recall power would give greater practical meaning to the notions of representation and accountability—or at any rate would provide a practical consequence for misrepresentation. It would also act as a counterbalance to the drag of the Whips.

There are several other questions about a recall power which would have to be answered. Would recall votes be cast solely on party lines? Of course they might be, especially in safe seats. But even if this did happen, would that be a bad thing? Even *without* a recall power the constituency party would retain a (democratized) selection and reselection process, and it could choose another candidate for the general election if it so wished. The recall power would speed up that process so as to bring about a more timely change of representation. In less safe seats, the threshold necessary for recall to be activated ought to mean that one party's view about the sitting Member would not of itself be enough to trigger a by-election. How, then, would a recall power mesh with a Member's parliamentary privilege of freedom of speech and action? The answer to that may be achieved through another question: how does the whip system truly and fairly mesh with parliamentary privilege? The honest answer is that it does not, and to the extent that a recall power would cause MPs to take care to conduct their affairs acceptably and to respond to constituency opinion, it would further diminish a Member's theoretical independence. But would voters be bothered to turn out to vote at what might be two further constituency polls—the recall vote and any resulting by-election?[22] This questioning of whether it is worthwhile establishing further formal opportunities for people to express their wishes because they might not use them is sometimes the last refuge of the anti-democrat. 'All these elections!', many politicians will cry. Governments in particular aver that people do not like being called frequently to polling stations, and that they will become bored by democracy if they are asked to participate in it too much.[23] What is nearer the mark is that Governments fear elections. So much is at risk in them—political power, the trappings of office, and keeping opponents where they belong. I believe that participatory democracy requires more elections,

---

[21] Those Members who joined the Social Democratic Party in 1981 did not fight by-elections; nor has any other MP who has subsequently changed party during the life of a Parliament.

[22] Actually three if the selection ballot is counted as well.

[23] A number of pilots have been held under the European Parliamentary and Local Elections (Pilots) Act 2004 to see if postal-only voting would improve the numbers voting. The results have been equivocal. More worryingly, allegations of fraud in some areas led to criminal convictions. Holding polls at weekends is also being considered: *The Governance of Britain*, Cm. 7170, paras 149–54.

not just the current rate of general elections plus a few random by-elections supported by candidate-selection procedures which occasionally produce unrepresentative candidates. The right to elect and to reject representatives is—or should
be—fundamental, and citizens should have proper and adequate opportunities to
do so.

Radical reformers will dismiss the idea of more elections—whether primary,
selection, or recall—as the equivalent of applying sticking-plaster to a comatose
patient, or will use some equally dismissive phrase. For they will say that it is not
the number but the method of elections which needs drastic change. So let me now
grasp the nettle of electoral reform. Anyone doing so ought to keep at the front of
his or her mind the facts that the Conservative Party is entirely opposed to voting
reform, that many Labour Party supporters are wedded to first-past-the-post (and
that the Labour Government is committed only to hold a referendum on electoral
reform at some unspecified time),[24] and that only the Liberal Democrats enthuse
about it. Persuading either—and certainly persuading both—of the two main parties to support radical changes to the voting system would be difficult, and perhaps
impossible in a normal parliamentary situation.

Quite understandably, for many people the only way to remove the disagreeable aspects of first-past-the-post is by applying the patent medicine of proportional representation.[25] The only point on which the purveyors of this remedy are
all agreed is the negative one that there must be no resort to the national party-
list method, as operated in the Israel and Netherlands. In that system there is one
national constituency in which seats are allocated to the parties in strict proportion
to the national votes achieved by the parties. Not only would such a system remove
British Members' constituency bases, but it would also give representation to a political party in the House of Commons on a mere 0.15 per cent of the national vote.[26]
Rather, proportional representationalists in the United Kingdom talk up, according to taste, either the regional-list system, or the single transferable vote, or the
additional-member system. A brief reminder of how they work may be helpful.[27]

The *regional-list method* allows voters in given areas to vote for the candidate of
their choice from his party's approved list of candidates. The votes cast in favour
of each of the party lists are then totalled and distributed proportionately to each
party. The order in which individual candidates on each list are voted for is used to
decide how many of those candidates are elected. A variant of this system is used in

---

[24] See Ch. 3 and below.

[25] For a comprehensive review of voting systems see the Jenkins Report (note 2 above), and the *Report
of the Working Party on Electoral Systems* (the Plant Report) (London: Labour Party 1993).

[26] See D. Butler, 'Electoral Reform', in J. Jowell and D. Oliver (eds.), *The Changing Constitution*
(Oxford: Oxford University Press, 3rd edn., 1994), 388. This could, of course, be avoided by requiring
a party to obtain a minimum threshold before it was awarded any seats, as is the case, for example, in
Germany.

[27] See the Jenkins Report for detailed analysis.

Finland, for example, and (more to the point) for elections in Great Britain to the European Parliament. At the latter, the voter is asked to put a cross against one political party, whose candidates are listed on the ballot paper. That system allows the individual party to put its listed candidates in its order of preference for election: the higher a name is in that list, the more likely it is that he or she will be elected if that party has success at the election. A disadvantage of that sort of scheme is the loss of the single-Member constituency. There is also the objection that candidates may be chosen by each party remotely from well-known Westminster constituencies, either at regional or even national level—the so-called 'closed' party list system. And Independents stand very little chance of election.

The *single transferable vote* method requires large constituencies, usually of about five Members, in which voters rank candidates in order of preference. A quota is arrived at in each constituency at each election by dividing the total number of votes cast by the number of Members to be elected plus one. As soon as a candidate obtains that quota in first preference votes he or she is elected; any votes of his or her over that quota are then allocated to the second preferences expressed, but at a lower value. If places then still remain to be filled, the candidates with the fewest votes are eliminated in turn and the second or subsequent preferences are reallocated until all vacant places are filled. The single transferable vote method is used in Ireland and for the Australian Senate. There is British experience of it in Northern Ireland, for local Government and European Parliament elections, and in elections to the Northern Ireland Assembly. Its use for elections to the House of Commons and to a new elected second chamber is currently urged by the Liberal Democrats. The drawbacks of the system include the complicated counting which is involved (how many electors would really understand and have faith in it?), and the necessity of having very large constituencies each of some 300,000 voters. Each party will put up at least as many candidates as the number of seats they hope to secure in each large constituency, and so ballot papers will be quite long. On the other hand, all that voters need to understand is that they will be asked to mark the ballot paper with the numbers 1, 2, 3, and so on against the names of candidates (whose party affiliations will be given), so indicating the voters' order of preference for individual candidates. The details of redistributions conducted by officials after the ballot, in truth, need not concern voters. The system is far more representative than first-past-the-post, and the notion of a wasted vote is eliminated.[28]

The *additional-member system*, used in Germany and for elections to the Scottish Parliament and the Welsh Assembly, gives each elector two votes. One is cast for the candidate of his or her choice, to represent him or her in a single-member constituency; the other is cast for the party of his or her choice. Seats are allocated from the party lists so that, taken together with the representatives elected from

---

[28] The Liberal Democrats strongly advocate STV to elect MPs: see *For the People, By the People* (London: Liberal Democrat Policy Paper No. 83, 2007), Ch. 3.

the candidates' list, each party has a number of representatives in proportion to the votes cast. There may be (as there is in Germany) a threshold to be achieved before a party obtains any seats in the legislature on the basis of the votes for the party lists. An objection to the additional-member method is that the choice of candidates is removed from the locality and taken by the parties at national level—but representation in proportion to votes cast is achieved, and the advantages of single-member constituencies are retained.

If a method of proportional representation were introduced for elections to the House of Commons, there might as a result be a lurch too far in the direction of the representative function and away from an efficient means of electing a Government. It is that possibility which gives some force to the view that proportional representation is undemocratic. Under first-past-the-post, a change of Government is normally brought about by the voters at a general election. But in systems which deny an overall majority to any one party—as any proportional method is likely to do—that elective function is removed from the voters and is given to the smaller parties which are represented in the legislature. The German experience of 1982 is often cited, in which the Free Democratic Party changed partners, withdrawing from one coalition Government and putting another in its place—all without any reference to the voters. So, too, in the United Kingdom smaller parties, such as (but not only) the Liberal Democrats, would have a similar power under a regime of proportional representation to alter Governments between elections, a Government-making and Government-breaking authority which would be wholly disproportional to the votes accorded them at the general election. Such a situation would be even more objectionable if the smaller parties refused to give any indication before a general election of which of the major parties they would favour. Indeed, the main third party refused to give such an indication before the 1983, 1987, or 1992 elections—although before the 1997 poll the Liberal Democrats said that they would not support the Conservatives in a hung Parliament, but subsequently reverted to 'equidistance' (as they expressed it) from the other parties. Voters would be denied what is perhaps the main advantage of the present voting method, the selection of a Government. In effect, voters would have to delegate that task to elected politicians. In choosing a coalition or minority Government, those delegates might have little regard to what voters had indicated about Government formation through the pattern of their votes. This is a serious constitutional objection to proportional representation, and in my view would amount to too great a tilt of the electoral scales in favour of the representative function and away from the voters' Government-choosing function. One unbalanced set of scales would be replaced by another unbalanced set, whereas the quality which needs to be aimed at is equilibrium, even though it is unlikely to be achieved perfectly.

Some misgivings about proportional representation can, it is true, be exaggerated. For instance, the advantage under first-past-the-post of returning a relatively stable Government has also been achieved in Ireland and in Germany, although of course by having coalition Governments in office. Even the phenomenon of revolvingdoor Governments in Italy rather co-ceals the fact that one party has dominated the administration since 1948.[29] Again, the local links which are preserved in single-Member constituencies are not necessarily lost: they are retained under the additional-member system in Germany (for the election of half the representatives), and in the Scottish Parliament and in the Welsh Assembly. In the latter legislature, for example, 40 of the 60 Assembly Members are returned by first-past-the-post. A proliferation of parties in the legislature does not follow inevitably: while it has happened in the Netherlands, Israel, and Italy, the number of parties in the Irish and German legislatures actually went down after the introduction of their current electoral systems. What *would* follow from the introduction of proportional representation in the United Kingdom would be the routine election of a hung House of Commons.

It is, perhaps, unnecessary to dilate on the implications for the British constitution of the demise of single-party majority Government, because detailed consideration has already been given to them.[30] Many settled constitutional and political practices would have to be reassessed and changed. Party manifestos would become no more than invitations to treat, formally published to the voters but in fact issued to the other parties for negotiation after the electoral verdict had been given. The formation of a minority or a coalition Government, and the question of granting dissolutions of Parliament, would be matters which could not be entirely settled without a reconsideration of conventions involving the Queen.[31] Party discipline in the Commons would become much more lax: Governments would have to inform and persuade Members in more than one party, rather than just relying on the Whips to deliver votes. The doctrine of ministerial responsibility would have to be modified to accommodate coalition Government. None of this represents an insuperable bar to proportional representation, but they are matters which would require very careful examination before any change was put into effect. How unattractive, however, all of this would be to the two main parties when set against the present certainties of elective dictatorship!

And so the tents are pitched in two entrenched camps. In one rest the immovable supporters of the electoral status quo, while in the other gather the hardy fighters for proportional representation. Proportional representation would only come about if the Labour Government's promised national referendum were to endorse

---

[29] Despite that, in 1993 Italy adopted the first-past-the-post system to fill three-quarters of each parliamentary chamber, leaving the remainder to be returned by the former proportional representation system. Full PR was, however, restored as from the 2006 elections, at which most parties campaigned as part of one or other of two umbrella groups, one of which achieved an overall majority in both Houses.

[30] See, e.g. V. Bogdanor, *Multi-Party Politics and the Constitution* (Cambridge: Cambridge University Press, 1983); R. Brazier, *Constitutional Practice* (Oxford: Oxford University Press, 3rd edn., 1999), Ch. 3; Oliver (note 2 above) 143–46.

[31] See Ch. 7.

a new voting system, or if the Conservative Party underwent a truly remarkable change of heart (involving the throwing away of the regular dose of unrestricted power which the present voting system brings), or if there were an electoral upset in which a small party obtained sufficient Members so as somehow to squeeze voting reform out of one of the larger parties as the price of vital parliamentary support. It is, of course, possible that the British electorate would opt for radical change at a referendum on the voting system—although in part that would depend on the alternative system which was on offer. But is there no option other than either staying where we are or changing to proportional representation? Might there not be a middle way down which the two sides might grudgingly travel? An answer to that question requires an examination of the second ballot, the alternative vote, and the system recommended by the Jenkins Commission in 1998, the alternative vote-top-up system.[32]

The second-ballot system is a very straightforward method of election which is used in France.[33] Voters cast their ballots in single-member constituencies, thus preserving the representative's local links. Any candidate who receives at least half the votes cast in his or her constituency is elected. If, however, no candidate has such absolute majority support there is a second ballot a week later, which is a run-off between the two candidates who came top of the original poll, together with any other candidate who obtained at least 12½ per cent of the votes in it. Often only the top two candidates qualify for the second ballot, in which case the subsequent winner is bound to receive an absolute majority of those voting in the constituency. The second-ballot system avoids the complicated redistributions which are a feature of any proportional representation method of election. It normally produces one-party Government. The second-ballot method is unattractive to proportional representationalists because it maintains the balance in favour of the Government-choosing function over the representative function. But if the second ballot were introduced for elections to the House of Commons, the days of MPs returned by only a minority of those who voted in their constituencies would usually be over, and there would be political upsets in numerous constituencies: no longer would a candidate who might, under the present voting system, expect only 40 per cent of the vote necessarily take the seat. For example, the Conservative candidate might poll 40 per cent of the votes, the Labour candidate 35 per cent, the Liberal Democrat 10 per cent, and other candidates 15 per cent. Today, the Conservative would win outright—even though 60 per cent of the voters preferred someone else. Under the second-ballot system, the Conservative and Labour candidates would fight it out in the run-off. Voters who had supported the Liberal Democrat might vote Conservative or Labour in the second round, and the seat could go either way. Those electors whose candidate did not survive the first ballot would be able to

---

[32] See note 2 above.
[33] It is used to elect the President of the Republic and the National Assembly.

vote again with all the other voters in the second ballot, and in that sense every-one's vote would count. The delay of a week between voting would allow the parties in each constituency where a Member had not been returned in the first round to consider how to recommend their supporters to vote in the second round. Majority Governments would at last often be worthy of that name: their legitimacy would be unquestionable, because it would be based on both a majority of seats in the House of Commons *and* on Members having the support of an absolute majority of voters in most constituencies.[34]

Objectors to the second ballot criticize the need for voters to return to the polls seven days after they have done their civic duty. Such an onerous consequence can be avoided (although the possible political benefits which may accrue in the hiatus will be lost) by opting for the alternative vote. This method, which is used for elec-tions to the Australian House of Representatives, has actually received the approval in principle of the House of Commons in 1918 and in 1931 for its own elections. And a variant of it, the supplementary vote, is used to elect the Mayor of London.[35] The alternative vote avoids the need for a physically separate second ballot by allow-ing voters to express their successive choices in one voting operation. The aim is to elect representatives by absolute majorities. Voters are asked to say which candi-date, again in single-member constituencies, they would support if their first choice did not receive an absolute majority. To do so, they number the candidates on the ballot-paper in order of preference. A candidate who gets at least 50 per cent of the first preference votes is elected. If none does so, the candidates with the least votes are eliminated in turn, and their second preference votes are redistributed, until one candidate has an absolute majority. While this does nothing to bring about national proportionality between votes cast and seats won, it has all the consider-able advantages of the second-ballot method without the inconvenient second visit to the polling-stations, although clearly the redistribution process (which is still much simpler than most proportional methods) would need careful explanation for voters.

The Labour Party in opposition promised an independent review of voting sys-tems, followed by a national referendum. The Independent Commission on the Voting System, chaired by Lord Jenkins, was established by the Labour Government after the 1997 election. Its terms of reference obliged it to recommend a system (or combination of systems) that satisfied four criteria. The system should be broadly proportional, deliver stable Government, extend voter choice, and keep the link between MPs and their constituencies. The Commission reported the follow-ing year.[36] It carefully considered the various voting systems on offer and, while acknowledging that the four criteria were not entirely compatible, recommended a

---

[34] For criticism of the alternative-vote and of the second-ballot systems, see E. Lakeman, *How Democracies Vote* (London: Faber, 3rd edn., 1970), 59–68.

[35] Greater London Authority Act 1999, s. 4 and Sched. 2.

[36] Cm. 4090 (1998). The Conservative member dissented from the main recommendation.

hybrid model which it dubbed the Alternative Vote-Top Up system (or AV Plus as it was to become known).[37] Under it each voter would have two votes. One would be cast by the alternative vote in a single-member constituency (of which there would be about 500). The other would be cast by the regional list system (which would return a further 150 MPs in larger, regional constituencies). The Commission thought that this model would have all of the advantages of the alternative vote and none of its drawbacks, while retaining the decisiveness of British general elections. The Commission asserted that if its system had been used at the general elections of 1979 to 1997 inclusive, only the 1992 poll (which had actually produced a Conservative majority of 25 seats) would have led to a hung Parliament.[38]

After the report was published the Government went rather cool over the whole idea of voting reform. At the 2001 general election Labour merely promised to review the Jenkins plan in the light of the experience of the new voting systems used for the Scottish Parliament and the Welsh and Northern Ireland Assemblies. It acknowledged that any proposed national change could only be validated by a referendum, but there was no commitment over when such a poll might be held.[39] The 2005 election manifesto took a similar view, but was even cooler in tone.[40] Members of the Government emphasized the complicated nature of the Jenkins top-up element. The Liberal Democrats were prepared to support AV Plus as a first stage towards a pure system of proportional representation. In his first statement to the House of Commons as Prime Minister, which he devoted to constitutional reform, Mr Gordon Brown promised that the Government's review of the voting systems used in the United Kingdom apart from those for the Westminster Parliament would be completed and published by the end of 2007.[41] In my view a major drawback with AV Plus would be the very complicated redistribution system at the heart of the PR element—a complication with which Mr Jack Straw as Home Secretary had some fun during a Commons debate on voting reform.

If the pressure for electoral reform became irresistible, the second ballot or the alternative vote or AV Plus might provide models which one of the two main political parties might support as a reasonable compromise, moving away from the first-past-the-post but falling well short of proportional representation. They might, at least, provide more defensible redoubts than does the current voting system. Radical reformers will reject those models and will continue to insist on the purity of proportional representation. But they need to show greater electoral realism: they are

[37] See Ch. 7 of the Jenkins Report.

[38] Critics asserted, however, that under AV Plus many of the elections between 1945 and 1974 would have produced hung Parliaments.

[39] *Ambitions for Britain* (London: Labour Party, 2001).

[40] *Labour: The Future for Britain* (London: Labour Party, 2005).

[41] See the Green Paper, *The Governance of Britain*, Cm. 7170, paras 155–6 (the context of that document is given in Ch. 3. There is also to be consideration of whether the voting age should be reduced: *The Governance of Britain*, para. 190), a policy to which the Liberal Democrats are already committed: see *For the People, By the People* (London: Liberal Democrat Policy Paper No. 83, 2007), para. 3.3.2.

not going to get proportional representation overnight from either of the main parties, and it might be better for them, as an interim measure in their terms, to support the second ballot or the alternative vote or AV Plus if either the Conservative or Labour Parties did so as well. Simple, decisive, producing stable parliamentary politics, providing governmental legitimacy, and fairer than the present method— these are qualities of the second ballot and the alternative vote and, to an extent, AV Plus which, in my view, deserve very close assessment. Those who resist change to the voting system for the Westminster Parliament have to acknowledge that PR is now used all around the United Kingdom for other elections. Regional party lists are used throughout Great Britain for elections to the European Parliament; STV is well-known in Northern Ireland; the additional member system is used in Scotland, Wales, and for the London Assembly, and the supplementary list is used to elect the Mayor of London. That perhaps throws the burden of proof on to supporters of first-past-the-post to argue why there should not be change to the method of electing MPs.

Whether, and if so how, to reform the British voting system would be questions for which a Constitutional Commission would be tailor-made.[42] It could take matters forward since the publication of the Jenkins Report in 1998. In such a gathering—which would include representatives of the political parties—quiet, calm deliberation, while perhaps not disentangling every knot, would at least bring the independent and the committed together. Research, evaluation, public consultation, and debate should all contribute to synthesis. Many issues would need to be addressed by the Commission. What theory (or theories) of representation are appropriate for the British House of Commons? What is the British electoral system designed to achieve? What are the practical advantages of the first-past-the-post system, and of proportional representation systems? What are the drawbacks in those methods, and to what extent might a different model overcome them—without introducing others? How satisfactory is the power of party over the selection of parliamentary candidates and over Members of Parliament? What value might there be, in an attempt to offset the influence of party, in the refreshing breeze of democratic primary elections, reselections, and recall, all governed by law? All that would amount to a wider-ranging inquiry than the Jenkins Commission was permitted or able to conduct.

The political parties will not be distressed that I have offered answers to such questions, but they might object that such matters are not the concern of any independent grouping such as a Constitutional Commission. Politicians, after all, are the experts who have to work British democracy; they have an intimate and unrivalled knowledge of its workings and they have to persuade voters to support them. The voting system and connected issues are, in a blunt politician's terms, no one else's business. It is, however, that very interest which politicians have which

---

[42] See Ch. 2.

makes it essential that informed and independent opinion should contribute to the development of parliamentary democracy. To take an analogy, independent machinery exists simply because the delimitation of parliamentary constituencies cannot be left entirely to the parties in Parliament (and certainly not the House of Commons alone), because they have a direct and vital interest in the result. It is not suggested for a moment that a Constitutional Commission should *decide* the rules of British parliamentary democracy, but it is proposed that the formulation of those rules should no longer be left entirely within the walls of Westminster. Such a proposition does not seem preposterous. Indeed, the Labour Party has accepted that politicians should not make a decision on their own about the future of the voting system, but that at some stage the people should speak on the issue at a referendum.

In the meantime piecemeal, but second-order, changes are periodically made. So for example the minimum age at which a person can stand for election as an MP is now 18, rather than 21.[43] And the independent Electoral Commission has done very useful work, including some on the nuts and bolts of electoral law.[44] It has recommended that the arguments for lowering the voting age from 18 should be seriously considered.[45]

[43] Electoral Administration Act 2006, s. 18.

[44] See, e.g. Electoral Commission, *Voting for Change: An Electoral Law Modernisation Programme* (London: Electoral Commission, 2003).

[45] Electoral Commission, *Age of Electoral Majority* (London: Electoral Commission, 2004).

5

The second-chamber paradox

A glance backwards

Rarely have Government plans for constitutional reform been formed in the agreeable setting of a golf course. But it was on Rye golf-links that the two-writ scheme was put to the Leader of the House of Lords in Mr Harold Wilson's Cabinet, Lord Longford, and where he became convinced of its efficacy.[1] The Cabinet, too, was subsequently taken by it, and in 1968 the Labour Government proposed that there should be two categories of peers, one made up of nominated life peers who could speak and vote, the other (mainly hereditary peers) having only the right to speak and having no right to pass membership on to their successors.[2] Despite such pleasant beginnings and the later gathering of all-party support for the scheme, all crowned by the approval of the House of Lords itself, the Bill to implement this major reform failed to pass the House of Commons.

House of Lords reform has proved immensely difficult for all Governments who have grappled with it. There has been no shortage of official analyses of the strengths and shortcomings of the upper House, or of attempts to improve it. The preamble to the Parliament Act 1911 set the scene for the replacement of the House by an elected chamber, but as the preamble lamented, 'such substitution cannot be immediately brought into operation'. That bare statement of intent was clothed with a detailed plan by the Bryce Committee after the First World War.[3] After the Second World War, a number of reform matters were settled in principle between the leaders of the political parties.[4] Twenty years later still, the comprehensive reform plan which had gained ground on the golf-links was placed before the House of Commons in the Parliament (No. 2) Bill, only to have backbenchers from both sides ensure its ignominious withdrawal.[5] Subsequently the political parties went their separate ways.

---

[1] See Lord Longford's revelations at 518 HL Debs. 606 (25 Apr. 1990). On Lords reform generally see D. Oliver, *Constitutional Reform in the UK* (Oxford: Oxford University Press, 2003), Ch. 10.

[2] In *House of Lords Reform*, Cmnd. 3799 (1968).

[3] *Report of the Conference on the Reform of the Second Chamber*, Cd. 9038 (1918).

[4] *Agreed Statement on the Conclusion of the Conference on the Parliament Bill 1947*, Cmd. 7380 (1948).

[5] For the text of that Bill see R. Brazier, *Constitutional Texts* (Oxford: Clarendon Press, 1990), 529–40.

The Conservatives decided that doing nothing was the best policy, the party leadership declining to adopt the scheme put forward by Lord Home and a Conservative Party committee in 1978 for a partly nominated and partly elected second chamber.[6] The Liberal Democrats, true to their radical traditions—exemplified in the preamble to Asquith's Parliament Act—wished to see a second chamber elected by proportional representation and possessing major legislative powers.[7] By the late 1970s the Labour Party had abandoned the two-writ scheme and had plumped for complete abolition of the House of Lords, a flirtation with unicameralism which was in its turn ditched in 1989. In that year the party opted to introduce an elected second chamber with limited legislative authority.[8] By the time of its 1997 general election victory the new Labour Government intended to reform the House of Lords in two stages.[9] In the first, the hereditary peers would be removed from membership, if necessary by relying on the Parliament Acts to overcome any intransigence from Conservative and other peers. That would leave an interim House made up of life peers. No one political party would have a majority in that interim chamber, and fresh creations of life peers would be recommended over a period of years so that the House would more accurately reflect the votes cast for the various parties at the 1997 general election. That situation was achieved under the House of Lords Act 1999, although 92 hereditary peers remained, as will be explained later. Then a joint committee of both Houses would set to work on the second stage of reform, to devise a scheme for a democratically elected second chamber. The Labour Government had clear electoral authority for that process, resulting from its manifesto pledge and its landslide general election victory in 1997. From the Labour Party's point of view a two-stage process made eminent political sense. But methodologically this was, in my opinion, a very bad way to go about constitutional reform. Voters were asked in 1997 to approve embarkation on a constitutional voyage to an unknown destination, throwing overboard in the early stages people (the hereditary peers) who, or some of whom, might—who knows?—have had a role if and when the final destination was reached.

But let us leave the 1997 Labour Government's work on Lords reform to one side for a moment. Over the years before 1997 paper plans were supplemented by legislative action over the composition and powers of the House of Lords—not, indeed, of a comprehensive or radical kind, but piecemeal and useful nonetheless. So the House of Commons was made pre-eminent in legislation, and omnipotent over

---

[6] For the Conservatives' case during the last quarter of the twentieth century see the then Leader of the House of Lords, Viscount Cranborne, at 573 HL Debs. 1581–89 (4 July 1996).

[7] See *Here We Stand: Proposals for Modernizing Britain's Democracy* (London: Liberal Democrats, 1993); see now *For the People, By the People* (London: Liberal Democrat Policy Paper No. 83, 2007), paras 5.2, 5.4.

[8] See Ch. 3.

[9] See Labour's manifesto *New Labour: Because Britain Deserves Better* (London: Labour Party, 1997).

money, by the Parliament Act 1911. After the invention of life peerages in 1958, the House of Lords gradually changed from being a thinly attended and rather sleepy place into a chamber with an average daily attendance of some 300 members which gets through a substantial amount of work. That transformation was enhanced by the introduction of attendance, travel, and office allowances and expenses. Peeresses in their own right and Scottish peers were made full members as recently as 1963, in the same year in which it became possible for hereditary peers to disclaim their peerages for life.[10] None of that has, however, touched the central anachronism that one House of Parliament had a large majority of members who were there only because they were the children of their parents, or who could claim some other line of descent in the hereditary peerage. And even the influx of life peers, untainted by the notion of heredity, has left the House of Lords unelected, unrepresentative, and unaccountable. Why, in a century in which democracy has burgeoned and flourished around the whole world, did the seemingly indefensible survive?

Those who have grappled with the problem of Lords reform might sympathize with Trollope's Plantagenet Palliser. He brought to politics, as seen through the Palliser novels, a burning passion to decimalize the Victorian currency. He failed. As Trollope put it, 'When in power, he had not succeeded in carrying his measure, awed, and at last beaten, by the infinite difficulty in arranging its details.'[11] Lords reform has, to the time of writing, beaten both Liberal and Labour Ministers, partly because of the complexities of arranging its details, but perhaps mainly because of a number of peculiarities and paradoxes which beset the upper House. Thus the hereditary composition of the House of Lords was stated to be temporary in the Parliament Act 1911, but it remained until the House of Lords Act 1999 was passed—and even then a rump of 92 hereditaries, as will be seen, were reprieved. The United Kingdom has exported to the nations of the Commonwealth large numbers of second chambers based on election, but she has been unable to create one for herself. Everyone (apart from unicameralists) believes that the House of Lords rightly has the power to delay Commons Bills in appropriate circumstances so that (for example) public opinion may be sounded on them; in effect, reliance is placed on an unelected and unrepresentative House to frustrate the wishes of the very chamber which is elected in order to represent public opinion. The Government majority in the House of Commons damns peers when they delay Commons Bills, but no House of Commons has been able to agree on how to replace such peers with elected representatives. Oppositions want the House of Lords to act against legislation passed at the request of an elective dictatorship, but do not want peers to interfere with *their* legislation when *they* are in office. Many Members of Parliament would like to see a reformed second chamber, provided that it did not exercise its new powers as a rival to the House of Commons; but a newly created second chamber

---

[10] See Life Peerages Act 1958, Peerage Act 1963.
[11] A. Trollope, *Phineas Redux* (London: 1874), Ch. 1.

would fairly assume that it had been given powers in order to use them from time to time, especially if it contained a significant elected element. A reconstituted second chamber could not be elected by the same method and at the same time as the House of Commons, because it would then be a pointless duplicate of that House; but if it were elected by a different method and at different times that could result in a chamber with a political make-up different from that of the Commons, thus making conflict between the two Houses inevitable. If the second chamber were to be elected by proportional representation, the objection that is currently made that the House of Lords has no political legitimacy would disappear; but if it *were* so elected the new House would have *greater* political authority and be more representative than the Commons which is merely elected by the first-past-the-post method. In view of all that, if Plantagenet Palliser had been given the option by his creator of either grappling with such peculiar traits and paradoxes or of trying to decimalize the currency, might he not still have elected to pit his wits against pounds, shillings, and pence?

Bicameralism, criticisms, and schemes

Most liberal democracies have legislatures consisting of two chambers.[12] Those that do not usually have small populations, such as Denmark, Sweden, or New Zealand. Even states which have been forced to embark on radical constitutional rearrangements, like Germany after the Second World War (and, indeed, in 1990), or France in 1958, have generally retained a second chamber. Perhaps that trend is explained as much by the forces of inertia and tradition as by any need to provide a legislative check on the lower chamber. Again, most second chambers are elected in one way or another, but in a minority of states some members are appointed by the Government and a few are entirely composed in that manner, the Canadian Senate being an example of the latter. The United Kingdom goes with the trend in being a bicameralist state; and the House of Lords on an average day, made up of a majority of peers who have been nominated to be there, is not a unique place in the parliaments of the world. What, of course, made it unique until 1999 was its potential majority of hereditary members who could turn up to alter the course of its proceedings. The question which should be addressed is not whether the House of Lords is unusual among world legislatures, but whether it is an effective and appropriate part of the parliament of a democratic country in the twenty-first century.

---

[12] M. Russell, *Reforming the House of Lords: Lessons from Overseas* (Oxford: Oxford University Press, 2000); D. Shell, *The House of Lords* (Hemel Hempstead: Philip Allan, 1988), 1–9. And for first-rate general analysis of the issues involved in changing the second chamber see Constitution Unit, *Reform of the House of Lords* (London, 1996).

It is possible to state the functions of the House of Lords with some precision, largely as a result of the deliberations of the several inquiries which have investigated it. The 1968 White Paper, for example, listed seven functions.[13] Undoubtedly the most important work of the Lords has for many years been its consideration and revision of public Bills sent up from the Commons. That work accounts for at least half of peers' time each session, and on average about 1,500 amendments are made by them every year. This is work well done, in that the vast majority of Lords amendments are accepted by the Government and the House of Commons—unsurprisingly, as most of them are proposed by Ministers in the Lords.[14] The legislative work of the House is complemented by the introduction there each session of about a dozen, usually uncontroversial, Government Bills. (The Constitutional Reform Act 2005 *was* controversial, but its parliamentary progress started in the House of Lords.) This reduces the pressure on the Commons, and gives work to peers while they wait for the first Commons Bills of the session to be sent up. The Government faces scrutiny through questions from peers, and through Lords select committees, of which those on the European Union and on science and technology are generally acknowledged to be outstanding successes. It is often claimed that the quality of debate in the House of Lords is higher than that in the Commons, a claim which in its nature cannot be proved. Debates are certainly of a *different* quality—much less party-political, joined by experts from many walks of life, not in general constrained by worries about whether a particular speech or point might upset the Whips, or might help or hinder the speaker's hopes for ministerial office. All this scarcely represents a picture of an otiose second chamber, but rather describes one which contributes usefully to the shape of legislation and to discussions of the issues of the day.

But critics of the House of Lords will no doubt come back to the central question of how appropriate it is in a democracy to have a chamber which is dominated by appointed life peers, supplemented by 92 hereditaries. It is worth pointing out that the pre-1999 objection had been to a chamber which was in the control of hereditary and mainly Conservative peers. But that earlier objection was occasionally exaggerated. Sixty years ago, the party composition of the House of Lords gave the Conservatives some 400 adherents, the Liberals eighty, and Labour a mere fifteen.[15] By 1997 and the onset of the Labour Government, that party mix had become very different. Leaving out of account those peers who had leave of absence and those

---

[13] Cmnd. 3799 (1968). They were: (*a*) to be the supreme court of appeal; (*b*) to provide a forum for debates; (*c*) to revise public Bills passed by the Commons; (*d*) to initiate less controversial public legislation; (*e*) to consider subordinate legislation; (*f*) to scrutinize the activities of the executive; (*g*) to consider private legislation.

[14] The 1988–9 session was unusual in that the House of Lords made 2,401 amendments to Bills, all but a handful of which were acceptable to the Commons: Lord Belstead, Leader of the House of Lords, at 518 HL Debs. 634 (25 Apr. 1990).

[15] See Shell, *The House of Lords*, 13.

who had no writ of attendance, the Conservatives could still claim some 480 supporters, while Labour had 126, and the Liberal Democrats 55. But another crucial difference from half a century ago was that there were over 300 cross-benchers, who on paper at any rate held the balance of power in the House between any likely Government and any likely Opposition. Of course, nothing like the maximum possible complement of some 1,100 peers, or anything like the maximum total of 780 hereditary peers, ever presented themselves. The average daily attendance was about 300, in which life peers and hereditary peers of first creation usually had a small majority over hereditary peers. In that working House the Conservatives were able to count on a small majority.[16] This transformation from a House overwhelmed by hereditary Conservatives was achieved by the inspired invention and conferment of life peerages.

Thus the House of Lords was not daily dominated by hereditary and, in the main, Conservative peers. But what of the backwoodsmen, caricatured as living deep in the shires, Conservative to a man, and ever ready to answer the summons from the Conservative Chief Whip to sweep to Westminster to save the nation—or at least to save the Conservative Party? The old, and largely accurate, jibe was that the House of Lords snoozed while a Conservative was in Downing Street, but sprang to life to thwart policies of Liberal, and later of Labour, Prime Ministers. But since the advent of Mr Edward Heath's Government the House of Lords has interfered with Conservative measures, too. It did so most spectacularly over the Bill to cancel Greater London Council elections in 1984 (the unelected House thwarting the elected chamber for acting undemocratically—another paradox), and over the War Crimes Bill in 1990. Although bare statistics about legislative defeats show nothing of their nature or importance, who would have even dreamt in 1979 that by 1989 Mrs Thatcher's Bills would have been amended against her wishes in the House of Lords on 125 occasions?[17] (The Conservative Government suffered its two-hundredth legislative defeat in 1992.) Labour Governments have endured numerically more setbacks, it is true. For example, from 1999 to 2005 the Labour Government was defeated 300 times on legislation in the House of Lords. But at least a degree of greater even-handedness with respect to both parties seems to have come about. The House of Lords can claim with some justice that it has forced Governments of both colours to think again over some of their legislation, in a proper exercise of the powers enshrined in the Parliament Acts.

And so, at present, we have an 'interim' second chamber made up of more than 600 nominated life peers, the 92 hereditaries, 26 Lords Spiritual, and the 12 Lords of Appeal in Ordinary.[18] What are the main benefits which are conferred on the constitution by this interim House of Lords? I will pick out two. One is the presence

---

[16] See the Conservative Government's figures at 451 HL Debs. 149 (26 Apr. 1984).

[17] Lord Belstead at 146 HL Debs. 534 (6 Nov. 1989).

[18] They will leave the House in 2009 to form the new Supreme Court: see Ch. 10.

of life peers. People outside the practice of politics, especially men and women rising in their careers, can be inducted into Parliament without having to become professional politicians or to embrace the burdens of elections and constituents. People earning their living, or living and working away from London, are not going to be attracted to Parliament if they have to commit themselves to being there regularly, and the paraphernalia of elections and the demands of constituents would scarcely be an added incentive. The expertise which they possess would not, by and large, be available in Parliament if the second chamber were based on any elective principle, because the political parties, quite naturally, would want to get as many of their own candidates elected as possible. By and large such people would be professional politicians rather than part-time members who could bring to the House experience of their outside lives. The other benefit is the unpredictability of the House of Lords in the matter of legislation. In its tendency to treat the legislation of both parties with something approaching an impartial rigour, the House of Lords has become the only counterweight in the British constitution to elective dictatorship.[19] That situation was reinforced by the removal of most of the hereditaries in 1999, because since that event no one party has had an overall majority in the House of Lords. While the Government can, in general, rely on the Commons to do as it is told, Ministers have no such felicity in relation to the Lords (although it is right that the elected House should normally get its way in the end). It could be very different if the second chamber were elected. Presumably if one party then held sway in both Houses, Ministers could sleep soundly at night in the knowledge that their Bills were sure of safe passages through Parliament; but when different parties dominated each House, disagreements between the two chambers would inevitably delay the Government's legislative programme.

Yet in two major respects the authority of the interim House of Lords is weakened. It is anomalous and unrepresentative. No modern state seeking to create a new legislature would devise anything as odd as a House most of whose members sat on the basis of the unrestricted patronage of the head of Government. Being an unelected House, it is not designed to be representative, but it is not even loosely representative of society. The House of Lords is dominated by well-off, well-educated men: it is not a cross-section of society, in the sort of way that we like to think that juries are. The greatest source of new personnel is the House of Commons, former Members being translated there as life peers for a kind of semi-retirement. The principle of having life peers is defensible: the way in which they are chosen is not. The non-statutory House of Lords Appointments Commission, it is true, has tried since its creation in 2000 to find non-party people to put forward to No. 10 for life peerages. The Commission vets all nominees for peerages for propriety, a task which the 2006 'cash for peerages' allegations shows is performed well, given that

---

[19] The bringing into domestic law of the European Convention on Human Rights may add an additional counterweight: see Ch. 9.

the Commission raised objections to certain nominees and thus sparked a police investigation. But the Commission has no role in choosing potential political life peers. (For the record, during his ten-year premiership Mr Blair recommended the creation of over 350 peers.)

So what is to be done about the House of Lords? Since the Labour Party abandoned a policy of abolition in 1989, we are all bicameralists. Abolition of the second chamber would not be a sensible way forward. Without a second chamber, elective dictatorship would be unfettered. Legislation, moreover, would become even worse than it is now: even at its present rate of overworking, the House of Commons manages to pass badly written legislation, tracts of which are immunized against debate and amendment by the guillotine (now prosaically called business motions).

The Conservative Party opposed radical reform of the Lords throughout the twentieth century. It opposed the Labour Government's two-stage reform. But in recent years it has sought to outflank Labour by arguing that the second chamber should be overwhelmingly elected. To change from defending the hereditary principle to the last moment, and then to espouse democratic election for most of the hereditaries' former chamber, must constitute one of the biggest shifts in constitutional policy ever seen in a major political party.

Without doubt the most radical scheme for reform emanates from the Liberal Democrats. There should, in their view, be a new Senate, which would consist of about 100 members, all of whom would be directly elected (naturally enough) by proportional representation. Scotland, Wales, Northern Ireland, and each of the English regions would return specified numbers of Senators, each of whom would serve for four years and with one-third retiring every two years. Commons Ministers would attend and participate as appropriate but without votes in Senate proceedings. Its powers would be broadly the same as the present House of Lords.[20]

That plan would establish a House of Parliament with the political legitimacy which popular election brings. The new chamber would be fully representative of the electorate—indeed, it would be more representative than the House of Commons itself. Because it would be elected by PR, it would most likely be a permanently hung chamber. Those would all be notable gains. But the scheme would have certain disadvantages. First, the pool of talented people prepared to make part-time contributions to Parliament as nominated peers would, without doubt, be largely lost, because most such amateurs would have no inclination to turn professional. Secondly, conflict between the House of Commons and the Liberal Democrats' Senate would be unavoidable, at least when the Government did not have a majority in it. And lastly the new second chamber would be overwhelmingly party-political, for how many independent members would be elected?

---

[20] See *Here We Stand* (note 7 above); 'Constitutional Reform' (London: Liberal Democrat Policy Briefing No. 22, 2005) *For the People, By the People*, para. 3.1.5.

As a first step towards the creation of such a redoubtable chamber the Liberal Democrats accepted, through the Labour–Liberal Democrat Joint Consultative Committee on Constitutional Reform,[21] Labour's two-stage plan for change. So what should we make of the Labour Government's desires to alter the House of Lords? The House of Lords Act 1999 was passed with little real difficulty, aided by the so-called Weatherill amendment which exempted 92 hereditaries from the legislative axe.[22] The Government had already established a Royal Commission on Reform of the House of Lords. It reported in 2000.[23] It recommended a mixed chamber of largely nominated and some elected members, although existing life peers would serve their terms. The nominated members would serve for fifteen-year terms and be found by a statutory, independent Appointments Commission. The Royal Commission gave three models for the elected membership, of which the largest proportion suggested would have been 35 per cent. The powers of the new chamber would be much the same as the House of Lords. Having accepted the broad outline of the Report the Government proposed that only 20 per cent of the new House should be elected,[24] and that the Appointments Commission should only look for independent, not political nominees. It became clear that Labour MPs would not support such a plan, which was at variance with the party's election promise to construct a more democratic and representative chamber. And so the Government set up a Joint Select Committee on House of Lords Reform, which reported in 2003.[25] It proposed among other things a range of options for the proportion of elected members. All of those options were voted down on a free vote in the Commons, while the House of Lords voted for a wholly-nominated chamber. In view of this shambles the Government waited until 2005 when the then Leader of the House of Commons, Mr Jack Straw, conducted private all-party talks to try to reach a consensus on membership. The Government also convened another Joint Select Committee to examine whether the conventional arrangements between the two chambers should be codified (a possibility to which it gave qualified support[26]).

The all-party talks led to a further White Paper in 2007.[27] It did not constitute a statement agreed by the parties. The Government expressed its preference for a half-elected, half-nominated chamber, whereas the Conservatives and the Liberal Democrats wanted a predominantly elected House. All parties agreed, however, that the Commons must remain the principal legislative chamber, with the second chamber complementing it: no significant changes were suggested over powers. All

[21] See Ch. 3.

[22] 1999 Act, s. 2.

[23] *Report of the Royal Commission on Reform of the House of Lords*, Cm. 4534 (2000). The Government had set the scene for the Commission's work in *Modernising Parliament: Reforming the House of Lords*, Cm. 4183 (1999).

[24] *The House of Lords: Completing the Reform*, Cm. 5291 (2001).

[25] *First Report*, HC 17 (2002–2003).

[26] Joint Committee on Conventions, *Conventions of the UK Parliament*, HL 265 (2005–2006).

[27] *The House of Lords: Reform*, Cm. 7027 (2007).

the parties agreed that no one party should have a majority in the second chamber, and that some independent members should have places in it: the Government wished at least 20 per cent of the total membership reserved for such people, with a further 30 per cent being party-political appointments. The Government suggested the party-list system to return the elected members, elections being held every five years at the same time as European Parliament elections. One-third of the elected membership would be elected at each election for a single, non-renewable, 15-year term. The nominated members would be chosen by an independent, statutory Appointments Commission: the Prime Minister's patronage would cease completely. The total membership would be 540 members—eventually: for the White Paper proposed that the life peers should remain until their death, or resignation, and elections would start in 2014 (with the following tranche in 2019, and the final third being elected in 2024, and so on). The remaining hereditaries would be removed; retired Justices of the new Supreme Court would be considered by the Appointments Commission for possible appointment. The bishops would remain, but reduced in number.

In early 2007 MPs, on a free vote, voted by a majority of 38 to support an 80 per cent elected House, and also by a majority of 113 in favour of a wholly-elected House. But within that large majority were MPs who opposed reform, and who hoped to goad peers into rejecting the plan. A week later the House of Lords in a free vote decisively supported an entirely appointed second chamber.

The Government committed itself in *The Governance of Britain* to holding further cross-party talks to work towards a comprehensive Bill on Lords reform.[28] The Government intends to commit itself in its next general election manifesto to introduce such a Bill, hoping that there will be much common ground by then between the political parties.[29]

The whole history of attempted reform of the Lords, however, presents troubling auguries: an elected second chamber will be difficult to achieve. In my view moderate change to the House of Lords is preferable to radical reform. After all, the importance of the second chamber must not be exaggerated. It is much the less powerful and the less significant House. The House of Commons is rightly pre-eminent and is the (admittedly somewhat worn) cradle of British democracy, which needs and deserves all the urgent reformist energy that can be mustered. The fair complaint that the House of Lords caused trouble only for non-Conservative Governments has been corrected to an extent. Several of the unacceptable incidents of the unreformed House have gradually been removed, such as its co-equal status with the Commons over legislation, its wholly hereditary basis, and its wholly male membership. Attempting to bring about radical change to the House of Lords may simply not be worth a Government's parliamentary time and any trouble involved

---

[28] Cm. 7170 (2007), paras 129–38.
[29] Mr Jack Straw at 463 HC Debs. *449* (19 July 2007).

in securing it against the objections of the Opposition; moreover, even if cross-party front-bench agreement were to be achieved, the events of 1968–9 show that such agreement may promise everything yet still deliver nothing. Rather, what should be done, I believe, is to continue in the gradualist tradition of limited and pragmatic reforms, ideally pursued through a Constitutional Commission and with multi-party support.

A notion of reduction

It is to the composition of the second chamber that gradualists should turn their minds especially if the Labour Government's latest proposals come to naught. Assuming that elections do not reach the House of Lords (as I suspect they will not), the ways in which people are nominated for life peerages are of central importance. As already noted the non-statutory House of Lords Appointments Commission seeks new cross-bench peers and vets nominations of all new peers for propriety before their names are recommended by the Prime Minister to the Queen. But lists of working party-political peers are compiled by the Prime Minister, having considered suggestions from his or her own party and from other political leaders. The procedures leading up to the publication of lists of working peers hold the key. At present these procedures are informal and based on barter between the parties: the leaders of the opposition parties try to get as many of their supporters as possible accepted for nomination as life peers, while the Prime Minister has ensured that people who will take the Government whip are in the majority in each list. It would be desirable if these discreet procedures could be made rather more formal, and if they could be based on a number of precepts. Thus the party leaders should acknowledge that all the parties represented in the Commons have a legitimate expectation of representation in the House of Lords (subject to some minimum number of Members of Parliament and votes obtained at the previous general election to qualify). They should accept that the active party strengths in the House of Lords, together with votes and seats won at the previous general election, should be taken into account in drawing up lists of working peers. A rough-and-ready formula for replenishing the Lords, with those aims in mind, would be preferable to a descent into tit-for-tat exercises of patronage. Part of a new compact between the leaders ought to be a concerted attempt to find more women, younger people, and members of ethnic minorities for nomination as life peers, together (if possible) with a strategy to ensure that all the nations and regions of the United Kingdom have active representation in the second chamber. There could be a role here for a revamped Appointments Commission. Voluntary groups and others could put in suggestions, and of course individuals could nominate themselves. Perhaps the party leaders might also agree that certain people should go to the House of Lords by virtue of their offices, such as the Governor of the Bank of England, the general secretary of the Trades Union Congress, and so on. It should not prove controversial to reduce the number of Bishops in the House—for it was agreed in 1968 to cut their presence from twenty-six to sixteen (still a remarkably generous number)—or to try to get leaders of other faiths into the Lords, perhaps ex officio.

What these more formalized procedures should aim at, in a word, is reductions— reductions in the gender and ethnic imbalance in the second chamber, reductions in the average age of life peers, and reductions in the over-representation of the Church of England. This notion of reduction is, in any event, being implemented with the removal of the Lords of Appeal in Ordinary. It is wrong in principle that judges are able to intervene in the process of legislation. Some legal expertise, which is of particular relevance to the form of legislation, would be lost by their going, but then as it has been estimated that 10 per cent of the House of Lords are qualified lawyers,[30] the loss of the Lords of Appeal will be of rather less significance than some might suppose.

A notion of reduction as a principle to guide changes in the House of Lords ought to apply so as to cut the number of peers entitled to attend its proceedings. Measures must be taken against those who are not seen at Westminster for months or even years on end. It is indefensible that a peer who is not able or prepared to present himself or herself for a certain number of parliamentary days should retain full voting rights. The 1968 White Paper envisaged a minimum attendance requirement of one-third of all sittings each session for voting peers. No one could object to reluctant peers keeping their rights to speak on their rare appearances (although it would be an interesting exercise to see just how many of the worst offenders actually have been moved to add their voices to their votes on such occasions). The Report by the Group on the Working of the House[31] recorded that, counting only those peers who attended at least one-third of the sittings, the party composition of the working House in the 1985–6 session would have been Conservatives 168, Labour 88 and Liberal–SDP Alliance (as they then were) 51, with 73 cross-benchers. On the same basis, there would have been 217 life peers and 163 hereditary peers entitled to vote. The cross-benchers would have held a balance of power between left and right. Now perhaps a one-third requirement would be too onerous, and a lower proportion might be agreed on. Younger or middle-aged life peers (and potential life peers) who are heavily engaged in earning their living perhaps nowhere near London are to be encouraged, rather than discouraged, from attending or becoming members. A careful balance would need to be struck. An additional advantage of a scheme based on an attendance requirement (or requirements) would be that the leave of absence procedure, invented over forty years ago to solve the backwoodsmen problem and having conspicuously failed to do so, could be scrapped.

[30] Shell, *The House of Lords*, 48.
[31] HL 9 (1987–8), table ii.

Given the increased pressure on the House of Lords to carry out its revising function,[32] it deserves to have more Ministers. Those who are there face a fairly heavy burden in being much fewer in number than in the Commons, having to answer for several departments, and having to face many peers (including former senior Ministers and civil servants) who are more knowledgeable than they could hope to be.

A final suggestion is that a Joint Select Committee on Parliamentary Affairs might be set up. One of its tasks would be to try to resolve, in private, conflicts on legislation between the two Houses when they arose. The idea is not new: formerly, a conference of both Houses might have been held in an attempt to settle disputes between the Houses,[33] and the Bryce Committee suggested that the mechanism should be revived. It might prove a useful, though no doubt not always successful, way of reducing disagreement between the two Houses in the matter of legislation.

These ideas will be criticized as being too timid. Certainly, when set against the bold nostrums put up by the Liberal Democrats and by the Labour Party, that is a fair adjective to use. Dreaming up schemes is a simple and agreeable pastime. But, as has been argued throughout this book, reform plans ought to be formulated with the realities of the political situation clearly in mind if they are to stand a reasonable chance of being implemented and of lasting. Most hereditary peers have been removed. As the subsequent ten-year delay after that event has shown, that was the easy part. The risk is that further progress may prove illusory.

---

[32] That pressure would be reduced in the second half of each session if more Bills were to be started in the Lords.

[33] See O. Hood Phillips, *Constitutional and Administrative Law* (London: Sweet & Maxwell, 7th edn., 1987), 139.

6

Ministers' powers

In his first statement to the House of Commons as Prime Minister Mr Brown outlined (in his description) a route-map towards a new constitutional settlement. This was accompanied by a wide-ranging and ambitious Green Paper, *The Governance of Britain*.[1] Its purpose was to help 'to forge a new relationship between Government and citizen...[through] a settlement that entrusts Parliament and the people with more power'.[2] Of particular relevance to this chapter is the Prime Minister's desire to transfer to Parliament certain powers which are enjoyed by Ministers under the royal prerogative. To put this surprising and welcome aspiration into context requires a brief consideration of that prerogative.

Ministers and harlots

A satisfactory definition of the royal prerogative has eluded very learned people. Yet the notion of the royal prerogative is one of major significance in British constitutional law and practice, because from it flow many of the most important powers possessed by Ministers and especially by the Prime Minister. Decisions on peace and war; the deployment of the armed forces within the United Kingdom and around the world; the diminution of national sovereignty through the conclusion of treaties; the Prime Minister's ability to appoint, reshuffle, and sack Ministers, to nominate the membership of one House of Parliament (so far, at any rate), and to precipitate a general election—all, and much more, is achieved by or through acts of prerogative.[3]

Statute law is also important. For well over a century Governments have derived very many of their powers from parliamentary authority. Royal prerogative powers have, however, survived the encroachments of statute—not for the benefit of the Sovereign, but because they are essential if Government is to function. Apart

---

[1] Cm. 7170 (2007).

[2] Ibid, p. 5.

[3] See further R. Brazier, 'Constitutional Reform and the Crown', in M. Sunkin and S. Payne (eds.), *The Nature of the Crown* (Oxford: Clarendon Press, 1999), Ch. 13. See also D. Oliver, *Constitutional Reform in the UK* (Oxford: Oxford University Press, 2003), Ch. 11.

from special cases where the Sovereign herself may use prerogative authority in her own discretion,[4] Ministers rely daily on the prerogative for what they do.[5] That Ministers can rely on that part of the common law known as the royal prerogative to give them authority to do what would otherwise be unlawful is highly convenient for them. In relying on the prerogative, Ministers are obviously not limited by the terms of any Act of Parliament. They do not have to pay heed to any safeguards for the citizen which Parliament might have included in any modern, statutory formulation of equivalent powers. They do not have to consult, or even inform, Parliament when they have it in mind to do things by virtue of the prerogative. They do not have to worry in every case whether the courts might review the manner in which they use such powers.[6]

These comments do not, I hope, echo the absurd diatribe against ministerial power which was unleashed over seventy years ago by Lord Hewart, the Lord Chief Justice.[7] Ministers cannot routinely rely on the prerogative to behave like irresponsible autocrats (even if they wished to do so), because there are some restrictions against misuse. Ministers are responsible to Parliament for their actions. The Government must be sure that parliamentary support will be forthcoming for things done under the prerogative, just as with things done under any other authority. Even so, for very much of that to be truly reassuring, the parliamentary safeguards against misuse of prerogative power must be such as to cause Ministers to pause and think, and perhaps occasionally to doubt whether they would carry the House of Commons with them. On some great national issues things may, indeed, work that way; but in most other things Governments know that the Whips will ensure that all is well, and they know that, over many minor, and indeed dull matters involving the use of the prerogative, Members of Parliament will be largely uninterested in what has been done. Indeed, it is unquestionably the case that Parliament has permitted the royal prerogative to grant to Ministers, in effect, power without responsibility, which, as Mr Stanley Baldwin reminded us, has been the prerogative of the harlot through the ages.

While the legislature has been lax in this matter, the judiciary have stirred themselves, especially in the GCHQ case,[8] so as to place some restraints on executive use of the royal prerogative. The courts will review the legality of Ministers' use of some prerogative powers. But not every prerogative power is justiciable: matters such

---

[4] See Ch. 7.

[5] For a ministerial defence of the use of prerogative powers see 223 HC Debs. 489–94 (21 Apr. 1993).

[6] These points are elaborated by the House of Commons Public Administration Select Committee, *Taming the Prerogative*, HC 422 (2003–4), paras 1–34 (which followed an inquiry for which I was the Specialist Adviser).

[7] In his book *The New Despotism* (London: Ernest Benn, 1929).

[8] *Council for Civil Service Unions v. Minister for the Civil Service* [1985] AC 374. See also, e.g. *R. v. Secretary of State for Foreign and Commonwealth Affairs, ex p. Everett* [1989] 1 All ER 655 (issuing of passports); *R. v. Secretary of State for the Home Department, ex p. Bentley* [1993] 4 All ER 442 (granting of pardons).

as the appointment of Ministers, the dissolution of Parliament, treaty-making, defence matters, and the grant of honours[9] are all still beyond judicial control. Even in relation to those aspects of prerogative which are justiciable, judicial remedies are often available only after the disputed action has taken place. It would be much preferable if some ministerial powers were to be surrounded by procedural and other rules which sought, for example, to ensure that the citizen was treated fairly before his or her rights were infringed.

The House of Commons Public Administration Select Committee reported on all this in 2003.[10] The Committee conducted the first-ever official inquiry into major aspects of the royal prerogative. As a result of the convention that the Sovereign must act, at least normally, on ministerial advice, the Committee concluded that prerogative powers had come, in effect, to be at the disposal of Ministers. That slow change had never been explicitly approved by Parliament or citizens. Because the regular use of such powers lacked adequate parliamentary safeguards, the Committee recommended that the Government should initiate a public consultation about Ministers' executive powers, which would include proposals for legislation to provide for greater parliamentary control over all such ministerial powers. The Committee also published in its report a draft Ministers of the Crown (Executive Powers) Bill[11] which, among other things, would surround with immediate effect legal and parliamentary safeguards three important uses to which the prerogative is put—that is, committing the armed forces to conflict, the conclusion of treaties, and the issuing of passports. But Mr Blair's Government rejected all of these ideas, essentially on the grounds that the case for change had not been made out, and that parliamentary accountability was already adequate.[12] The Constitution Committee of the House of Lords subsequently focused solely on the prerogative war-making power, reporting about it in 2006.[13] It fully accepted that this power should not continue to be used as it has up to now. But the Committee thought that legislation carried the risk of being too restrictive in unforeseeable cases in which the forces had to be deployed quickly. And so the Committee's main recommendation was that a parliamentary convention should be explicitly agreed by both Houses which would set out Parliament's role in such decision-making, and indicate some of the elements which such a convention should contain.[14] My difficulty with that approach is that constitutional

---

[9] Mr Brown confirmed his predecessor's commitment not to alter lists of honours passed to him for transmission to the Queen by the Main Honours Committee: *The Governance of Britain*, Cm. 7170 (2007), paras 82–85. This is wholly separate from the grant of peerages.

[10] See note 6 above.

[11] Ibid, Appendix 1.

[12] Government Response to the Public Administration Select Committee Report, Cm. 6187 (2003–4).

[13] Select Committee on the Constitution, *Waging War: Parliament's Role and Responsibility*, HL 236 (2005–6).

[14] Ibid, paras 108–110.

conventions can—in all good faith—be broken, leaving no real safeguard at all. True, the Government obtained parliamentary votes in favour of deploying the armed forces in Iraq in 2003, and Ministers have claimed that a convention exists as a result that Parliament must approve any such future deployments. I will return to that power, and some other prerogative powers, at the end of this chapter.

This current state of the prerogative shows yet again that when Ministers acquire power they are, on the whole, perfectly content to keep it to themselves, and that Parliament is quite happy that this should be so—although the 1997 Labour Government deserves full credit for its constitutional legislation (such as the Human Rights Act 1998) which makes life harder for the British Government. It does not seem too radical to suggest that at least a review is called for, to establish precisely what powers are conferred by the royal prerogative, what legal restraints already attach to them, and what prerogative powers (if any) might sensibly be abolished. Such a review, suggested in the first edition of this book in 1991, has been in important respects carried out by two parliamentary committees, but as the Public Administration Select Committee recognized, a wider and deeper review is needed. Such an examination should not be such a utopian and remote prospect as it at first appears, because the Labour Party in opposition committed itself to a review of the royal prerogative when it was next in Government.[15]

That commitment survived the transition to new Labour in the 1990s,[16] although unfortunately there was no reference to it in the 1997, 2001, or 2005 general election manifestos. How disappointing it was that Ministers chose to forget the proposal after winning power, until Mr Brown revived it in 2007.

I again put in a plea for the use of a body such as my suggested Constitutional Commission.[17] At the heart of these technical questions about the present scope of the royal prerogative are important issues of constitutional power. The proper delimitation of constitutional power is a matter of such importance that it ought to be resolved, wherever possible, on a multi-party basis. The Constitutional Commission might endorse the abolition of any obsolete prerogative powers: candidates are several, and include the cataleptic prerogative powers to impress men into the Royal Navy, and to create courts to administer the common law. The Constitutional Commission might also identify and confirm that handful of powers which the Sovereign should retain in her personal discretion, such as the appointment of the Prime Minister, and the dissolution of Parliament.[18] By far the greatest burden of work, however, would be borne in deciding how all those other prerogative powers, Ministers' executive powers, which are necessary for efficient Government,

---

[15] *Meet the Challenge: Make the Change* (London: Labour Party, 1989), 56.

[16] *A New Agenda for Democracy* (London: Labour Party, 1993), 33. The Liberal Democrats also support radical reform of such powers: *For the People, By the People* (London: Liberal Democrat Policy Paper No. 83, 2007), paras 5.8.2–5.8.3.

[17] On which see Ch. 2.

[18] See further Ch. 7.

might be reformulated in modern language, in statute, and be made subject, where appropriate, to new safeguards. While the Interception of Communications Act 1985 should not by any means be held up as a model statute, the process of making prerogative powers subject to statutory limitations which was illustrated by the enactment of that Act at least indicates the general approach. The legally doubtful power of a Secretary of State to issue warrants under the royal prerogative to allow telephone-tapping and to permit the interception of mail was confirmed in that Act, but was made subject both to the satisfaction of criteria upon which any warrant may be issued, and to policing by a statutory Tribunal and a Commissioner. (I do not think for a moment that those safeguards adequately protect the citizen against improper interference with his or her rights; but it is the *process* which is relevant.) The Security Service Act 1989 and the Intelligence Services Act 1994 illustrate a similar process. In the more comprehensive review and reformulation of the royal prerogative which I am suggesting, it would be much better if each particular prerogative power were expressly abolished, and any equivalent power and attendant safeguards were enacted. Doubts which have surrounded more ambiguous statutory interventions into prerogative ought thereby to be avoided,[19] and the courts could then be relied on to keep Ministers within the four walls of the new statutory powers. Multi-party consideration of what powers, currently based on the royal prerogative, should continue to exist, all culminating in the enactment of perhaps a number of statutes precisely defining the continued powers and subjecting them to safeguards, should produce a proper balance between appropriate ministerial authority and the rights of the citizen.

I want to turn now to the personal powers of the Prime Minister. Most of the powers to be discussed derive from the royal prerogative, while the others are based on constitutional convention and political practice.

Every Prime Minister needs, and is entitled to have, a degree of personal authority over the Government. He or she must, for instance, be able to reconstruct the administration from time to time so as to bring in new blood, or to fill posts quickly following a sudden resignation, or to promote people who seem to have ministerial potential. As in any large organization, someone must provide a sense of direction and momentum, and in a Government that can only be done by the Prime Minister. To do all this, and much more, a Prime Minister needs personal authority, which is amply given to him or her by the British constitution. But that personal power is enhanced by other things, too. The Prime Minister's profile is much higher than that of any other Minister. The Prime Minister is frequently news. He or she has the chance to shine once a week at Prime Minister's Questions, and that shining may be seen on television. A Prime Minister's visits and speeches in the country, enhanced by carefully arranged photo-opportunities, concentrate attention on his

---

[19] For these doubts and difficulties, see S. A. de Smith and R. Brazier, *Constitutional and Administrative Law* (London: Penguin Books, 8th edn., 1998), 139–40.

or her doings and sayings. A Prime Minister's many visits abroad representing the United Kingdom, meeting major political leaders, attending European Council gatherings, economic summits, biennial Commonwealth heads of Government meetings, and so on, all mean that the electorate may be forgiven for concluding that the Prime Minister *is* the Government.

It would be silly to suggest that matters of personality and style would be amenable to much change through new constitutional rules. None the less, post-war Prime Ministers have acquired disproportionate power in relation to the House of Commons and to the Cabinet. To adapt the famous 1780 resolution of the House of Commons tabled by George Dunning, the influence of the Prime Minister has increased, is increasing, and ought to be diminished. Indeed, an alarming picture can be painted of the consequences of that power, and Mr Tony Benn, notably, has painted it in vivid colours.[20] His canvass shows that Prime Ministers have used prerogative powers so as, for example, to invite United States military forces to be based in the United Kingdom (Mr Clement Attlee in 1945), to commit troops to battle (Sir Anthony Eden and Suez in 1956, to which may be added Mrs Margaret Thatcher and the Falklands in 1982, and Mrs Thatcher and Mr John Major and the Gulf in 1990–1 and Mr Blair with several deployments, notably and so controversially in Iraq in 2003), to conclude treaties of the highest constitutional importance (Mr Edward Heath and the 1972 Treaty of Accession to the European Communities), to appoint and sack Ministers, to create peers (827 in the period 1945 to 1979), and to make hundreds of other appointments. Other specific examples which have occurred since he wrote include the banning of trade unions at GCHQ (a ban lifted in 1997 by the new Labour Government), and the giving of consent to the President of the United States to use airbases in the United Kingdom to bomb Libya. Critics of Mr Blair as Prime Minister allied themselves with this point, painting his premiership as more 'presidential' even than Mrs Thatcher's. They pointed not only to 'his' foreign wars, but also to the concentration of major policy-making in No. 10 Downing Street, in the main accepted by compliant departmental Ministers.[21] It is not necessary to accept Mr Benn's solution—the adoption of a republican form of Government with what are now prerogative powers conferred afresh, as necessary, by Parliament[22]—to recognize some truth in his assertion that the premiership in Britain is, in effect, an elected monarchy. We should, in my view, consider whether the total consecutive period for which a person can be Prime Minister should be limited. Perhaps there should be a constitutional convention that, normally, no one should serve for more than the equivalent of two Parliaments—a maximum, that is, of ten years (which is precisely the time, in the event, which was served by Mr Blair). As Parliaments are usually dissolved after about four years, the maximum would in

---

[20] *Arguments for Socialism* (London: Cape, 1979), 125–6.

[21] His informal style of Government was criticized by Lord Butler of Brockwell (a former Secretary of the Cabinet) in his *Review of Intelligence on Weapons of Mass Destruction*, HC 898 (2003–4), 148.

[22] See, e.g. his Commonwealth of Britain Bill (HC Bill 161 (1990–1)).

practice be about eight years—by coincidence, the most that by law a person can be President of the United States.

I want now to select five areas in which rearrangement of ministerial power would be highly desirable. The first two concern patronage in one form or another; the other three involve a Prime Minister's working relationship with the Cabinet.

Restoring cabinet Government

In a draft for the introduction to Bagehot's *The English Constitution,* Mr Richard Crossman wrote that a Prime Minister can liquidate the political careers of his rivals as effectively as any Soviet leader. This was written long before *perestroika* had been thought of, but even so, his publishers (who must have been very nervous souls) insisted that the sentence be deleted. Crossman obliged, and three years later, after Cabinet experience, that deletion was his only regret about the Introduction.[23] The use which is made of ministerial patronage varies from Prime Minister to Prime Minister. No one could accuse Mrs Thatcher of having been other than single-minded in her reshuffles. After only two years as Prime Minister five 'wets' had been shuffled out of the Cabinet. Fifty-seven people joined and left Mrs Thatcher's Cabinet and following Sir Geoffrey Howe's cathartic resignation Mrs Thatcher enjoyed a few weeks before her own departure as the sole survivor from the original formation from 1979. Mr Blair's premiership also witnessed more or less annual reshuffles of Ministers. It is easy to see that if Ministers have to work hard to master new departments to which they are sent, they will lack time to consider and debate the general position and policies of the Government. If, in addition, they are ambitious for higher ministerial office, they will also lack the inclination to oppose the Prime Minister's wishes effectively. Taken together, that lack of time and inclination to challenge the Prime Minister must entrench his or her power.

Although political limitations on a Prime Minister's patronage do exist, must power over colleagues really be so wide in order to maintain a Prime Minister's proper position as chief of Government? The Labour Party constrains its new Prime Ministers by the party rule that, when the first Labour Cabinet is formed after coming to power at a general election, places must be found in it for the elected members of the Shadow Cabinet.[24] Labour Prime Ministers have followed that requirement very closely,[25] and although as a consequence they have found themselves with some Cabinet colleagues who are not congenial to them, it cannot be said that this element of democracy in Cabinet-making has had a deleterious effect on efficient

[23] J. Mackintosh, *The British Cabinet* (London: Stevens & Sons, 3rd edn., 1977).
[24] Standing Orders of the Parliamentary Labour Party, No. E.
[25] Although Mr Tony Blair broke the rule on coming to power by not including Dr David Clark, Mr Michael Meacher, or Mr Tom Clarke in his new Cabinet.

Government. This is partly because the obligation to elected Shadow Cabinet members does not continue after the first Cabinet reshuffle, and because there are no elections to Labour Cabinets once formed. Thus Mr Blair was able to drop four Cabinet Ministers in his personal discretion in his first reshuffle in 1998. Should the system of elections for Labour Shadow Cabinets by the Parliamentary Labour Party be extended to actual Cabinets when Labour is in power? Should the Conservative Party adopt elections by Conservative Members of Parliament at least to its Shadow Cabinet? It would not be sensible to restrict a Prime Minister to the extent of electing individuals to particular ministerial portfolios, and the Prime Minister should retain his or her discretion to decide who should be sent to which department, and over reshuffles within the Cabinet, a discretion which he or she would continue to exercise on his or her knowledge of the people concerned and their particular strengths and weaknesses. Cabinet elections would certainly deprive a Prime Minister of one of his or her most significant powers, and would induce Cabinet Ministers to have greater regard to the opinions of the parliamentary party which would elect them, and less to the wishes of the Prime Minister.

When Mr James Callaghan was asked in 1977 to list all the public appointments for which he was responsible as Prime Minister his written answer ran to four columns of *Hansard*.[26] Even that list was not complete, because (as Mr Callaghan explained) he had omitted ministerial, ecclesiastical, and civil service appointments. This is the second area of prime ministerial patronage—the dazzling range of jobs outside the Government which is at a Prime Minister's disposal. The Chairman and governors of the BBC, the Governor and directors of the Bank of England, officers such as the Comptroller and Auditor-General, the Parliamentary Ombudsman, and the Chairman of the Public Accounts Committee, Regius Professors, members of Royal Commissions and committees of inquiry—all require the Prime Minister's blessing for appointment. In the civil service, senior officials need the approbation of the Prime Minister for appointment and promotion, approbation which Mrs Thatcher used selectively over choices for Permanent Secretaryships. In the Church of England, nearly 400 appointments are made by the Queen on the Prime Minister's advice. In the judiciary, the Lords of Appeal in Ordinary, the Lords Justices of Appeal, the Master of the Rolls, the Lord Chief Justice, the Vice-Chancellor, and the President of the Family Division, all owe their positions to the Queen on the Prime Minister's advice (although the Lord Chancellor's approval is also most important, as are now the recommendations of the independent Judicial Appointments Commission[27]). Because of her amazing longevity in office, Mrs Thatcher had to appoint the entire judicial House of Lords, all the Court of Appeal, and all the four heads of division. There are, inevitably, restraints on the choices: for example, the numbers which are involved alone mean that the

---

[26] 932 HC Debs. *232–6* (written answers 19 May 1977).
[27] See Ch. 10.

Prime Minister must rely on advice about possible candidates. Individual Ministers, too, possess wide powers of appointment. The adoption of numerous new non-statutory principles and practices concerning public appointments, recommended in 1995 by the Committee on Standards in Public Life,[28] and known as Nolan principles after its first Chairman, is warmly to be welcomed.

There is a case for subjecting most major public appointments to a parliamentary confirmation process. The public has a right to expect that the fitness of candidates to hold important public jobs will be fully and properly investigated by their representatives in Parliament. Members of Parliament are entitled to discover the attitude to the office under consideration of those who might be appointed to it, and, in particular, to explore the nominee's political, economic, and social beliefs where they are relevant. Such a confirmation process could be conducted by the relevant departmental select committee, and a report would be published. That sort of examination would also provide a further safeguard against corruption in public life. Governments could not rely on their arithmetical majorities on the departmental select committees to deliver the goods, for the history of those committees since 1979 shows that they do not routinely report along party lines, and unanimous reports strongly critical of the Government have been published. This principle has now been accepted in the Government's 2007 Green Paper.[29] A list of posts would be drawn up with a view to pre-appointment hearings being held by the relevant departmental select committee. Mr Brown also accepted that the Prime Minister's role in ecclesiastical appointments should be greatly reduced, so that, for example, the Crown Nominations Commission would in future submit just one name for senior appointments in the Church of England to the Prime Minister who would forward it to the Queen for her approval.[30] The Government will also consider Ministers' role in judicial appointments in the light of the operation of the Judicial Appointments Commission, 'including conceivably a role for Parliament itself…'.[31] Civil service appointments, too, might be removed from any allegations of bias by giving the Civil Service Commissioners a much more decisive role.[32] Mr Brown has promised that the 'core principles and values' of the civil service will be enshrined in legislation,[33] probably in the 2007–2008 parliamentary session. The independence of the Civil Service Commissioners would be protected by it. Such legislation will be welcomed by many who have called for such a change, not least parliamentary committees such as the Public Administration Select Committee.

---

[28] *First Report of the Committee on Standards in Public Life*, Cm. 2850 (1995).

[29] *The Governance of Britain*, Cm. 7170 (2007), paras 72–79.

[30] Ibid, paras 62–66.

[31] Ibid, paras 69–71. Mr Jack Straw, as Secretary of State for Justice and Lord Chancellor, is opposed to parliamentary involvement because of the risk of 'politicization' of judicial appointments: *The Times*, 12 July 2007. See further Ch. 10.

[32] The Prime Minister's patronage powers in relation to the House of Lords were considered in Ch. 5.

[33] *The Governance of Britain*, Cm. 7170 (2007), paras 40–48.

But what of the Prime Minister's relationship with the Cabinet? There are, I believe, three areas in which changes are needed, with the aim of tilting the balance back towards Cabinet Government. They concern recommendations for a dissolution of Parliament, the control of economic policy through, in particular, the annual Budget, and the use of extra-Cabinet decision-making.

The Prime Minister's ability to dissolve Parliament has often been described as an important element in his or her political authority. Of course, if he or she can avoid it, no Prime Minister unleashes a general election if the Government's fortunes are at a low ebb: every Prime Minister naturally goes to the country at the most advantageous (or least disadvantageous) time for his or her party. That gives the Prime Minister an obvious advantage over the other political parties, who must make the best they can of the election date chosen for them. Leaders of the Opposition imagine themselves reaping the benefit of that advantage one fine day, and so they are unlikely to be attracted any more than a Prime Minister to the notion of having a fixed-term Parliament of (say) four or five years' duration, followed by an automatic dissolution. It is, however, an idea which deserves further consideration. It may be, indeed, that we have all exaggerated the freedom of manoeuvre enjoyed by Prime Ministers in the matter of dissolution dates. Most Prime Ministers since 1945 seem to have worked on the basis of a four-year parliamentary term, and have tried to put their Governments in the best possible light within that period. That was Mr Blair's and Mrs Thatcher's preferred timing. This may well be because it is risky business for a Prime Minister to allow a Parliament to survive into its final year of life, because things might go wrong for the Government during that year as the inevitable appointment with the electorate rushes towards it (as Mr John Major found to his cost in 1997). Equally, we might have assumed too readily that fixed-term Parliaments would end the unfair electoral advantage enjoyed by Prime Ministers. Only the Liberal Democrats have taken the criticisms of the present dissolution system to the logical conclusion of demanding automatic dissolutions, and the principle operates in the Scottish Parliament, the Northern Ireland Assembly, and Welsh Assembly.

But what of the present dissolution decision? Sixteen Prime Ministers since Mr David Lloyd George have had the power which he assumed to recommend a dissolution off his own bat without feeling bound to obtain Cabinet agreement. The constitutional legitimacy of a Prime Minister having the sole right to obtain a general election, rather than seeking it on the basis of collective Cabinet advice, has been challenged,[34] but in practice the Prime Minister *can* make the recommendation without consulting the Cabinet. A restoration of the pre-1918 position would not, however, result in such a major reduction in prime-ministerial authority that Prime Ministers would necessarily oppose it tooth and nail, and I propose that the Prime Minister should have to present this advice as the collective advice of the whole

---

[34] Notably by G. Marshall, *Constitutional Conventions* (Oxford: Clarendon Press, 1984), Ch. 3.

Cabinet. In the light of the way in which Prime Ministers have actually made up their minds about general election dates at least since the end of the Second World War, this would not be a very great departure from current practice. Since that time the Prime Minister has consulted senior Ministers and party officials both to help pick a date *and* to involve them in the responsibility for it. It is obviously better for a Prime Minister to involve at least some senior colleagues in the decision so that they are implicated if all goes wrong. (If all goes right, the Prime Minister's political acumen is applauded and few seem to care that others played a part in picking the date.) This process contradicts the idea that a Prime Minister has unrestricted personal power in the matter. In view of this process, which has been followed for decades, it would be but a small step for the Cabinet's formal position to be restored in it. An attribute of traditional Cabinet Government would thereby be restored. On becoming Prime Minister Mr Brown stated that the Prime Minister should be required to seek the approval of the House of Commons before asking the Queen for a dissolution of Parliament. There would, he accepted, have to be provision for the case in which a Government could not be formed but in which the House of Commons declined to support dissolution. The Government would consult on this idea and, if it were accepted, Mr Brown would make a formal statement to Parliament which, when acted on, would produce precedents and a constitutional convention governing the process.[35] Perhaps unsurprisingly, Mr Brown did not say whether any such vote would be whipped (for if it were, the Prime Minister would be likely to obtain compliance), or whether he had any intention of submitting a dissolution request to the Commons and the Queen as a collective Cabinet decision of the pre-Lloyd George variety. There is, perhaps, rather less to this initiative than meets the eye.

The Cabinet's role in the formulation of economic policy is limited by several factors. In particular, the personality and style of the Prime Minister, and, as Mr Gordon Brown was to show to an unprecedented degree, the Chancellor of the Exchequer, may diminish the Cabinet's collective contribution: the more authoritarian the Prime Minister, and certainly the more successful the Chancellor, the less will the Cabinet feel disposed to intervene in economic and financial decisions. Mr Brown was the most powerful Chancellor in history. Fully supported by the Prime Minister, he extended the authority of the Treasury into individual departments, insisting that Treasury-set targets be met in return for funding allocated to them. In any case, the annual Budget has for many years been presented to the Cabinet as a fait accompli. The Chancellor's Budget proposals are of major economic and political importance, but, regardless of the Cabinet's relationship with him or her, those proposals are first disclosed to the Cabinet on the morning of

---

[35] *The Governance of Britain*, Cm. 7170 (2007), paras 34–36. The Liberal Democrats favour fixed-term Parliaments lasting for four years: *For the People, By the People* (London: Liberal Democrat Policy Paper No. 83, 2007), paras 3.1.7–3.1.8.

Budget day. There is no time for any significant changes to be made. It was not ever thus. As late as the 1930s, four or five days would elapse between the Budget Cabinet and the Chancellor's delivery of his proposals to the House of Commons, giving ample time for Ministers to suggest or insist on alterations. The modern cavalier treatment of the Cabinet is justified by the need for secrecy: the less time there is between a Cabinet Minister hearing these secrets and their publication, the less chance there will be of a damaging leak. The *effect* of this procedure is to put economic and fiscal policy firmly in the hands of the Chancellor and the Prime Minister. What is astonishing is that no Cabinet seems to have rebelled at a system which both calls into question Ministers' honour and largely removes the Cabinet from a central area of policy. But why should not the Cabinet consider key Budget proposals in draft, no doubt enjoined by warnings about the need for secrecy of information and the safety of documents?

The exclusion of the Budget from unhurried, full, and collective debate is but a particularly notable example of the way in which Prime Ministers can remove matters from the reach of the Cabinet. The use of Cabinet committees and informal groups of selected Ministers has permitted more general side-stepping of the full Cabinet. A system of sub-Cabinet decision-making is essential: the days are long gone when the full Cabinet could adequately deal with all questions which have to be addressed by the most senior Ministers. Small groups of Ministers can settle preliminary issues so as to leave only fundamental points, or points of disagreement, for higher authority. Yet extra-Cabinet decision-making has undoubtedly enhanced prime-ministerial power. The Prime Minister has absolute authority over Cabinet committees. He or she alone decides to set them up, which Ministers should serve on them, who is to chair them, and what the terms of reference will be. The Prime Minister may lay down rules which restrict access from committees to the Cabinet. He or she can give committees executive authority. The Prime Minister decides when to wind them up. Mrs Thatcher *reduced* the number of Cabinet committees, but only because from the earliest days of her Government she held discussions with small, informal groups of Ministers. Such flexibility has advantages; but the looseness of such arrangements means that prime-ministerial packing of such gatherings with supporters is quite easy, and that the Cabinet—and even Cabinet committees—are circumvented. Mr Blair went further. As Prime Minister he effectively took many decisions in meetings with just the departmental Minister concerned, and/or with other advisers hand-picked by him. Cabinet meetings were largely formal and brief—often less than an hour. Mr Blair robustly justified this approach in terms of efficiency. But his informal style of governance earned the title of 'sofa Government', which was not meant as a compliment. There is a balance to be struck between, on the one hand, efficiency, and on the other collegiality and proper record-keeping.

The public is entitled to know the organization of the Cabinet committee system, given its central place in the way the country is governed. But it was not until 1992 that the publication of the composition and terms of reference of Cabinet committees and subcommittees was ordered, by Mr John Major, thus ending the previous complete secrecy which had surrounded them. That secrecy had been attacked and defended for many years.[36] Mr Major had also directed the official publication in 1992 of *Questions of Procedure for Ministers,* which is the nearest we have to a ministerial rule-book in the United Kingdom. Mr Blair republished it in 1997 as the *Ministerial Code.* Mr Brown's version includes provision for a new independent adviser who will be able, at the Prime Minister's request, to investigate alleged breaches of the Code.

The Cabinet is responsible to Parliament for the Government's tenure of office. As a result, all the members of the Cabinet are, I suggest, entitled to take part in all important decisions which they think ought to be decided by the Cabinet as a body. Conclusions of issues by the Prime Minister, or by Cabinet committees, or by ministerial groups, necessary as that may be for most governmental decisions which are not settled by individual Ministers, must often be second-best to a full Cabinet debate, even though it is less efficient. A restoration of Cabinet Government is what should be aimed at, a form of Government which did not suddenly start to wane in May 1979. The question of whether to risk the Government's life by calling a general election, strategic economic and fiscal decisions epitomized in Budget judgements, and other major matters should all be brought back, so far as is practicable, to where they ought to be discussed, at the Cabinet table with all the seats occupied.

The ability of any newcomer to the premiership to have complete authority over the future of his or her colleagues results largely from the failure of his or her party to impose rules about the matter. Such rules might, for example, require either elections by Members of Parliament to the membership of the Cabinet (as Labour has for the Shadow Cabinet), or at the very least wider consultations within the party about who should be included in the administration.

The ability of a Prime Minister to decide on how the Government shall be run results from a series of abdications of authority by Cabinets in favour of the Prime Minister, based on the simplistic notion that the leader must lead, and that efficiency always trumps collective decision-making. There has been a failure to insist that those who will, together, bear the responsibility for the Government's performance (mainly Ministers, but also the parliamentary party) have a right to a greater say in how that Government is conducted and how its decisions should be arrived at. It is not the case that the political changes outlined in this chapter are unattainable, or that any Prime Minister would have an unbreakable veto over them. Mr Brown is to be applauded for beginning his premiership by emphasizing the importance which he attaches to Cabinet Government.

---

[36] For these defences and attacks, see R. Brazier, *Constitutional Practice* (Oxford: Oxford University Press, 3rd edn., 1999), 121–24.

Naturally, there are disincentives to such changes being canvassed. In particular, hardy souls who wished to insist on new arrangements would be threatened with the withholding of the patronage of party leaders. Certainly, if changes such as those suggested were thought to be appropriate in any party, those who sought to bring them about against the leader's wishes would have to hang together, or, most assuredly, they would all hang separately. But any Prime Minister's authority rests in the end on his or her party electorate and on the Cabinet. In the end, that fact was dramatically illustrated when the Cabinet and Conservative Members of Parliament forced Mrs Thatcher to abdicate in 1990; and party pressures forced Mr Blair in September 2006 publicly to confirm that he would resign within a year (having announced before the 2005 general election that he would serve a full third term as Prime Minister before retiring). We may not see another Prime Minister toppled like Mrs Thatcher for decades, but the memory of it should be etched in the minds of all Mrs Thatcher's successors—and in the minds of Cabinets and parliamentary parties. It is up to them to bring about reductions in prime-ministerial authority and to redress the balance back towards more traditional forms of Cabinet Government. Mr Major arrived at more decisions through collective discussion than Mrs Thatcher did. In doing so, however, he only restored matters to what they were before 1979. Mr Blair set the clock back; we must wait and see exactly how collegiate Mr Brown turns out to be.

So far I have written mainly about matters over which the Prime Minister has authority. I now want to return to some issues over which the Cabinet and individual Ministers have clear authority. What is to be repeated, in more detail, is that the existing parliamentary safeguards over the use of the royal prerogative for certain purposes should be supplemented by more effective parliamentary and legal controls.[37] The Brown Government reversed in bold terms the dismissive response of its predecessor to the Public Administration Select Committee's report *Taming the Prerogative*. The Government now believes that, in general, ministerial executive powers should be put on to a statutory basis, and should be brought under stronger parliamentary scrutiny and control.[38] Some powers might be placed under greater parliamentary scrutiny by the adoption of new constitutional conventions or parliamentary resolutions, although a wider review of all such powers will consider whether, in the long term, they should all be codified or put into statute.[39] The Government accepted the analysis of the Committee which had traced the history of the executive powers, demonstrated how they had been put into the hands of the executive without any explicit parliamentary or popular authority, and accepted that new safeguards were required.[40] Where legislation was required for particular

---

[37] See Public Administration Select Committee, *Taming the Prerogative* (see note 6 above).

[38] *The Governance of Britain*, Cm. 7170 (2007), para. 24.

[39] Ibid.

[40] Ibid, paras 14–17, 20–22.

powers, this would be introduced as soon as possible. In my view this approach deserves much praise.

On several occasions since 1945 the Cabinet has committed large military forces to actual or possible armed conflict, although not, in legal parlance, to war. In most of those cases Parliament was not formally consulted before the decision to send forces was made. Suez, the Falklands, the Gulf, the former Yugoslavia, Afghanistan, and Iraq all received British armed forces on ministerial direction under the royal prerogative power to dispose those forces as the Crown thinks fit. How odd—perhaps bizarre—it is that the approval of both Houses of Parliament is required for pieces of technical, and often trivial, subordinate legislation, whereas it is not needed at all before men and women can be committed to the possibility of disfigurement or death. Speed of military response may, of course, be vital. Indeed, the quick deployment of British forces in the Gulf in 1990 might have been in small part responsible for Saudi Arabia being made safe from aggression. To insist on prior approval of all military deployments would be absurd, especially when Parliament is in recess, as it was at the start of the Gulf emergency. But the commitment of military forces is an act which may have such terrible consequences that the approval of Parliament ought to be required within a specified period. Even under the present arrangements, no British Government is going to take the country to the brink of, or to actual, fighting unless it is reasonably confident that it can carry Parliament with it. Any Government will need general political support, and perhaps legislation and certainly appropriations, to wage what ordinary people will call war. Of course that is so: and these facts make the proposal all the more reasonable. The United Kingdom needs a War Powers Act of some kind, under which Parliament would have to be informed and its consent obtained within a specified number of days in order that the armed services could be deployed lawfully overseas. Mr Brown has proposed that a convention, adopted by parliamentary resolution, should govern every deployment of the armed forces abroad, although he has not ruled out legislation on the matter at some stage. Through this Parliament would be able to vote on each deployment. He has emphasized the need for flexibility so as to continue to allow rapid military responses.[41] Such a shift of responsibility to Parliament is long overdue.

The relationships between the United Kingdom and other states involve, among other things, the power or influence which other states are to have in relation to the United Kingdom: in short, they involve relationships of national sovereignty. If any rearrangements of sovereignty are contemplated through new treaty obligations, Parliament ought not to stand like a spectator on the sidelines. Some treaties are highly technical and others are arrived at as delicate compromises after tricky negotiations; no sensible Parliament would wish to amend them, or to pick and choose which parts it liked and which it would reject. But why should Parliament

---

[41] *The Governance of Britain*, Cm. 7170 (2007), paras 122–23.

not have the formal authority to approve all treaties in draft before they can, in English law, be ratified and become effective? That would be a simple rule, conditioned in the use Parliament were to make of it by the precise circumstances in which the draft had been arrived at.[42] The Government's decision in 2000 to refer the text of treaties where possible to the relevant departmental select committee for consideration, and to provide parliamentary time to debate them if a committee so requested, was a very welcome development.

Mr Brown's Government is to consult on whether there should be a statutory rule about the approval of treaties. The question would be whether all treaties that require ratification must be laid before Parliament at least twenty-one sitting days before ratification is effected under the prerogative, so that Parliament could vote upon the most important treaties.[43]

There are, of course, other matters which Ministers must decide through the use of the royal prerogative but which have no connection with the great issues of peaceful or warlike relations between states. None the less they require better regulation than surrounds them today. Just one may be mentioned by way of example: the grant of passports. In any review of ministerial powers, it is clearly for consideration whether the right to a passport should become a right enshrined in statute which contains procedural rules to ensure fair decision-making. Now that the exercise of the prerogative power in connection with passports is subject to judicial review,[44] and given that (within the European Union) citizens are entitled to identity documents or passports enabling them to leave and re-enter the country, this would be a step which should not cause Ministers too much distress. The Government, happily, is considering whether, in the longer term, the issue, refusal, revocation, or withdrawal of passports should be placed on a statutory footing.[45]

We can, again, only wait and see the result of the consultations and deliberations about Ministers' executive powers initiated by Mr Brown in the summer of 2007. With luck they should result in the rebalancing of constitutional power away from Government and to the legislature. It is a rebalancing which is long overdue.

---

[42] For one of a number of unsuccessful attempts along those lines see the Treaties (Parliamentary Approval) Bill (HL Bill 27 (1995–6)).

[43] *The Governance of Britain*, Cm. 7170 (2007), paras 31–33.

[44] *R. v. Secretary of State for Foreign and Commonwealth Affairs, ex p. Everett* [1989] 1 All ER 655.

[45] *The Governance of Britain*, Cm. 7170 (2007), para. 50.

7

A constitutional guiding light

Why not a Republic?

The Golden Jubilee of the Queen's accession to the throne was celebrated in 2002. In view of the criticisms of the monarchy and the royal family that had been made in the preceding few years, especially following the death of Diana, Princess of Wales in 1997, it was surprising to some people that the occasion produced substantial public thanks for the Queen's work over those 50 years. Although she turned 80 in 2006 the Queen's robust health makes it wise for plans to be laid for the Diamond Jubilee in 2012. Concentrating on the Queen in this way underlines a unique point about the headship of state when considering its possible reform: it is the only major constitutional institution composed of just one person. Even politically powerful Prime Ministers, such as Lady Thatcher or Mr Blair at their zeniths, are members of and dependent on the Cabinet and political party for continuance in office. Not so the Sovereign. In considering any changes to the monarchy it is unrealistic to expect people to ignore who is the present and the next Sovereign.

The Queen, as the possessor of the Crown, performs many legal and constitutional functions as head of state. As a matter of law, her direct or indirect participation is required in a large number of governmental acts, such as the granting of the royal assent to legislation, the making of Orders in Council, the issue of royal proclamations, the appointment of officers such as ambassadors and high commissioners, and the appointment of Ministers by the delivery to them of seals of office. In limited circumstances, the Queen's legal power might have to be used in a direct intervention in politics. No Prime Minister will hold office unless appointed by the Queen and, although the choice is usually determined for her, the choice of one person rather than another could still require the exercise of her own judgement. The Queen retains a number of reserve powers, for example to refuse her consent to a requested dissolution of Parliament. Even if the scope of the royal prerogative were to be cut drastically, as was suggested in Chapter 6, all of those legal and constitutional, routine and reserve, powers would have to remain vested in someone or some body.

The Crown, or constitutional monarchy, should be no more immune to fundamental reconsideration than any other part of the constitution. It has no immunity against reform merely because it is ancient, or because consideration of other systems of Government might be taken as some kind of attack on the Queen personally. Nor is the wholehearted acceptance of the monarchy by the political parties conclusive of the issue whether the headship of state should continue to be discharged on a hereditary basis. Republican sentiment is said to be weak in the United Kingdom especially given the Queen's personal popularity, although the Prince of Wales seems to enjoy a much more equivocal position with the public. That is certainly the case, in the sense that relatively few people would vote to replace the Queen by an elected President. Yet there is undoubtedly criticism of royalty, whether as to the personal behaviour of some younger members of the royal family, or the number and cost of royal residences, or to the number of royal and related persons dismissively described as 'hangers-on'. (The Queen's agreement in 1993 to pay direct taxes, and to remove most members of the royal family from the Civil List, took much of the heat out of arguments about the cost of royalty.) It is, I believe, important to state a number of fairly trite points in order to make a sharp distinction between what is necessarily required in a monarchy as part of a constitution and what is not. First, the Queen as head of state has legal and constitutional duties to perform. As with any head of state, the Queen must have the means of discharging those duties. That requires, at the least, expenditure of a certain amount of public money, a supply of information from Ministers to the Queen, and opportunities for the Queen to exercise her conventional rights in relation to Ministers. By contrast, the rest of the royal family has no such legal or constitutional duties, except one.[1] *Constitutional* considerations do not apply to members of the royal family other than the Queen (and, to the extent that he is the next head of state, and potential Regent, the Prince of Wales). As a matter of constitutional law and practice, the United Kingdom does not need an extended royal family supported by substantial sums to help them with where they live, where they go, and what they do. They do, however, support the Queen in the monarchy's social welfare functions.[2]

A second obvious point is that in a parliamentary democracy like that of the United Kingdom it is essential that someone or some body is able to act, if necessary, as a constitutional umpire. There have been, for example, competing claims to political power following inconclusive general elections, and such claims could recur, especially if a more proportional system were to be introduced for elections to the House of Commons. They may continue to be settled by politicians themselves, as on the whole they have been, but there can be no guarantee of that. Or, to take another case, there must be a mechanism to ensure that the political parties perform within the constitutional rules. Such an umpire cannot be appointed from the ranks of the players. He or she may not be called upon to intervene very often,

---

[1] Specified members may be required under the Regency Acts 1937–53 to act as Counsellors of State in the event of the Queen's absence or illness.

[2] F. Prochaska, *The Republic of Britain* (London: Allen Lane, 2000).

but every constitution should, like any Scout or Guide, be prepared for foreseeable, even though unusual, happenings. If the United Kingdom were to adopt a presidential system of Government, with the headships of state and of Government merged in one person, the functions of umpire would have to be located elsewhere, perhaps in a Supreme Court with the legal power to hold the actors within the rules of the constitution. On the safe assumption that there will be no such merger, the head of state must retain legal powers.

Yet even arriving at those far from elusive conclusions does not address the question of the attributes which would be best for a head of state in the United Kingdom. His or her duties could be discharged by a President, elected directly by the voters or indirectly by Parliament, with the Prime Minister remaining as head of the Government. A powerful case can be made for such a radical break with the past.[3] Several points form the basis for that case. One is that it would extend democracy to the pinnacle of the state, sweeping away both heredity as a basis of influence, and any succour which monarchy gives to class divisions. The person elected would enjoy a constitutional legitimacy based on popular or parliamentary will, not on the privilege of birth. Another point is that the creation of a new office of head of state, proceeding as presumably it would from a blank sheet of paper, would require a fresh statutory formulation of the powers and duties of that office. The present monarchical powers, imprecise as some are, with many only to be seen at all accurately through layers of convention, would be replaced by an unambiguous code of rights and obligations, although no doubt along with some discretionary authority as well. Again, the office of President would be supported by such financial and other arrangements as might be appropriate, but no more. Criticisms which are voiced about the high cost of the whole monarchy would cease.[4] Those would be not inconsiderable benefits from a constitutional point of view. But, for better or worse, the British constitution is not based on logic alone. To abolish the monarchy would require the setting aside of forces which are no less powerful for being intangible. The Queen is, on any measure yet devised, very popular. She remains a potent symbol of national identity, national loyalty, and national pride. She personifies the nation, a representation made glorious through occasional splendid pomp and ancient ceremonial. By the accounts of those best able to know, the Queen has punctiliously discharged her constitutional rights to be consulted, to encourage, and to warn. That would be a hard act for an elected President to follow, and there is little

---

[3] What follows is developed in my article 'A British Republic' [2002] *Cambridge Law Journal* 351 at 364–70. For the republican case see S. Haseler, *Britain's Ancien Regime* (London: Cape, 1991); A. Barnett (ed.), *Power and the Throne* (London: Vintage Press, 1994); J. Freedland, *Bring Home the Revolution* (London: Fourth Estate, 1999).

[4] There would be several consequential matters to be settled, such as the Queen's place as Head of the Commonwealth and as Supreme Governor of the Church of England. On those roles, and for a generally conservative critique of the monarchy, see V. Bogdanor, *The Monarchy and the Constitution* (Oxford: Clarendon Press, 1995), esp. Chs. 9, 10.

doubt that most voters do not want the Queen to quit the stage. At root, the question is: would an elected head of state exercise the office any better than a monarch? A President would be democratically chosen and would possess clearly formulated powers:[5] but what would he or she make of them? It could be that the President's authority was so circumscribed by Parliament that the risk of the President having to exercise a personal discretion would be almost non-existent. The point of having such a weak officer would be hard to comprehend. If, on the other hand, he or she were to be endowed with as many discretionary powers as the Queen, the President's impartiality might well be called into question when they were used, especially if, in an earlier existence, he or she had been a politician.

In any systematic and fundamental re-examination of the British constitution, the future of constitutional monarchy should be as proper a question as any other. The political parties (apart from the Liberal Democrats) have refused to touch the issue with a bargepole, no doubt mainly because they recognize the Queen's popularity and consequently fear the electoral unpopularity involved in raising the question. I have little doubt that root-and-branch reconsideration would support the continuance of constitutional monarchy. But that should not preclude inquiry. Such an investigation—never attempted in our modern constitutional history—would be beneficial. It would, in particular, provide the occasion to decide what should be the Sovereign's appropriate constitutional powers, and I will say more about that shortly. It would also allow a clear delineation of the constitutional duties of royalty from the social attributes of royalty; in the process, a cost-benefit analysis might be carried out into the royal family. As part of that, the manner of financing the head of state should be looked at again. Walter Bagehot's injunction that we should not let in daylight upon royalty, because daylight should not be let in upon magic, was uttered in a more deferential age, and in any case the curtains have been opened; more importantly, it also confused the social characteristics of monarchy with its constitutional aspects, which is precisely the distinction that I believe ought to be made as sharply as possible.

A possible compromise between hereditary constitutional monarchy and an elected President would be to institute a periodic referendum on the continuance of monarchy. That would combine some of the features of an hereditary system tempered by an elective element.[6] The timing of such referendums would certainly be tricky to arrange so as to avoid taking a snapshot at one of the temporary ups and downs of the monarchy.

Assuming the continuance of the monarchy, a number of limited changes are worth considering.[7] The Liberal Democrats, for example, favour transferring the Queen's responsibilities for choosing a Prime Minister and for dissolving

[5] The indirect method of electing a President of Australia offered in a referendum there in 1999 proved unpopular, and the proposal was rejected.

[6] Brazier (see note 3 above) at 384–85.

[7] See generally Fabian Society, *The Future of the Monarchy* (London: Fabian Society, 2003).

Parliament to the House of Commons itself.[8] An objection to that would be the politicization of that office, in that each party would be keen to get its candidate elected to it. Again, the Royal Marriages Act 1772 is indefensible: why should everyone in the line of succession to the throne require the Sovereign's consent to make a valid marriage? And how can the common-law rule that males are preferred to females in that line be justified when male primogeniture has been expunged from the rest of the law, except for hereditary peerages? More radically, it should be pondered whether the rules, in the Bill of Rights 1689 and the Act of Settlement 1701, should be retained which require the Sovereign to be a communicant Anglican and which debar the Sovereign from marrying a Catholic (a prohibition applying to all in the line of succession). Reconsideration of those rules would really depend on whether the Church of England should remain as the established church, which is a broader issue than the position of the monarchy.

None of that directly affects those aspects of the royal prerogative—Ministers' executive powers—which were examined in the previous chapter.

Subjecting power to democracy

There is no controversy or difficulty surrounding the Sovereign's place in the workaday constitution. Indeed, ample evidence has been published by former Prime Ministers attesting to the advantages which they obtained from the Queen's use of Bagehot's trinity of rights, exercised within the cardinal convention of the constitution that the Sovereign acts on ministerial advice. Yet the Sovereign continues to possess powers which might have to be exercised when no ministerial advice is available, or when that advice is so constitutionally repugnant that she feels obliged to reject it. Those powers are concerned with the appointment (and dismissal) of the Prime Minister, the dissolution of Parliament, and the granting of royal assent to legislation. What I wish to suggest is that, because the British constitution is based on parliamentary democracy (however imperfect that democracy may be), the opportunity for the use of royal discretion in constitutional affairs ought to be cut to an irreducible minimum. To do that new conventions would have to be worked out so as to ensure that political decisions were arrived at by politicians, who would take responsibility for them. Such a process would mean that in a future political crisis there would be no room for criticism that a non-elected head of state had imposed a particular solution on the elected House. It should also enhance the Queen's perceived impartiality as between the political parties, which would

---

[8] Liberal Democrats, *For the People, By the People* (London: Liberal Democrat Policy Paper No. 83, 2007), paras 3.1.9, 5.1.6. See also R. Blackburn and R. Plant, 'Monarchy and the Royal Prerogative' in Blackburn and Plant (eds.), *Constitutional Reform: The Labour Government's Agenda* (Harlow: Longman, 1999).

be especially important if no compromise could be arrived at by politicians on their own. A guiding light of political decisions, politically arrived at, might largely remove the need for royal power tò be exercised on the Queen's personal initiative in three situations: the appointment of a new Prime Minister following the incumbent's resignation on personal grounds; the return of a hung Parliament; and the appointment of a coalition Government to cope with a national emergency. I will take each of those situations in turn.

No Government would wish to see a repeat of the events which took place in Blackpool in the autumn of 1963, when Mr Harold Macmillan caused his impending resignation as Prime Minister on the grounds of ill health to be announced to an assembled Conservative Party which had no formal mechanism for electing a new leader.[9] While this *démarche* provided high drama for onlookers, it required the Queen to choose a successor to Mr Macmillan based on customary processes of consultation which he activated from his hospital bed, and controversy has surrounded the accuracy of the consultations ever since. The adoption by the Conservative Party in 1965 of a secret ballot to elect its leader, so bringing itself into line with the other parties, was an example (although no doubt an unwitting one) of the guiding light which I am proposing. Now a new Prime Minister will have to be found occasionally from an existing and continuing Government, as we were reminded before the 2005 general election when Mr Blair announced that it would be the last he would fight as Prime Minister. Prime Ministers fall ill, or grow very old and have to accept the inevitability of leaving politics, or decide to retire, voluntarily or otherwise. In such circumstances there is no reason why the decision about who is to take over the reins of the Government should be taken by anyone other than the political party concerned, through its leadership election machinery. When that machinery had produced a new leader, the Queen would merely appoint formally the successful candidate as the new head of Government. Such a convention is, in my opinion, in practice already in place and would benefit from formal enunciation. After all, in both 1957 (on the resignation of Sir Anthony Eden) and in 1963 the Queen *did* carry out the wishes of the Government party, as those wishes were (however amateurishly or inaccurately) represented to her. The convention worked superbly well in 1976 when Mr Harold Wilson announced his intention to resign as soon as the Labour Party had elected a new leader. On the election of Mr James Callaghan, Mr Wilson resigned and his party successor was appointed Prime Minister. And in 1990 it ensured that all went equally smoothly even in the exciting circumstances of Mrs Margaret Thatcher's withdrawal from the Conservative leadership contest. When she decided to drop out of the race she informed the Queen that she would resign as Prime Minister as soon as her party had completed its election for her successor, and Mr John Major kissed hands as

---

[9] See A. Horne, *Macmillan 1957–1986* (London: Macmillan, 1989), Ch. 18; Geoffrey Marshall, *Constitutional Conventions* (Oxford: Clarendon Press, 1984), 29–32.

Prime Minister on Mrs Thatcher's subsequent resignation. That convention was followed in 2007 when Mr Blair announced his intention to resign as Prime Minister. The Labour Party elected Mr Brown (unopposed), who was appointed to succeed Mr Blair by the Queen upon his resignation as Prime Minister.

A practical difficulty might arise in the context of such a convention as a result of party leadership elections being sometimes very slow affairs. The current Conservative Party leadership election rules require a two-stage ballot. Conservative MPs elect two of their number who are acceptable to them, and then party members in the country elect one in a postal ballot. Labour's procedure is more complicated. A leadership contest is conducted in an elaborately-elected and conducted electoral college. Speed might be said to be of the essence in some cases, a point of view which would certainly have been pressed had Mrs Thatcher been killed in the Brighton bombing in 1983, and it might also be urged if a Prime Minister were laid low by serious illness at a time of national emergency. There is, happily, a way round this problem which would result in the democratically based convention being upheld. During the transfer of authority between one Prime Minister and the next, the Prime Minister's deputy (or, if there were no such Minister, the number two in the Cabinet pecking-order) could be authorized by the Cabinet to take charge of the Government, but keeping only his or her existing ministerial portfolio. This caretaker would be chosen automatically by his or her place in the dead or ailing Prime Minister's Government. This is precisely what happened in both 1957 and 1963, when Mr R. A. Butler was asked in turn by Sir Anthony Eden and by Mr Macmillan to take over the Government temporarily. As soon as the party election was completed, the formal transfer of power could take place. The democratic ideal would be preserved; no Government, during the interim, would be without a pilot to weather the storm; and the Queen would remain isolated from party politics.

British electors return hung Parliaments from time to time. It cannot be said that this has caused major constitutional problems in the last hundred years. But it would be unwise to brush aside the possible consequences of such an election. The precedents which might engender complacency, such as those from 1923, 1929, and 1974, must be approached with caution. They amount to little more than political accommodations arrived at both as a result of the political realities of the day and the personal relationships between the party leaders. They should certainly not be taken as rule-constitutive precedents.[10] Caution is also needed before suggesting that new rules should be worked out in advance to prescribe both how a Government should be formed in a hung Parliament and the circumstances in which a dissolution of that Parliament should be permitted. It *might* be possible to produce such rules by consensus, but the seemingly intransigent positions of the

---

[10] For a fuller discussion, see R. Brazier, *Constitutional Practice* (Oxford: Oxford University Press, 3rd edn., 1999), Ch. 2; V. Bogdanor, *Multi-Party Politics and the Constitution* (Cambridge: Cambridge University Press, 1983).

party leaders make the prospect of success seem rather bleak. The leaders of the Conservative and Labour Parties have refused to discuss hung Parliament issues, on the ground that (as they would be expected to say) they would win an outright victory at the next general election. If cornered, they have insisted that in the wholly unlikely event of a hung Parliament being returned, the leader of the largest single party would be entitled to form a minority Government. By contrast, leaders of the Liberal Democrats—who might hold the balance of power—have followed the stance taken by earlier third-party leaders in asserting that only a coalition Government (or at the least a formal inter-party pact) would do in a hung Parliament. To complicate matters, more recent Liberal Democrat leaders, notably Mr Charles Kennedy and Sir Menzies Campbell, have expressly ruled out unconditional co-operation with any minority Government.[11] In such unpropitious circumstances, the laying down of new conventional rules might prove difficult. Therefore, procedures need to be described which would keep the Queen's contribution (which might be highly controversial) as near as possible to zero. As a consequence, politicians would have to take responsibility for Government-making and election-timing in a hung Parliament. What might those procedures be?

In order that the guiding light of political decisions, politically arrived at, should burn brightly after the election of a hung Parliament, it would be important that no precipitate action be taken from Buckingham Palace. The Prime Minister might wish to inform the Queen of the political situation, as Mr Edward Health did in 1974 after losing his parliamentary majority at the first general election of that year.[12] But I suggest that the Queen should take no part in the resolution of the political crisis. Such a royal disinclination would mean that the political parties would be forced to decide what to make of the electorate's ambiguous judgement. In 1923, 1929, and 1974 the party leaders did, indeed, resolve the succession crises themselves. In each case, a minority Government was formed. It may be that that pattern would be repeated, or it may be that the parliamentary arithmetic, the personal relationships of the party leaders (or any two of them), the wishes of the parliamentary parties, and of the parties in the country all came together to cause a coalition to be formed. I do not think for one minute that the party leaders would be averse to taking the initiative themselves in order to keep their destinies in their own hands, and an intimation from Buckingham Palace that no royal intervention should be expected would come as music to their ears. Such a procedure could be communicated to the parties at any time (but preferably when a hung Parliament was only a theoretical possibility), and in an informal way (such as by the Queen's Private Secretary explaining it privately to the party leaders).

---

[11] This was partly a reaction to Mr Blair failing to implement his pre-1997 offer to the then Liberal Democrat leader, Mr Paddy Ashdown, of a coalition Government even if Labour were to win the 1997 election outright. See P. Ashdown, *The Ashdown Diaries: vol. 1: 1988–1997* (London: Allen Lane, 2001), passim.

[12] E. Heath, *The Course of My Life* (London: Hodder & Stoughton, 1998), Ch. 18.

In a confused parliamentary situation, however, things might not proceed with the practised ease of a mature constitution. What if agreement between the parties were not forthcoming? What if (say) two parties were prepared to co-operate with each other, but a third (perhaps the largest party in the House of Commons) were to insist on its right to form a minority Government? Small parties such as the Liberal Democrats always gloss over the fact that their power in a hung Parliament may be more theoretical than real. It is never easy for politicians to admit to possible political impotence. But if no other large party were prepared to vote with them (because, say, it did not want to risk an immediate, costly general election so near to the previous contest), a minority Government might be fairly secure from defeat on a vote of confidence, and a coalition or some other inter-party arrangement might remain pie in the sky. Even if a coalition were to be agreed on in principle between two parties, the third, if it were the largest single party, might still insist on its right to form a minority Government. And behind both of those possibilities would lurk the prospect of a prime-ministerial request for another dissolution of Parliament. (As was noted in Chapter 6, Mr Brown is consulting on whether a prime-ministerial request for a dissolution should be conditional on the approval of the House of Commons, but he is mindful of the possible difficulty of obtaining such a vote if the Government were in a minority in that House.)

If Government formation in a hung Parliament were likely to take more than a few days, it might be common ground that the incumbent administration should continue in office as a caretaker Government, overseeing affairs on a care and maintenance basis in so far as circumstances permitted. The political negotiations—especially if they were aimed at coalition—might be lengthy, but essential administration during the hiatus could be carried out by the caretaker Ministers. Speed in forming the successor Government would not then be of the essence: no hasty decision would have to be taken by the Queen or by anyone else about the nature of the new Government or the identity of the next Prime Minister. While there should be little dispute about that, the decisions of substance might produce differences which the politicians were unable to reconcile. Suppose that a Government lost its majority at a general election, but was the largest single party in the new Parliament. The Prime Minister might insist on his right to continue as head of a minority Government. The main opposition party and another, smaller party might state publicly that they wished to form a majority coalition. Agreement between all three parties as to what should happen might prove impossible. In advance of any royal action, I suggest that it should be made known on the Queen's behalf that before she would consider taking any action, proof would have to be made public that a coalition Government would be viable. There would have to be a copper-bottomed agreement between the prospective coalition partners, including the name of the proposed Prime Minister, disposition of Cabinet offices, an agreed Queen's Speech, and a guarantee that the coalition would not seek a dissolution within a stated minimum time. That agreement would have to be published. These political negotiations would take place where such matters belong—at Westminster, not at Buckingham Palace. If such an agreement were not forthcoming, the Queen should do nothing to obstruct the continuance of the minority administration in office.

It could be argued that, in the spirit of my suggested royal reticence, the Queen should not intervene in such a case even to the extent suggested. Rather, it might be argued that the minority Prime Minister and his rivals for power should resolve the issue by meeting Parliament. If that happened, and if the minority Government survived a vote of confidence, that would be that. But would we be any nearer to a solution to the succession crisis if the Government were defeated? The precise nature of any alternative Government, and hence its parliamentary viability, would remain unclear. Further, the suggestion that the whole problem be deferred until after the State Opening of Parliament would substitute a second constitutional problem for the first. Few things would be more natural than for the minority Prime Minister to dare the opposition parties to defeat him or her on the Queen's Speech, just as, for example, Mr Wilson did in 1974. If they accepted the challenge (as they did not even try to do in 1974), the Prime Minister would then presumably ask for an immediate dissolution. An inchoate coalition might, however, be in the wings, claiming the right to take over without a further general election. Would ministerial advice be accepted—or would a person who might have the ability to secure a majority in the existing Parliament be appointed Prime Minister?

There is no doubt that a request for a dissolution can be refused in appropriate circumstances. The rub lies in the words 'in appropriate circumstances'. There are three propositions which I think should be considered for formulation as constitutional conventions.

(a) If a Government continues in office after an inconclusive election obtained by its Prime Minister, and is defeated on its Queen's Speech, any request for a second dissolution by that Prime Minister should be rejected. No such request, in effect for a recount, has ever been made: the precedents all require that the Prime Minister thereupon resign (as did Mr Stanley Baldwin in 1924).

(b) If a new Government is formed in a hung Parliament which is subsequently defeated, a request for an election from its Prime Minister—his or her first such—should be granted (provided, as will be mentioned in a moment, it had been made with clean hands). The 1974 precedent is in point. Mr Heath had asked for the February election, and lost it. Mr Wilson's request (some months later) for a dissolution was his first, and was granted. The request will be the more apt the longer was the delay in seeking the election, for the Government will have been seen to have done its best in an awkward parliamentary situation.

(c) If a Prime Minister in a hung Parliament were to ask for an election, even for his or her first time, in order to forestall another majority grouping from supplanting the administration, then refusal would be right if that grouping actually existed. Such a royal stance would require one of two conflicting constitutional principles to be preferred, one being that the Queen must accept ministerial advice (here, to dissolve), the other being that a person with a parliamentary majority behind him or her is entitled to be Prime Minister (here, the head of the proposed coalition). In favour of the Queen giving preference to the second principle would be the Prime Minister's improper motive in trying to thwart his or her rivals, and the existence of a viable alternative Government in the existing House of Commons which could be installed without the need for another election.

Inherent in (c) is the question of the presence of a viable alternative administration. One reason for the discredited 'automatic theory' of dissolution—that a dissolution must be granted to every Prime Minister in all circumstances—was that its application would avoid any allegation of royal bias. Such an allegation could otherwise be made if the Queen (like Lord Byng as Governor-General of Canada in 1926) were to refuse in the mistaken belief that another Government could be formed, and could carry on without an election, when in the event that proved incorrect and the new Government had to be granted the very thing which had been denied its predecessor. As with the primary decision of whether a minority or a coalition Government should be formed immediately after the return of a hung Parliament, so here the politicians who were anxious to form a new Government from the existing House should be obliged to make public an agreed package concerning the majority Government in waiting. Nothing less than that would do if the Queen were to be expected to reject ministerial advice and bring about a new Government. Once again, such a process would enable the head of state to give effect to the unambiguous wishes of Members of Parliament: once again, the proposed guiding light of political decisions, politically arrived at, would shine out.

Fortunately, grave national emergencies which can only be met by a grand national coalition Government composed of all the political parties are rare events. When such dangers have unleashed themselves, the identification of the person who is to lead the coalition has not proved difficult—Mr David Lloyd George in 1916, Mr Ramsay MacDonald in 1931, and Mr Winston Churchill in 1940. If, however, an emergency coalition were needed but agreement on its leader could not be quickly reached, it would be convenient to have in place an understanding of how a new Prime Minister could be chosen through a democratic process rather than through the use of the Sovereign's prerogative. What I suggest is that the House of Commons as a whole should choose the new Prime Minister.[13] The existing Government should continue as a caretaker until candidates are nominated and a secret ballot is held under (say) the superintendence of the Speaker. The person receiving the most votes of Members would be formally appointed Prime Minister. Even at a time of national emergency, the ideal of election could still take precedence over

---

[13] See also Brazier, *Constitutional Practice* (see note 10 above) at 20–23.

royal nomination—assuming, of course, that Parliament were sitting at the onset of the emergency.

Thus far the whole thrust of the argument has been that British parliamentary democracy needs to be made more complete by agreements to reduce the potential scope of royal discretionary power to an absolute minimum. The Queen's power to refuse a dissolution has been examined, and procedures have been indicated which ought to ensure that any refusal should have the support of the House of Commons. But the Queen has other reserve powers: to *insist* on a dissolution, to refuse royal assent, and to dismiss a Government.[14] These powers remain shrouded in mystery, not because of any legal doubt that they exist, but because they have lain unused for so long. Sovereigns and Prime Ministers have obeyed what they have taken to be the constitutional rules. Governments have not behaved in outrageous or illegal ways that have invited the exercise of royal reserve powers to check them. Should not the realities of contemporary constitutional and political conduct therefore be recognized by the formal abolition of all, or at least a majority of, those powers? The power to refuse a dissolution might be exempted from such abolition, for it might be relevant in some future hung Parliament. I think that caution dictates that the other powers should also be maintained—but, again, I want to suggest that decision-making be diverted to political authority.

Any royal insistence that Parliament be dissolved would throw the final judgement on a Government to the electorate, exactly where such judgements belong. If a Government were to refuse to recommend an election, or to resign, following its defeat in the House of Commons on a vote of confidence, or if a Government were to ask for a mass creation of peers in order to overcome an obstructionist House of Lords, but declined to follow precedent and allow the electorate's opinion to be tested first—unlikely though such astonishing turns of events would be—the Queen would be justified in requiring that a general election be held. Perhaps any case in which refusal of assent to legislation were contemplated might be met more appropriately by insistence on a dissolution, especially as it is very hard to postulate realistic examples of conduct which might invite such refusal. If, for example, a Government were to procure the passage of legislation to prolong the life of Parliament for an improper reason, the House of Lords could use its absolute veto to block the Bill's passage: no question of refusal of assent would arise in that case.[15] Or, to take another example, a Government might persuade Parliament to pass a Bill subversive of the democratic basis of the constitution which the Queen might feel justified in vetoing in her capacity as the ultimate guardian of the constitution; but she could more appropriately insist on a general election to test the electorate's attitude to the Bill, and leave the question of royal assent until that verdict was available. Vigorous private protest, perhaps followed by a general election forced

---

[14] See also Brazier, *Constitutional Practice*, 189–97.

[15] Parliament Act 1911, s. 2(1).

by the head of state if the Government persisted in its plans, would be a safer royal reaction, for it would throw the final decision to the voters. Similarly, the power to dismiss a Government might also be better left dormant in favour of a forced dissolution. If a Government declined to budge after defeat on a vote of confidence, might it not be wiser for its fate to be decided by the voters at a general election brought about by the Sovereign? (Admittedly, in such extraordinary circumstances, that Government might refuse to bow to the wishes of the electorate, in which case dismissal would be the only weapon left to dislodge it.)

Royal power in the United Kingdom is (or should be) the handmaiden of parliamentary democracy, not its master. If understandings along the lines of those outlined here were to find support, the supremacy of the political authority in the British constitution (whether the House of Commons, or the electorate) would be made clear beyond doubt. In highly charged political circumstances the Queen's personal discretion would be made subject by and large to the resolution of political questions by politicians. Only if the political process were to fail would the head of state, as final arbiter of the constitution, have to act on her personal responsibility. The working-out of new conventions, and the further development of older ones, would be best done in an authoritative body such as the suggested Constitutional Commission.[16]

Constitutional continuity[17]

A final aspect of constitutional monarchy which needs consideration is the constitutional relationship between the Queen as head of state and the Prince of Wales as the next head of state. As the Queen moves further into her eighties Prince Charles is understandably representing her more often on visits around the United Kingdom and especially in tours in the Commonwealth and around the wider world. The public expects nowadays to see an outward and visible monarchy, and might not accept fewer public appearances which might result from old age or infirmity. The constitutional status of the Prince of Wales could easily continue for another fifteen years or more. He has little prospect of attaining the Crown until he is over sixty, and he could be over seventy; his accession will not be accelerated by the Queen's abdication. Her concept of monarchy as being hereditary, and therefore for life, has induced in her a profound sense of duty towards the throne, sanctified by her vows at the Coronation, and strengthened by the unhappy memories of Edward VIII's quitting of his responsibilities in 1936. Accordingly, the United Kingdom and those

---

[16] See Ch. 2.
[17] See R. Brazier, 'Royal Incapacity and Constitutional Continuity: The Regent and Counsellors of State' [2005] *Cambridge Law Journal* 352.

Commonwealth realms in which the Queen remains head of state face the prospect of elderly monarchs for the foreseeable future. That fact makes it important that effective constitutional provisions exist to provide for any future royal infirmity or incapacity.

Prince Charles has some limited experience of the role which he will one day exercise as king, for example through periodic appointment as Counsellor of State. The appointment of Counsellors of State, and provision for a Regency, are two mechanisms through which the Sovereign's functions in Government may be discharged when he or she is unable to fulfil them as a result of illness, absence, or minority.[18] Counsellors are appointed if the Queen intends to be absent from the United Kingdom, and would be appointed if she were suffering from an illness which was not, however, so serious as to require a Regency (although, remarkably, to date no Counsellors have been appointed since 1952 on account of any illness of the Queen). The Counsellors have delegated to them such royal functions as are specified in Letters Patent issued for the purpose; they are, however, statute-barred from dissolving Parliament (except on the Sovereign's express instructions) and from creating peers. The Letters Patent always require Counsellors to act in pairs, but it may be that the law actually permits one person to act alone.[19] A Regent would be appointed if a Sovereign succeeded under the age of 18, or if the Sovereign were by reason of infirmity of mind or body incapable for the time being of performing royal functions, or if he or she were for some definite cause unable to perform them. If a Regent were required today, he would be Prince Charles. A Regent could perform all the functions of the Sovereign, except consenting to Bills to alter the succession to the throne, or which would repeal the Acts securing the established Church in Scotland.

The present law was not designed to allow any substantial transfer of functions from a relatively fit Sovereign to an heir apparent so as to give the latter greater experience of constitutional matters, or to ease the burden on an ageing head of state (whether the Queen or a future King Charles III). I believe that a new Regency Bill should be contemplated within the next few years, in order to ensure that constitutional continuity was assured in all foreseeable circumstances. Such legislation could retain the present provisions for Counsellors of State and for a Regency, but it should also permit the Sovereign to put a Regent into office by Letters Patent whenever he or she thought fit. Such a mechanism should be flexible enough to permit a Regency for specified periods, such as the Sovereign's lengthy absence abroad; it should also allow the Sovereign, as old age made it more difficult to fulfil all the duties of modern monarchy, to begin to delegate duties to the next in the line of succession (whether Prince Charles or, in the next reign, Prince William) as Regent. An objection to dividing royal functions in that way would be the constitutional

---

[18] Regency Acts 1937–53.
[19] Brazier, 'Royal Incapacity and Constitutional Continuity', 378–80.

oddity of having both a Sovereign and a Prince Regent, when the former was not incapacitated. That might be compounded if the Queen were to choose to retain her personal, important constitutional duties, such as opening Parliament each year, giving royal assent to legislation, and appointing a new Prime Minister when required. That minor difficulty could be met by the invention of a new title for that role—perhaps that of Chief Counsellor of State, or Viceroy. If this idea found favour at Buckingham Palace (and it would obviously require an initiative from, and the full-hearted consent of the Queen and the Prince of Wales), the Prime Minister and the Cabinet would need to be informed of the Queen's wishes, and there is no reason to suppose that they would wish to do other than to cooperate in preparing legislation. No doubt the Leader of the Opposition and the other party leaders would be told of the development by the Prime Minister so that the changes might receive cross-party support in Parliament.

Possible Regency provisions are not of the first order of importance in the British constitution. But because the Sovereign possesses governmental and other responsibilities, the law ought to be so framed as to ensure that those responsibilities can be discharged as efficiently as possible. The Queen may be naturally reluctant to accept the idea of the Prince of Wales as Regent (or any alternative title), because to do so might smack of a dereliction of her duty. But she might be advised that her duty also includes the need to prepare Prince Charles for kingship, and ensure the full discharge of the responsibilities of the monarchy in her old age.

8

Union, dissolution, or federation?

The constitutional structure of the United Kingdom was radically altered at the end of the last century.[1] The Labour Government believed that the devolution settlement enacted in 1998 would be an enduring constitutional edifice.[2] A major purpose of this chapter is to question whether that settlement will, or should, last.

The Union and devolution

The United Kingdom of Great Britain and Northern Ireland is usually described as a unitary sovereign state. At least for the purposes of statutory interpretation the phrase 'United Kingdom' means 'Great Britain and Northern Ireland'. The United Kingdom, with the Channel Islands and the Isle of Man, together constitute the British Islands,[3] which thus form a larger geographical and constitutional concept. But to what extent is the United Kingdom still a unitary state now that devolution of constitutional authority to Scotland, Wales and (with vital qualifications) Northern Ireland has been completed? To answer that question, and to see what the future may hold for the United Kingdom, requires a glance backwards through several centuries of constitutional history, and then a look at some of the effects of the devolution legislation.[4]

The union between England and Wales is the oldest and most complete in the United Kingdom. Effective integration came about with the passing of a number of English statutes, notably the Laws in Wales Act 1535. Under that Act England and Wales were declared to be united, with Welshmen and Englishmen subject to the same laws. In the following year Welsh Members of Parliament were returned to the

---

[1] See generally D. Oliver, *Constitutional Reform in the UK* (Oxford: Oxford University Press, 2003), Chs. 13–15; J. Jowell and D. Oliver, *The Changing Constitution* (Oxford: Oxford University Press, 6th edn., 2007), Chs. 9–11; R. Brazier, 'The Constitution of the United Kingdom' [1999] *Cambridge Law Journal* 96.

[2] For its plans see *Scotland's Parliament*, Cm. 3658 (1997), *A Voice for Wales*, Cm. 3718 (1997), *The Good Friday Agreement*, Cm. 3883 (1998) (sometimes known as the Belfast Agreement).

[3] Interpretation Act 1978, s. 5 and Sched. 1.

[4] The Scotland Act 1998, the Government of Wales Act 1998, and the Northern Ireland Act 1998.

English Parliament and the English system of local Government was extended to Wales. So complete, indeed, was the annexation in practice that the word 'England' in Acts of Parliament was later deemed to include Wales, a slur which was not removed by statute until 1967; moreover, administrative and departmental devolution was to come to Wales much later than it was to Scotland. Thus it was not until 1951 that a Cabinet Minister (the Home Secretary) was given responsibilities for the principality with the additional title of Minister for Welsh Affairs, and only in 1964 was the separate Welsh Office with its own Secretary of State established.

The union between England and Scotland began and was completed very differently. The accession of James VI of Scotland to the throne of England in 1603 constituted a personal union of the two crowns; only when the still separate countries agreed more than a century later to coalesce was a constitutional union born. The Articles of Union, given legislative effect by the Union with Scotland Act 1706 and the Union with England Act 1707, created a United Kingdom of Great Britain, involving the merger of the Scottish and English Parliaments. Despite that union Scotland retained and nurtured her own church, legal and judicial systems, criminal and civil law, local Government, and educational system. That long history of Scottish institutions, in the main unaffected by the union, must help to explain why nationalist, or at least devolutionary, sentiment has been stronger in Scotland than in Wales. A Secretary of State for Scotland was first appointed in the British Government in 1709, and, with gaps, has remained ever since. Administrative and departmental devolution—in itself a recognition that Scotland had been a separate and effective state before 1707—was firmly rooted in Scotland long before the devolution debate caught fire in the 1960s. Indeed, as the Prime Minister was to write in the Scottish devolution White Paper, 'Scotland is a proud historic nation in the United Kingdom'.[5]

Union between Ireland and England began and has continued differently again. The attempts by the Plantagenet Kings of England to subjugate Ireland met with limited success. Despite the repression under Cromwell and William III, by 1783 the British Parliament gave up the fight when it purported to relinquish jurisdiction over Ireland. From that date until the union in 1801, in Maitland's well-known phrase, 'Ireland was no more subject to England than was England to Ireland'.[6] In 1801 the Parliament of Ireland entered into union with Great Britain, and one hundred Irish MPs were returned to the House of Commons, along with twenty-eight Irish representative peers to the House of Lords, in the new Parliament of Great Britain and Ireland. That union survived the Government of Ireland Act 1920 which separated South from North and which established two Parliaments, in Dublin and Belfast. With the recognition of the Irish Free State in 1922 by the

---

[5] *Scotland's Parliament*, Cm. 3658 (1997), v.

[6] F. W. Maitland, *Constitutional History of England* (Cambridge: Cambridge University Press, 1908), 335.

British Parliament, Northern Ireland, and the United Kingdom of Great Britain and Northern Ireland, came into being. The trappings of a semi-independent state with which the Government of Ireland 1920 Act endowed Northern Ireland—a Prime Minister, Cabinet, Privy Council, a Supreme Court, and a Senate and House of Commons with executive and legislative authority over internal affairs—survived as a Protestant unionist-dominated regime until disintegration set in in 1968. As a result of that climacteric the Stormont constitution was abrogated by the Northern Ireland Constitution Act 1973 to be replaced by direct rule from London through a Secretary of State for Northern Ireland. The efforts which then began to find a workable constitution were marked by tragedy and occasional (but illusory) successes.[7] Hopes for a serviceable constitutional settlement currently rest on the multi-party agreement reached in Belfast on Good Friday, 1998, the Good Friday Agreement, and on the power-sharing coalition Executive Committee headed by Dr Ian Paisley as First Minister and Mr Martin McGuinness as Deputy First Minister which took office in May 2007.[8]

Thus the union between the countries, nations and regions of the United Kingdom was originally achieved by England through treaty-making with Scotland and by force in Wales and in Ireland. The whole union came to rely on the consent of the majorities in the constituent parts of the United Kingdom. But the United Kingdom is still a unitary state. The whole of that state, and all the parts that comprise it, remains—at least ultimately—under the jurisdiction of the Parliament of the United Kingdom and through it of Her Majesty's Government in the United Kingdom. Local power, of course, remains vested in traditional local authorities throughout the United Kingdom, and much power has been diffused to the new institutions in Scotland, Wales and Northern Ireland. But the critical constitutional point remains that those new institutions owe their authority and, indeed, their existence to the Westminster Parliament. It established them; it could, as a matter of law, amend or take away their powers at any time through ordinary legislation; it could, legally, abolish any of those institutions at any time. Executive and legislative authorities outside the British Parliament enjoy no specially-protected position in the state, secure from easy interference from the national legislature, as they would in (say) a federal structure.

But, as is so often the case with the British constitution, these matters are not quite as simple as the letter of the law implies. While British parliamentary sovereignty over the whole of the United Kingdom is legally absolute, obviously it is conditioned in its operation by other factors. The place of Ireland, and later of Northern Ireland, in the British state has been, and for reasons to be explained later remains, all too clearly an unstable one. The guarantee obtained by unionists

---

[7] For an excellent analysis of the history from 1886 to the early 1990s see C. McCrudden, 'Northern Ireland and the British Constitution since the Belfast Agreement' in J. Jowell and D. Oliver (see note 1 above) at Ch. 10.

[8] Cm. 3883 (1998).

that the province would only cease to be part of the United Kingdom with the consent (originally) of the Parliament, and (subsequently and now) of the people of Northern Ireland expressed through a referendum[9] would not have been necessary had Northern Ireland's manifest destiny been as a permanent and unequivocal part of the British constitutional system. In Scotland the Scottish National Party (SNP) has sought independence for decades, and it is taking a full part in the Scottish Parliament because the party sees devolution not as an event, but as a process towards independence. Indeed, the SNP achieved office in 2007 in a minority Scottish Executive headed by Mr Alex Salmond as First Minister. And in August of that year the Executive issued a paper *Choosing Scotland's Future* which set out its aspirations for Scotland's constitution. The Executive wanted a 'national conversation' about it, its own strong preference being for a referendum to authorize the Executive to negotiate with the British Government independent statehood for Scotland. The paper also indicated areas in which new powers could be granted to the Scottish Parliament, including economic and fiscal policy (including taxation), oil and gas reserves, pensions policy, and broadcasting. The other parties in the Parliament (except the Green Party) rejected the referendum idea, but all accepted that the authority of the Scottish Parliament should be extended. Clearly, for so long as the SNP continues to represent a substantial portion of opinion in Scotland, it is impossible to assert that Scotland's final system of Government has been achieved. To Scotland, Northern Ireland and (possibly) Wales the granting of legislative and executive authority emphasizes the fact that the legal absolutism of British parliamentary sovereignty is not as settled throughout the United Kingdom as it was once taken to be. Indeed, while orthodox legal doctrine will continue to assert that that authority could be retaken at any time, as a matter of political reality any such action might well be out of the question, and a further important limitation on parliamentary sovereignty will have slid into place.

The Labour Government intended that the creation of the Scottish Parliament should strengthen the union between Scotland and the rest of the United Kingdom by giving practical expression to the aspirations of the Scots to run their own affairs. The Government believed that this would be the basis for a final constitutional settlement. It is well known, however, that the late Conservative Government vigorously opposed devolution to Scotland largely on the ground that devolution of power would mark out a slippery slope down which the United Kingdom would unavoidably slide to break-up. And it is that slope on which the SNP wishes to ride. The Government's task has been to ensure that the terms of the Scotland Act 1998 deliver an acceptable form of home rule while preserving the unitary nature of the state. The philosophy underlying the Act is to give Scotland the greatest degree of autonomy consistent with national matters remaining in the hands of the British

[9] Ireland Act 1949, s. 1(2); Northern Ireland Constitution Act 1973, s. 1; see now the Northern Ireland Act 1998, s. 1 (which will be examined later).

Government and Parliament. To do that the Act reserves to the United Kingdom only specified matters, so that all other powers (subject to stated exceptions) are devolved. So, for example, the United Kingdom Parliament reserves to itself authority over such matters as the constitution, foreign and European Union affairs, and defence, while the Parliament has legislative authority over such matters as local Government, health, education, housing, economic development, transport, law and home affairs, and so on. Vast areas of Scottish life, therefore, are subject to laws made by Scots in Edinburgh, and Westminster's writ no longer runs over them. But what constitutional and legal mechanisms exist to preserve the sovereignty of the United Kingdom Parliament over Scotland? That question is highly relevant to any discussion about further reform of the structure of the state. The Scottish Parliament is elected every four years, by the additional member system; it has chosen a succession of First Ministers and Scottish Ministers, until 2007 leading to a Labour–Liberal Democrat coalition, and since then a minority SNP Scottish Executive. And Scottish legislation flows. But the United Kingdom Parliament still has full legislative authority over Scotland. By convention, styled the Sewell convention after the Minister who articulated it in the Westminster Parliament, the British Parliament will not legislate for Scotland on devolved matters. Yet that Parliament retains its sovereignty through a triple lock.

First, the Scottish Parliament is a devolved legislature within the United Kingdom, and remains subject to the legal sovereignty of the British Parliament. The only authority enjoyed by the Scottish Parliament stems from an ordinary Act of the British Parliament, the Scotland Act 1998. That which the British Parliament has conferred it could take away. Indeed, as a matter of strict law the line between reserved and devolved matters could be altered at any time by the British Parliament. This could be done in order to fine-tune the devolution settlement,[10] or even so as to render nugatory a piece of Scottish legislation, or even by a complete taking back of devolved authority. Secondly, the Scotland Act 1998 states in terms that it does not affect the power of the Parliament of the United Kingdom to make laws for Scotland.[11] That provision is unqualified: the sovereignty of that Parliament over Scotland, despite anything else in the Act, continues. Of course, there are non-legal guarantees which underpin the 1998 settlement, especially the Labour Party's clear 1997 general election pledge to set up the Parliament, and approval of it by the people of Scotland at the referendum by a substantial margin. Scottish electors voted in favour of setting up a Parliament by 74 per cent to 26 per cent (and for it to have a tax-varying power by 64 per cent to 36 per cent), on a 60 per cent turnout. Perhaps it follows, politically, that the settlement should not be altered to the prejudice of Scotland without the approval of its Parliament, or another referendum, or

---

[10] Provision is made in the Scotland Act 1998, s. 63, for the devolution of further authority by Order in Council.

[11] S. 28(7).

both. Yet the Scotland Act is not *legally* entrenched, in the sense that the term is understood in constitutional law: there is no special amending formula; there is no mention in the Act of a further referendum for any purpose; it could be amended or repealed by a British statute enacted in the ordinary way. Thirdly, there are express limitations which the Scotland Act places on the power of the Scottish Parliament to legislate. The matter may be approached through questions. As a matter of law could the Scottish Parliament enlarge its own powers? Could it even pull itself up by its own bootstraps and achieve independence without the legislative consent of the Parliament of the United Kingdom? After all, the SNP has committed itself to holding a referendum on independence, although the current minority SNP Scottish Executive faces a Scottish Parliament majority against such a move. Law-making power is conferred on the Scottish Parliament by ss. 28 and 29 of the Scotland Act. So, the Parliament passes Acts of the Scottish Parliament, which require royal assent. Such Acts constitute primary legislation in Scotland. But it is clear in those sections that any attempt by the Parliament to alter the Scotland Act outside the permitted provisions without the co-operation and legislative consent of the British Parliament, or any Scottish legislation on a reserved matter, would not produce a valid Scottish Act.[12] Under the Scotland Act 'the constitution' is a reserved matter wholly within the authority of the Parliament of the United Kingdom.[13] The phrase 'the constitution' is a novel one to find in a British statute: the phrase includes the Crown, the succession to the Crown, a regency and the Parliament of the United Kingdom. More specifically, the phrase 'the Union of the Kingdoms of Scotland and England' was added at a late stage to Sched. 5. The Scottish Parliament, of course, might persuade the British Government to legislate for an independence plebiscite; the Scottish Parliament might express a view through a parliamentary resolution about the matter; the British Government might, however reluctantly, choose to enact the necessary legislation to test opinion in Scotland. Who can say whether, one day, the Parliament of the United Kingdom might agree to relinquish its authority over Scotland? But the Scottish Parliament can achieve none of those things under its own powers.

Nothing in the Labour Government's policy plans for Wales or in the Government of Wales Act 1998 itself was intended to give Wales anything that would approach the degree of autonomy granted to Scotland or, as will be seen, to Northern Ireland. This is reflected, in part, symbolically: the Welsh legislature is an Assembly,[14] not a Parliament; that Assembly has at present no power to enact primary legislation. This situation resulted from the early and complete union between Wales and England, and the development of Welsh civil society as an integral part of England's. There was less of a distinctly Welsh system of Government and political

---

[12] A similar analysis applies to the Northern Ireland Act 1998: see especially s. 6 and Scheds 2, 3.
[13] S. 30 and Sched. 5, para. 1.
[14] Its formal title is the National Assembly for Wales: Government of Wales Act, s. 1(1).

life to carry forward into that union and therefore less to which subsequent nation-alists could point for reclamation in an independent Wales. On political tests, too, the balance of opinion in Wales has remained against independence or (until 1997) even devolution, and therefore, it seems, in favour of the continued union. So, on first being offered an Assembly in 1979 the Welsh electorate rejected it by a margin of four to one. The Government of Wales Act 1998 was implemented on the basis of a referendum result that came perilously close to rejection: 50.3 per cent voted for a Welsh Assembly and 49.7 per cent against it, on a 51.3 per cent turnout. And Plaid Cymru only achieved representation at Westminster as late as 1966. Plaid's policy, indeed, takes account of Welsh history: it aims to achieve self-Government for Wales within the EU, although occasionally it advocates independence rather more bullishly. Not surprisingly, therefore, the Labour Government's arrange-ments for Wales were always going to be much less ambitious than for their Scottish counterparts, with Wales remaining more closely integrated within the union and subject to a greater degree of British authority than Scotland (or, it was planned, in Northern Ireland). In the Government's view, therefore, the main need was to transfer as much responsibility as possible from the Secretary of State for Wales and the Welsh Office to a Welsh Assembly as a directly-elected body, while reserving to Westminster responsibility for functions which currently operate on a common basis throughout the United Kingdom.

Quite unlike the Scottish Parliament (and, indeed, the Northern Ireland Assembly), the Welsh Assembly was given no powers in 1998 to enact primary legislation. Primary law-making for Wales continues to be done in the United Kingdom Parliament. The Assembly has the functions that were transferred to it by or under the Government of Wales Act 1998.[15] The essence of this process was to give to the Assembly the powers previously and mainly enjoyed by the Secretary of State for Wales to enact subordinate legislation. The Assembly legislates by means of Assembly subordinate legislation, as voted by the Assembly.[16] This delegation of authority represented a significant transfer of democracy to Wales.

Given that the clear legislative purpose of the Government of Wales Act 1998 was to endow the Welsh Assembly with the power to make secondary legislation over transferred matters, in no sense could the Assembly rival the United Kingdom Parliament. The Welsh Assembly represents an extension to Wales of local democ-racy at the expense of the Government and Parliament in London, but not so as to affect the place of Wales in the United Kingdom. As with the Scottish Parliament, the Assembly is a devolved legislature within the unitary state, and one which (unlike the Scottish Parliament or the Northern Ireland Assembly) enjoys no primary law-making powers—at least at present. For further reform is at hand. A multi-party inquiry in Wales recommended radical changes—such as the granting of primary lawmaking powers to the Assembly, and the election of that Assembly by the single

---

[15] S. 21.   [16] Ibid, s. 66.

transferable vote rather than the additional member system.[17] The Government's response, however, was more cautious. The Government of Wales Act 2006 gives the Assembly authority to pass Assembly Measures within its own competence, although the Measures still need the formal approval of the Privy Council. At some future time the Assembly may get primary legislative powers, but only if three votes so decree—the Assembly itself, by at least a two-thirds majority, Welsh voters at a referendum, and a vote in each House of the Westminster Parliament. The 2007 Labour–Plaid Cymru Welsh Assembly Government has a two-thirds majority in the Assembly. Is it too cynical to suggest that the Labour Government's triple lock over a slower approach in Wales comes from a fear of a consequent reduction in Westminster of constituencies in Wales, which are minded to return in the main Labour MPs?

For well-known historical, political and religious reasons the relationship, and therefore the union, between Great Britain and Northern Ireland has been very different from the union between the United Kingdom and the other countries and regions within it. The latest version of a constitution for Northern Ireland is enshrined in the Northern Ireland Act 1998. That Act was brought into operation by the Secretary of State for Northern Ireland under the authority of the statute, but the institutions so created—especially the Northern Ireland Assembly and the Northern Ireland Executive—were suspended by the Secretary of State on three occasions since, and they were only reinstated in 2007. The suspensions were the result of continuing tensions between the political parties and communities in Northern Ireland. Throughout the second half of the last century—again for clear historical reasons—the union of Northern Ireland with Great Britain has been underpinned by a guarantee enacted by the Parliament of the United Kingdom, first in the Ireland Act 1949, then in the Northern Ireland Constitution Act 1973, and now in the Northern Ireland Act 1998, s. 1. That guarantee, of course, is not itself entrenched. The Parliament of the United Kingdom could therefore quite lawfully ignore such constitutional guarantees and legislate in the ordinary way to alter the status of Northern Ireland without a referendum. It is true that that Parliament might well consider itself bound as a matter of political morality to obey what is really a statement of a constitutional convention which was born in 1949. But as with any other convention there would be no breach of the law if its terms were broken. In any event, the terms of the guarantee have been altered under the Good Friday Agreement. The British and Irish Governments undertook in that agreement to recognize the legitimacy of whatever choice is freely made by the majority of the people of Northern Ireland over its status, whether that be to continue the union with Great Britain or to support a sovereign united Ireland. Moreover, if the people of the island of Ireland were to decide that they would prefer a united Ireland it would be a binding obligation on both Governments under the agreement to

---

[17] *Report of the Independent Commission on the Welsh Assembly* (Cardiff: Welsh Assembly, 2004).

introduce legislation in both Parliaments to give effect to that wish.[18] The existence of that obligation may have more importance than is indicated by the bare wording of the 1998 Act. For it raises, as it were, a statutory doubt about the continuance of the union between Great Britain and Northern Ireland. Uniquely in the legislation which binds all parts of the country together as the United Kingdom, it is in relation to Northern Ireland that a dissolution of that union is recognized as a possibility in the Northern Ireland Act. No such query exists, in law, in relation to Scotland or to Wales. To the contrary: in the Union with Scotland Act the union is expressed to be 'for ever', and in the Laws in Wales Act 1535 Wales was declared to 'continue for ever ... incorporated united and annexed to' England. Political reality overlays the law: the union of England and Scotland may well not last for ever: but only in the Northern Ireland Act does an explicit mechanism exist to test the will of the Northern Ireland people, and is a duty placed on the British Government to ask the Westminster Parliament to cede the province to Ireland if that is the wish of the people of Northern Ireland.

The Northern Ireland Assembly has authority under the Northern Ireland Act to pass primary legislation about agriculture, economic development, education, the environment, finance, and social services. The Northern Ireland Act is identical to the Scotland Act in preserving the sovereignty of the United Kingdom Parliament, while transferring executive and legislative powers to the Northern Ireland Assembly. The Act is entrenched in the same sense that its Scottish and Welsh counterparts are entrenched—through the wishes of the people of Northern Ireland expressed so clearly in the 1998 referendum, in which 71 per cent voted for the settlement and 29 per cent against, on an 81 per cent turnout.

Like the Scottish Parliament, the Northern Ireland Assembly has the power to enact primary legislation on devolved matters, but despite that power it is denied the title of 'Parliament'. No doubt this is in recognition of nationalist memories of the Stormont Parliament of Northern Ireland which still rankle. But the Queen is given functions in relation to the Northern Ireland Assembly. Thus, while the Assembly (like the Scottish Parliament and the Welsh Assembly) is elected for a fixed, four-year term it may be dissolved earlier in specified circumstances by the Queen, but (unlike in Scotland) under the authority of an Order in Council approved by both Houses of Parliament and by two-thirds of the members of the Assembly. As in relation to Scottish Bills, Bills passed by the Northern Ireland Assembly require royal assent.

Possible devolution of legislative authority to England outside London is still a long way off.[19] The Labour Government's strategy has been to proceed cautiously with the English dimension of constitutional reform and, with the exception of

---

[18] Northern Ireland Act 1998, s. 1(2). See B. Hadfield, 'The Belfast Agreement, Sovereignty and the State of the Union' [1998] *Public Law* 599.

[19] See generally R. Hazell, *The English Question* (Manchester: Manchester University Press, 2006).

London, its policy initiatives have failed. The Government pinned its hopes on individual regions of England expressing the wish to have an elected regional assembly, Ministers having ruled out an English Parliament or Assembly. A start was made through the enactment of the Regional Development Agencies Act 1998. This was followed by the Regional Assemblies (Preparations) Act 2003, which provided for referendums in designated regions to see if the public there wanted an elected regional assembly. The first (and last) was held in the North East in 2004: the result was a crushing rejection of the idea by 78 per cent to 22 per cent, on a 50 per cent turnout. The Government, not surprisingly, abandoned any plans for further such referendums for the indefinite future. Do people in England consider the Westminster Parliament to be their Parliament? Is there a greater resistance in England to an additional, devolved, layer of Government, along with a refusal to offset it by abolition of old and respected (or at least tolerated) English counties? Even if there is some truth in all that, the West Lothian question remains. Why should MPs from Scottish constituencies be able to legislate at Westminster for England on matters such as health, education, and so on, while MPs from English constituencies cannot legislate for Scotland over such devolved matters? Indeed, Mr Gordon Brown presides over a Cabinet which cannot initiate legislation over a vast range of matters which would affect his Kirkaldy constituency. The Conservative Party's answer is, in effect, that only MPs representing English constituencies should vote on legislation affecting only England. That is entirely logical, and it would be a more convincing solution than reducing the number of MPs returned to Westminster from Scotland. Their number was cut from 72 to 59 as from the 2005 general election. But the constitution and politics are intertwined. Everyone knows that if the Conservative answer were adopted a Labour Government might well lose its majority in the House of Commons over 'English' legislation because of the large number of Labour MPs returned from Scotland. And so the Labour Party continues to decline to offer any convincing answer to the West Lothian question.

But London leads England, at least in the sense of having voted at a referendum in 1998 in favour of a directly-elected Mayor of London and a twenty-five member London Assembly.[20] Together they constitute the Greater London Authority, under a statute of that name, with responsibility for economic and industrial development, strategic planning, public transport co-ordination, and for the emergency services. While it is clear that the Labour Government does not want the Authority to be like the former GLC, it wished the Mayor to have significant executive power, and the Government would be happy for other English cities to copy the new London model. Indeed, several cities in England have instituted directly-elected mayors.

---

[20] Held under the Greater London Authority (Referendum) Act 1997. See *A Mayor and Assembly for London*, Cm. 3897 (1998).

Governments in the UK

In 1998 the United Kingdom had one body of Ministers, Her Majesty's Government in London. By 2000 there were four groups of Ministers located in the capitals of the constituent parts of the United Kingdom.

As befits executive officers drawn from a Parliament, members of the Government in Scotland[21] are known as Ministers and are headed by a First Minister. The Scottish Ministers are supported by junior Ministers and by the Lord Advocate and the Solicitor-General for Scotland. The First Minister, Scottish Ministers and the two Scottish Law Officers collectively (but excluding junior Ministers) collectively form the Scottish Executive. Similar nomenclature is used for the Northern Ireland ministerial arrangements. Executive authority is discharged on behalf of the Northern Ireland Assembly by a First Minister and a Deputy First Minister, together with up to ten Ministers with departmental responsibilities and supported by junior Ministers, forming the Executive Committee. The Northern Ireland Assembly is elected by the single transferable vote, and elaborate statutory rules in the Northern Ireland Act 1998 ensure that the Executive will always be a coalition based on power-sharing. In Wales the Assembly chooses an Assembly First Minister, who in turn appoints Assembly Ministers, collectively forming a Welsh Assembly Government. The three executives are responsible to their legislatures, in constitutional relationships designed to be similar to that which exists between the British Government and the United Kingdom Parliament. Each executive depends on the confidence of its legislature, and if that confidence is lost the executive will have to resign or may be removed by the legislature.

In general terms the responsibilities of British Ministers have obviously been reduced following devolution of legislative and executive power. In terms of personnel, it might be thought that question marks could exist against the continuance of the offices of three Secretaries of State for the three countries and regions, many of whose duties have been assumed by the devolved authorities. But the British Government has been keen to stress that although the duties of those offices have changed, they will remain. Thus all three Secretaries of State continue to represent the interests of Scotland, Wales, and Northern Ireland in the Cabinet especially in relation to reserved areas, and they argue for resources; they have duties in relation to the devolved legislatures.[22] The Scottish and Welsh Secretaries, however, each hold other Cabinet posts as well, in recognition of their reduced territorial duties. There is a case for the merger of the Scotland Office and the Wales Office into a

---

[21] For a full treatment of the Scottish Executive see R. Brazier, 'The Scottish Government' [1998] *Public Law* 212.

[22] *Scotland's Parliament*, para. 4.12; *A Voice for Wales*, paras 3.33–3.35. The Secretary of State for Northern Ireland has many duties under the Northern Ireland Act, and that Secretary of State will be required for the foreseeable future.

revived Department for Constitutional Affairs, a point to which I will return in Chapter 10.

The future of the United Kingdom

What, then, of the future? Does the future of the United Kingdom as a constitutional entity lie in continued union, or in dissolution, or in federation?

In the long history of the British Islands the United Kingdom has existed for barely two hundred years. The West Lothian question is dwarfed by a much larger constitutional possibility. Current tensions make the continued existence of the United Kingdom as a constitutional entity uncertain. It is, of course, the consent of the Parliament of the United Kingdom which would be needed for any further alterations to the status of the constituent parts of the United Kingdom. Any foreseeable United Kingdom Parliament, however, is likely to contain a unionist majority. The maintenance of the union between England, Wales, Scotland, and Northern Ireland (subject in the latter case to any contrary expression of the people's wish) is the firm policy of the Labour Party and (even more emphatically) of the Conservative and Unionist Party. That stance no doubt reflects the preference for the union which exists in England and elsewhere, possibly shored up by the forces of inertia, by a view that the United Kingdom has come through much together, and by the belief that the larger unit is a bigger player in the world than would be any of the individual parts alone. (That said, there is a view in England that Scotland benefits disproportionately in financial terms from the union.) The Labour Party also reaps the benefit of large numbers of MPs who are returned to Westminster from Scottish and Welsh constituencies: moreover, at the 2005 general election the Conservatives won more votes in England than did the victorious Labour Party. It seems unlikely that either party would do other than argue passionately for the constitutional benefits which they say the union brings to the countries, nations, and regions of the collective whole, and will resist separatist movements. Both parties are now committed to the terms of the Scotland Act. The force of unionism between England and Wales is stronger. The Government's commitment to the Welsh Assembly has been underpinned by the Government of Wales Act 2006, which could see the Assembly looking more like the Scottish Parliament. Conservative support appears lukewarm at best for Welsh devolution, and the Assembly itself was initiated on the least certain expression of popular desire for greater autonomy anywhere in the United Kingdom. Probably the Welsh Assembly will prove to be a permanent feature in the United Kingdom constitution. But it is at least possible that it might be abolished if, in the light of experience, it failed to function in a manner satisfactory to Wales and the United Kingdom. Any such collapse would strengthen, not undermine, the union between Wales, England, and the United Kingdom.

Yet—of course—there are stresses which pull against union. The consistent policy of the SNP has been to strive for an independent Scotland, using whatever legitimate means come to hand. The party worked hard at the 1997 referendum for Scottish approval for a Parliament with tax-varying powers as a sort of down-payment on independence—the very process about which the Conservative Party had warned so consistently in recent years. It went on to become the largest party in the Scottish Parliament in 2007, and the party wants a referendum on independence as soon as possible. While the constitutional and legal mechanisms are patently in place to continue the supremacy of the United Kingdom Parliament over Scotland's future, *if* the view takes hold in Scotland (perhaps expressed unambiguously through a referendum if one were permitted by the United Kingdom Parliament, or demanded by a majority of the Scottish Parliament), would it be a credible or viable policy for the unionist parties at Westminster to resist such demands, presumably by all means not excluding the use of force? A bold step which the Government might consider would be to extend the new form of the Northern Ireland unionist guarantee to Scotland. It might be better for the Government to seize the initiative, to guarantee the continued union for so long as the people of Scotland wanted it, but to agree to respect any expression of a wish for independence. The advantages for the British Government of such a step would be that it could set the terms in which any such expression might be deemed to be valid (perhaps including a threshold which had to be achieved, and perhaps with minimum periods to elapse between referendums), and it would be seen to grant (in the possibility of a referendum) the very thing which it would otherwise merely determinedly resist despite nationalist demands in Scotland.

In Northern Ireland all the political parties are committed to abiding by the wishes of the majority as to union with Great Britain or with a united Ireland. At the last expression of opinion on the border issue in 1973 nearly 600,000 people voted for Northern Ireland to remain in the United Kingdom, while only some 6,500 voted for union with the Republic—but in a poll in which the Social Democratic and Labour Party (SDLP) and 41 per cent of the population abstained. Under the Northern Ireland Act 1998 a border poll may now be ordered by the Secretary of State if it appears likely that a majority would vote for union with Ireland, although any such polls must be seven years apart. That there is a significant nationalist population in Northern Ireland can be seen, for example, by the fact that at the 2007 Northern Ireland Assembly elections nationalist parties secured almost as many seats as did unionists. (Indeed, at the 2005 general election more Sinn Fein MPs were returned than SDLP ones (five to three respectively).) Looking ahead, therefore, while it is possible that the 1998 settlement and institutions will endure, it is equally plausible that, one day, the people of Northern Ireland might opt to join the Republic of Ireland, as provided for in the guarantee. The absolute certainties of permanent union which existed from 1922 until the abolition of the Stormont Parliament in 1973 seem very remote today. It must be added, in the light of history, that an equally plausible outcome might be the collapse of the 1998 settlement.

But even if the Labour Government's constitutional settlement does endure, there would remain a case for taking matters one step further, towards formal federalism.

It is notorious that the word 'federal' can be made to mean what the user wants it to mean: the word has no fixed, legal meaning.[23] It is that elasticity that has allowed friction to enter the debates about the development of the European Union. Federalism can embrace a strong central executive and legislature, with subordinate local units enjoying only specified authority but who nonetheless have constitutional protections against the centre (as, say, in Canada); or it may imply strong local units with a limited central Government (as in the United States). And between those two extremes there are various other balances which can be struck in a federal system. There are, too, various reasons why a federal constitution may be created. Local units will wish to retain certain rights. There will be perceived advantages in taking action collectively in certain matters within a federation (invariably including defence, external relations, and so on), while establishing rules to keep the federal authorities within those collective purposes. Sometimes there may be an initial distrust of strong central Government, as was the case with the American colonists, and in post-war Germany. Occasionally that concern may be reflected in a federal constitution which ensures that local rights cannot be taken away, even by constitutional amendment. Despite those variable factors, a federal constitution will contain three principal features, namely, (a) the delimitation of federal and local powers, (b) the protection of that delimitation by making constitutional amendment difficult (requiring more than a bare parliamentary majority in the federal legislature); usually this will include the consent of the local legislatures or populations, and (c) the policing of the delimitations by a supreme constitutional court.

The case for moving towards a federal constitution for the United Kingdom, in brief, may be expressed this way. Significant powers exist in the countries and regions of the United Kingdom (although not in England): the old, centralized British state has passed away: it follows that the next step to a federal constitution would be a much smaller one to take than would have been the case as recently as (say) in 1995. It may be that a de facto federal constitution is in place, if the United Kingdom Parliament and Government leave the devolved authorities in peace—as the Northern Ireland Parliament was for fifty years. A reasonably settled division of responsibilities between London and the other capitals is emerging. This amounts to a practical expression of subsidiarity within the United Kingdom. A new federal constitution would ensure that the devolved systems would be protected

---

[23] For a good short account see E. Barendt, *An Introduction to Constitutional Law* (Oxford: Oxford University Press, 1998), Ch. 3.2; see also G. Sawer, *Modern Federalism* (London: Watts, 1976); Sir Kenneth Wheare, *Federal Government* (Oxford: Oxford University Press, 3rd edn., 1953). For the Liberal Democrats' case for a federal United Kingdom see *For the People, By the People* (London: Liberal Democrat Policy Paper No. 83), Ch. 6.

from easy infringement by the Parliament of the United Kingdom:[24] never again could a Government, relying on its parliamentary majority, abolish tiers of local Government contrary to their wishes. A final advantage would be that representatives of the various parts of the kingdom could meet and collectively decide the settlement: this did not happen in 1998. Federal constitutions usually spring from a truly national constitutional assembly or process.

What, then, might be the prospects for the adoption of such a federal solution for the United Kingdom? Strangely, perhaps, it might be those who champion local rights the most strongly who would oppose a federal structure for the United Kingdom the most vigorously. Nationalists in Scotland (and usually in Wales) want independence, not the freezing of Scotland (or Wales) within a permanent federation. Nationalists in Northern Ireland, too, would be loath to enter a federation, because they see the destiny of Northern Ireland in a unified Ireland. An obvious compromise might be to include a mechanism for local resignation from the federation. Under it the federal constitution would operate with its advantages until any component part succeeded in activating the dissolution mechanism (just as, under the (probably defunct) draft EU Constitution, a member state could resign its membership). British antipathy towards constitutional theory, preferring that institutions be allowed to develop pragmatically, would also hinder the adoption of a federal constitution. That attitude may also explain in part the Labour Government's disinclination to present its constitutional reform programme as a related whole, driven by any constitutional theory. The 1998 devolution settlement, which provides for separate and different development in Scotland, Wales, and Northern Ireland, fits better with that approach. In any event, there is a case for establishing a review mechanism to examine how successfully the whole devolution legislation has worked. (It is, however, notable that Mr Brown's ambitious Green Paper, *The Governance of Britain*,[25] is deeply conservative on the structure of the United Kingdom.)

The immediate aspirations of the people of Scotland, Wales, and Northern Ireland may be met through the new democratic assemblies and Governments that have been established. Very many matters of daily importance to citizens, such as housing, education, and health, are now the responsibility of those new and accessible authorities. In arriving at that new disposition a revised United Kingdom constitution—neither federal, nor as purely unitary as it was—has been developed. It has produced a politically weaker central Government. Edinburgh, Cardiff, and Belfast have gained substantial legislative and executive authority at the expense of the United Kingdom Parliament and the British Government. Because those powers are underpinned by the popular sovereignty expressed through the referendums, it would be difficult (albeit legally possible) for the United Kingdom Parliament to

---

[24] On entrenchment, see Ch. 9.
[25] Cm. 7170 (2007), paras 141–44.

take back those powers without a similar expression of popular sovereignty. While the Scottish constitution has been limited in law by the Westminster Parliament, that constitution provides a new and continuing means for Scots, if they wish, to express their national aspirations. Northern Ireland has been moved nearer to the joint suzerainty of the United Kingdom and the Republic of Ireland, and a mechanism now exists in law which would require the cession of Northern Ireland to the Republic if the majority in the North so wish.

For the moment constitutional power is redistributed within the United Kingdom. It is quite possible, however, that within the next few decades the state known as the United Kingdom may disappear, to leave Scotland independent once more, a whole island of Ireland, and—after a three hundred year diversion— England and Wales alone.

9

Defending rights

How best to protect rights?

Now that the United Kingdom has a Human Rights Act may we not simply put a tick against the words 'reform human rights law' in any list of constitutional changes which still need to be carried out? I think not. Rather, we need to see whether the best regime for human rights now exists in the United Kingdom. To do that we need to evaluate how rights were safeguarded before that statute was passed, analyse the strengths and weaknesses of the Act, and consider the so-called problem of entrenchment—which for so long got in the way of change, and continues to do so. In any case, political debate about the protection of human rights did not stop when the Human Rights Act was passed. Indeed, Ministers whose own Government sponsored the Act have occasionally criticized the uses to which their own statute has been put by judges and others. And, as will be seen at the end of this chapter, Mr Gordon Brown as Prime Minister has described the enactment of the Human Rights Act as the first step on a journey: a review has been initiated to judge whether the United Kingdom needs (in his words) a new Bill of Rights and Duties. Moreover, Mr David Cameron as Conservative leader has pledged that the next Conservative Government will consider the repeal of the Act and the replacement of it with 'a British Bill of Rights'.[1] And we live in a more dangerous world today than we did in 1998: balancing public safety and individual liberty has become a harder task given the horrors of international terrorism.

It was not only Victorian worthies in the pages of fiction who spoke disparagingly of foreign constitutions.[2] The great A. V. Dicey himself dismissed with scorn the way in which the rights of the citizen were defended abroad. As he put it, 'most foreign constitution-makers have begun with declarations of rights. For this they have often been in no wise to blame.'[3] What Dicey seems to have had uppermost in his mind was the futility of setting out ringing declarations of human freedoms without underpinning the rhetoric of liberty with effective means to protect them.

---

[1] 'Balancing Freedom and Security: A Modern British Bill of Rights' (London: Conservative Party, 2006).

[2] See Ch. 1, note 3.

[3] Dicey, *Introduction to the Study of the Law of the Constitution* (London: Macmillan, 1959), 198.

To the extent that, in England, matters have always been very different—precise, legal remedies being available through which the citizen can secure his or her freedoms, but without any general statement of rights—Victorian commentators naturally took it for granted that, once again, England had got things entirely right while all foreigners had got them completely wrong.

But in the final decades of the twentieth century many people in the United Kingdom came to believe that human rights were much better protected in many foreign legal systems than they were in Britain. The old Victorian certainties had been swept away. How did this happen? Two things had changed. Abroad, states had incorporated in more modern declarations of rights highly effective, and usually judicial, means to guarantee that rights are enjoyed against all comers, including Governments which might be avaricious for greater powers. Rights obtained sanctions for breach. At home in the United Kingdom, elective dictatorship[4] allowed British Governments either to be careless whether their legislative and administrative acts derogated appropriately from human rights, or (according to taste) permitted Governments deliberately to infringe the rights of the citizen in favour of increased power for central Government. In my view, although personal liberty lost ground during the last Conservative Government (and during Mrs Thatcher's reign in particular), the setbacks to freedom did not start in 1979; moreover, I think that the extent of the loss since 1979 has occasionally been exaggerated. Hyperbole unleashed in the debate about civil rights by those on the political left against the privations of a right-wing Government are fair enough,[5] but even some academic commentators have been rather carried away in anti-Thatcher diatribes.[6] Be that as it may, it came to be argued that legislative, and perhaps institutional, change was urgently needed in order to improve the lot of civil liberties in Britain in the late twentieth century.

At first sight the omens in favour of any such reform might have seemed to be bleak. Many of those who most need guaranteed and effective rights, such as the poor, or the badly educated, or the unpopular, are the least able to secure them. There may well be few votes to be gained by a political party in proposing an extension of rights to such people. And more rights for the individual mean less power (or at the least great inconvenience) for any Government. Against such a background both the Liberal Democrats and the Labour Party deserve full credit for having committed themselves—in different ways—to extending civil rights.

---

[4] See Ch. 1.

[5] See the dismal catalogue listed by the then Shadow Lord Chancellor, Lord Irvine of Lairg, in the House of Lords debate on the state of civil liberties under Mrs Thatcher's administration: 519 HL Debs. 904–9 (23 May 1990).

[6] See esp. P. McAuslan and J. F. McEldowney, 'Legitimacy and the Constitution: The Dissonance between Theory and Practice', in P. McAuslan and J. McEldowney (eds.), *Law, Legitimacy and the Constitution* (London: Sweet & Maxwell, 1985), 1–38.

Of course, to argue that civil rights in the United Kingdom are not what they once were or are not what they ought to be requires some litmus-test against which the assertion can be measured. One such serviceable test has been provided in the judgments of the European Court of Human Rights, which have registered against the state of liberty in Britain. By late 1997 that Court had found against the British Government in fifty cases. As a result many things which the courts, Parliament, and successive Governments in the United Kingdom had accepted as being perfectly proper were declared to violate the European Convention on Human Rights, and action had to be taken to bring British law and practice into conformity with the European Convention. The regime for tapping telephones; birching in the Isle of Man; discriminatory Immigration Rules; the law on homosexuality in Northern Ireland; the law of contempt; the rights of prisoners; the rights of the mentally ill: all these things, and many others, were in a perfectly acceptable state in the eyes of British judges and politicians, but fell below the standards insisted upon by the terms of the European Convention. The shaft of liberty's light cast by British judges by means of the progressive development of judicial review of administrative action, it is true, illuminated to an extent the gloom of those European condemnations.

Many on the political left in Britain have claimed, not unfairly, that most civil rights have been secured in the United Kingdom by legislation, and not by the courts. They suspect that the judiciary on its own would not have developed the law in favour of the rights of the individual, and therefore have argued that the parliamentary process should be allowed to continue. In that way further rights must be established through democratic means, and as little reliance as possible should be placed on the judges who, for various reasons, are ill-equipped for the task of securing and extending freedoms. Individuals with grievances about civil rights must, on this view, put pressure on Members of Parliament to change the law. There are, though, difficulties with this approach (leaving aside the observation, made with the luxury of hindsight, that the judges have been more robust in enforcing rights in recent years than might have been imagined in (say) 1990). There are limits on what the individual can be expected to achieve in securing a change in the law from Parliament for an alleged wrong. The citizen is, in effect, asked to pursue a mere possibility that the Government might deem it expedient to take action. Yet it may be that it was the Government's own action which raised the grievance in the first place, thus making Ministers judges in their own cause. The attitude of the Government's own backbenchers to the situation, the inconvenience for Ministers which might result if it were to take steps to correct the injustice, the pressure on the legislative programme, and perhaps the general unpopularity of the complainant, might very well all persuade the Government that no action was the best action—or, indeed, in relation to people suspected to be dangers to society, to move to *restrict* their rights. Whatever might have been Parliament's historic place in securing individual rights, the realities of contemporary politics mean that more people tended to look for help, not to their Members of Parliament, but to the courts (especially through applications for judicial review), and if need be to the European Court of Human Rights.

What, then, was to be done to put matters right? The policies of the political parties, were, as always, very important, because the party in power sets the framework for the protection of rights. Demands that action be taken to improve individual rights counted for little before the intransigence of the last Government. Everything in the Conservatives' garden was rosy: I suppose that, having been in power for so long, they perhaps viewed things through rose-tinted spectacles. The general satisfactory condition of the garden was due to the loving attention, as required, of judicial gardeners; the occasional weed was removed by parliamentary action; from time to time parts of the display received low marks in the European competition, but maintenance work was then speedily carried out to bring the exhibits up to the mark. Outside that garden the other political parties saw matters very differently. The Liberal Democrats believed that radical change was necessary, and urged the incorporation into municipal law of the European Convention, together with the protocols to it, as a new United Kingdom Bill of Rights.[7] The legislation which would do that should, in their view, require United Kingdom courts in applying it to have regard to the judgments of the European Court of Human Rights. That policy had been supported for a long time by pressure groups, including Liberty and Charter 88.

The Labour Party has undergone a radical change of mind towards the question of a Bill of Rights.[8] For most of its life the party has opposed the ceding of the protection of rights from Parliament to the courts. In the late 1980s, however, Labour took a tentative step towards a greater protection of individual rights by advocating a series of new civil rights statutes, collectively to be known as the Charter of Rights. That would have amounted to an attempt to pass legislation in detailed language on discrete topics, leaving as little opportunity as possible for judicial meddling in Parliament's intentions. Labour at that time continued to reject the case for a Bill of Rights on the grounds that it could not be entrenched (a point which I will consider in a moment), and because such a Bill—cast in statements of general principle—would be open to interpretation by the judges, with no certainty that they would give adequate protection to the most vulnerable members of society, or, to be frank, those to whom the judiciary was perceived as being antipathetic, such as the trade unions. There was an objection in principle to be made to Labour's Charter of Rights approach. At least some rights exist—or ought to exist—independently of the wishes of Governments. A Government and Parliament should not be able to select certain rights to protect, and pass statutes to establish them, while leaving other rights outside the ambit of the law. Rights ought to exist above and beyond the reach of any Government, Parliament, or party: the availability of rights should

---

7 For a Liberal Democrat peer's attempt to achieve this see 560 HL Debs. 1136–74 (25 Jan. 1995).
8 See Ch. 3.

not vary according to whether a particular Government finds them convenient, or acceptable, or compatible with its electoral aims. That suspicion of any coherent and comprehensive code of individual rights echoes disagreements which existed in the post-war Labour Government. Sir Stafford Cripps urged the Cabinet not to ratify the European Convention on Human Rights because he thought that its provisions would make it impossible, or certainly very difficult, for the Government to achieve a fully planned economy. The Cabinet decided against him, but Cripps's reservations remained in Labour's subconscious for a long time.

By the time of the 1997 general election the Labour Party had committed itself to incorporate the European Convention on Human Rights into English law.[9] In the autumn of 1997 the Labour Government published a White Paper to explain how this would be done,[10] together with the Human Rights Bill to give effect to the proposals. In summary, it will be recalled that under the Human Rights Act 1998 it is unlawful for any public authority (a concept which is widely defined) to act in a way incompatible with Convention rights. A victim of such unlawfulness is able to challenge the authority in the courts, and at any appropriate level of court. The courts are bound to take account of relevant decisions of the European Court of Human Rights (but these decisions are not binding on English courts). As far as interpretation is concerned, Acts and secondary legislation are to be interpreted by the courts as far as possible so as to be compatible with the Convention, a requirement that applies to future as well as to existing legislation. If a court finds that a rule of statute law conflicts with Convention rights it does not have the power to strike it down, but it may issue a declaration of incompatibility. The Government and Parliament are thereby placed under political pressure to alter the statute law. Legislation to be so amended may be changed by an Order in Council, so the usual delay in passing an ordinary Bill can be avoided. Ministers are under a duty, in introducing any Bill into Parliament, to declare whether its provisions are compatible with the Convention.

The Human Rights Act 1998 is a welcome and subtle mechanism which makes it easier to get the protection of Convention rights.[11] It saves an alleged victim the commitment, time, and money which were previously required to get to the European Court of Human Rights (although that ultimate route is preserved by the Act). The statute maintains the legal supremacy of Parliament, which remains the final arbiter of whether any statute, found by the judiciary to be incompatible with Convention rights, should be changed by legislation. To date Ministers

[9] See Ch. 3. See also Constitution Unit, *Human Rights Legislation* (London: Constitution Unit, 1996).

[10] *Rights Brought Home: The Human Rights Bill,* Cm. 3782 (1997).

[11] Oliver, *Constitutional Reform in the United Kingdom* (Oxford: Oxford University Press, 2003), Ch. 6; Lord Irvine of Lairg, 'The Development of Human Rights in Britain' [1998] *Public Law* 221, and 'The Impact of the Human Rights Act: Parliament, the Courts and the Executive' [2003] *Public Law* 308; Klug and Starmer, 'Standing Back from the Human Rights Act' [2005] *Public Law* 716.

have acted to alter the law following an adverse declaration—a political fact which should make the strongest proponents of parliamentary sovereignty and opponents of entrenchment pause for thought. This does not mean that Ministers have invariably acted in a slavish fashion in such situations. Indeed, the Government's reaction when the House of Lords ruled that the power to detain certain people indefinitely under the Anti-Terrorism, Crime and Security Act 2001, s. 23, was incompatible with Convention rights,[12] was to pass the Prevention of Terrorism Act 2005. This introduced control orders, designed to restrict the freedom of movement of those deemed to present a risk of terrorism.

But there are defects in the scheme of the Human Rights Act. First, the powers of the Government to derogate from the European Convention on Human Rights remains. Such a derogation from fundamental rights is impossible in some legal systems, such as under the United States Bill of Rights. Should derogation—at least from core rights such as the right to liberty—be permitted at all, or at least only subject to stronger safeguards than exist under the European Convention? Secondly, Ministers are not bound as a matter of law to respond positively following a declaration of incompatibility—still less do the courts have the kind of strike-down power possessed by, say, the United States Supreme Court. Thirdly, some rights are not protected specifically at all under the Human Rights Act. There is, for example, no general right protecting against discrimination, nor are social or economic rights, such as to housing, employment, or healthcare, mentioned. Any more detailed, newer, British Bill of Rights might identify those, and other, rights for recognition and defence. Fourthly, the Human Rights Act is, of course, an ordinary statute, and as a matter of law could—as Mr David Cameron has noted—be repealed (although, without more, the machinery of the European Convention on Human Rights would remain in place). It is that last point that I want to pursue next. Could a Bill of Rights be entrenched in the United Kingdom, or does the doctrine of parliamentary sovereignty mean that the sort of regime—clever as it is—in the 1998 Act is the strongest that could be devised?

A red herring

One of the Labour Party's reasons for its former policy of spurning both the adoption of a new Bill of Rights and the incorporation into English law of the fairly old European Convention was that no such document could be entrenched against amendment or repeal. For others, that was *the* conclusive reason against adopting a Bill of Rights. Much was made of the point in a House of Commons debate in 1990 on a possible Bill of Rights, and for most Members who spoke that was the

---

[12] *A. & Others v. Secretary of State for the Home Department* [2005] 2 AC 68.

end of the matter. Every first-year law student knows what Dicey said about parliamentary sovereignty: that Parliament can make or unmake any law whatever.[13] So how would rights in a new declaration of rights be any better protected against the rapacity of elective dictatorship, given that fresh legislation could encroach on the rights declared in it? The Government could easily get Parliament to amend, or indeed entirely repeal, any inconvenient provisions with the assistance of the Whips. Now there are several ways in which the entrenchment argument (or rather the *lack* of entrenchment argument) can be answered. It is possible that an entrenchment could result from a legal revolution which, through the adoption of a comprehensive new constitutional settlement including a written constitution and a Bill of Rights, would overthrow the present constitutional order and with it the doctrine of absolute parliamentary sovereignty. A codified constitution, even on optimistic assumptions, is a long way off,[14] and so discussing it as a method of entrenching a Bill of Rights would not be time well spent. I will, however, summarize five other solutions.[15]

The first is to concede the argument outright and accept that the uniquely odd nature of the British constitution means that entrenchment would, indeed, be impossible. Let it be acknowledged that not only is the United Kingdom Parliament unique in being unable to enact effective entrenched legislation, but also that it is unique in having no power to alter that fundamental rule of the constitution by legislative means. It would be quite possible to leave all of that unchallenged, and to pass a new Bill of Rights as an ordinary statute, amendable and repealable in the usual way, but to include a requirement in it that a Minister report formally to Parliament if any subsequent draft legislation appeared to be inconsistent with the new Bill. This is what happens under the Human Rights Act 1998. Such a Bill of Rights might acquire a special place in British constitutional legislation. It might come to possess a moral force of its own, with Governments loath to introduce any measure which would derogate from it. The rule that any Government wishing to do so would have to declare its intention openly ought to place a particular responsibility on Ministers to explain why they wished to act in that way, so exposing them to criticism and perhaps to political unpopularity. If, as the years rolled by, the Bill of Rights remained unamended (or perhaps amended in only minor ways) it might be protected as a matter of political reality, although not (it is true) as well as if some special method were required as a matter of law to amend it. As a result, the United

[13] Dicey, *Introduction*, 39–40. That view is now subject to the supremacy of European Community law.

[14] See Ch. 11.

[15] On the question generally see the excellent analysis in J. Jaconelli, *Enacting a Bill of Rights: The Legal Issues* (Oxford: Clarendon Press, 1980), Ch. VI. For an excellent survey of recent developments in the doctrine of parliamentary sovereignty see A. W. Bradley, 'The Sovereignty of Parliament—Form or Substance?' in J. Jowell & D. Oliver (eds.), *The Changing Constitution* (Oxford: Oxford University Press, 5th edn. 2004), Ch. 2.

Kingdom would retain an unsullied doctrine of parliamentary sovereignty while also acquiring some political protection against easy amendment of its new Bill of Rights.

A second answer to the entrenchment question would be to adopt what might be called the football-pools solution.[16] The new Bill of Rights might contain an entrenchment mechanism, say a requirement that special majorities be obtained in both Houses before any amendment were duly passed. But—as with the football pools—that arrangement would be binding in honour only. The orthodox view of parliamentary sovereignty would remain; as a matter of practice, though, Governments and Parliaments might consider themselves honour-bound to follow the amendment mechanism given the special nature of legislation designed to secure fundamental rights and freedoms. If the mechanism were ignored by Parliament on any occasion, that would be a lawful manifestation of parliamentary sovereignty (although, over time, the judges might adapt their attitude to that sovereignty and ascribe to the entrenchment provision the attributes of a binding rule). Parliaments and Governments might not wish, however, to incur the odium of breaking the amendment terms of the Bill of Rights, just as football-pool companies do not welsh on winning bets; and the Bill would, in effect, have achieved a degree of special protection which Dicey and others would say was impossible to achieve.

Then, thirdly, there are the various interpretative devices which have been suggested over the years. So, a Bill of Rights might state that any earlier Act which was inconsistent with it was, to the extent of that inconsistency, repealed, and that any inconsistent common law rule was abrogated. It might also contain a direction to the judges that any legislation passed *after* the Bill of Rights was to be interpreted consistently with it, if that were possible; it might also state (to bow the knee to parliamentary sovereignty) that if such an interpretation were not possible, the later provision must override the Bill, as would any later Act which stated expressly that it was to have effect despite any inconsistent language in the Bill of Rights. Again, that is the general approach which applies in the Human Rights Act 1998. There is, of course, much judicial and other authority which urges that a line be drawn there in seeking to defend civil rights legislation against amendment or repeal. Both the Standing Advisory Committee on Human Rights in Northern Ireland and the Select Committee of the House of Lords on a Bill of Rights[17] have reported— consistently with academic and judicial opinion—that any attempt (by interpretative provisions or otherwise) to override *future* inconsistent Acts would be nugatory. Even if the line were to be drawn short of such an attempt, a Bill of Rights which contained interpretative sections such as those just indicated would none the less be before the judges frequently and would require them to compare and

---

[16] This is my label for a suggestion made by Hood Phillips, *Constitutional and Administrative Law* (London: Sweet & Maxwell, 7th edn., 1987), 437.

[17] Cmnd. 7009 (1977); HL 176 (1977–8).

contrast other statutory provisions with it. It is hard to think of any other single Act to which reference might be made so frequently in court. Older statutes would be checked to see whether they had suffered implied repeal; newer statutes would be scrutinized for consistency with the Bill of Rights; judges would become immersed further in the language of rights. That process would inevitably give it a rather special place in the scheme of British legislation.

Fourthly, it would be possible to choose a parliamentary solution to the entrenchment problem. One has been suggested by Lord Scarman.[18] He thought that having incorporated the European Convention into English law, a new Parliament Act should be passed which would give the House of Lords an absolute veto over Bills to amend or repeal that Parliament Act and any statutes scheduled to it, which would include the incorporation Act. (Other scheduled Acts suggested by him might include the Habeas Corpus Acts, Magna Carta, and specified Acts aimed at achieving equality.) Thus, in relation to the new Parliament Act and to scheduled Acts, the Lords would have restored to it the absolute legislative veto which it enjoyed before 1911. A variant on that might be centred on any new second chamber that might be created one day.[19] An elected second chamber might be given the power to delay legislation designed to amend the new Bill of Rights. That delay could last (if the second chamber desired it) for the whole life of a Parliament, thus providing the electorate with the chance to pass judgement at the following general election on the Government which was proposing to derogate from fundamental rights. The chamber's constituent Act would give it an insurmountable legislative veto. The orthodox doctrine of parliamentary sovereignty would have to give way. For it would then be absurd to suggest that the House of Commons could ignore the new chamber's constituent Act and any veto imposed by that chamber of a Commons Bill, and seek to assert that that Bill had become law despite the veto. To do so, the Commons would be relying on some mysterious, fundamental, and unalterable rule of parliamentary sovereignty which referred to a Parliament which by then would no longer exist in the form upon which that rule had been based.[20] That said, there would be two political difficulties inherent in such a scheme if it were put into being. It assumes a party in effective control of the second chamber which would be minded to oppose any Commons Bill which would derogate from the Bill of Rights. That would not necessarily be so. Obviously, whenever the *same* party was in control of both Houses, it would be unlikely that a veto would be used against the Government—although as the House of Lords under the late Conservative Government showed us, that could not be taken for granted. Moreover, it is unlikely that a general election campaign could be fought on the single issue of a proposed

[18] See 'Bill of Rights and Law Reform' in R. Holme and M. Elliott (eds.), *1688–1988: Time for a New Constitution* (London: Macmillan, 1988), 109–10.

[19] See Ch. 5.

[20] See further on this point S. A. de Smith and R. Brazier, *Constitutional and Administrative Law* (Harmondsworth: Penguin Books, 8th edn., 1998), 81–84.

amendment to the legislation on fundamental rights. Such simple things rarely happen in general elections, however much the political parties urge the voters to concentrate on one question. Despite those points, such a plan, if enacted, might tame the Leviathan of parliamentary sovereignty.

Lastly, there are judicial solutions to difficulties of entrenchment. Sir William Wade has argued that it is time the United Kingdom grew up and stopped mumbling feebly that nothing can be done to entrench legislation. His 'easy way out' would be to secure recognition of any entrenched provisions through a new judicial oath of office. An Act would discharge the judges from their existing oaths, and would require them to re-swear in terms obliging them to recognize and give effect to the terms of entrenched legislation (such as a new Bill of Rights).[21] Provided that the provision relating to the new oath was itself immunized against amendment, this would be a simple and effective means through which a Bill of Rights could be safeguarded.

And so entrenchment may be exposed as a red herring in the debate about civil rights, and, indeed, over a possible codified constitution trailed across the way of those wishing to map out a path towards further legislation. There are several ways of negotiating any obstacle caused by entrenchment. It might be—for who, other than the judges, can say?—that only a fairly weak form of entrenchment of rights would be possible in the United Kingdom. Even if that proved to be so, however, that should not mean, in my opinion, that all further discussion of fresh statutory rights would be a futile exercise. On the other hand, it might be that greater protection of rights would be possible. Entrenchment should not be the beginning and end of the Bill of Rights debate.

But what is the case for continuing the British tradition of safeguarding rights through the courts and Parliament, thus eschewing the adoption of a brand-new Bill of Rights? Some arguments should be dismissed with derision, or possibly with contempt. We are assured that individual rights in the United Kingdom are already adequately protected, and that, to the extent that adjustments prove to be necessary, ad hoc legislation can be passed for the purpose, all within the framework of the Human Rights Act. Now, while the British do unquestionably enjoy better rights than citizens in several other countries, assertions such as these fly in the face of the evidence. Then we have been told that a formal declaration of rights would be contrary to British tradition. That argument has been weakened, perhaps fatally, with the passage of the Human Rights Act, which constitutes an (admittedly malleable) code of rights. And we are threatened with a flood of litigation if a Bill of Rights were adopted. This is no more than the old floodgates argument which is resurrected, usually in desperation, by many who oppose some change or other in the law. There is more food for thought in other strands of argument. The first runs that a Bill of Rights which is entrenched (whether as a matter of law or through its

---

21 Sir William Wade, *Constitutional Fundamentals* (London: Stevens & Sons, 1989), Ch. 3.

own moral force) is undemocratic, for it can prevent a Government implementing parts of the programme which had been approved by the electorate. This argument becomes stronger the older any Bill might be, and the more representative the House of Commons might become, for Parliament would then be thwarted by tablets of stone carved by long-dead legislators. Another strand queries whether any Bill of Rights could, or even should, achieve finality. The meaning of legislation can only be definitively divined by judges who, in doing so, establish precedents. But what of awkward precedents established on a Bill of Rights? The courts might, for example, uphold legislation as being compatible with an exception in the Bill. The Opposition might view that as an indefensible use of such an exception. When they were next in power, should they put things right by securing an amendment to the Bill of Rights? If they cannot satisfy any amendment requirements, the Bill is undemocratic in the sense just indicated; if they *can* obtain an amendment, the value of having a measure whose purpose was supposed to be to secure rights indefinitely might be doubted.

That is not really an argument against judicial power as much as an argument that a draft Bill of Rights is strengthened if it has wide, and preferably cross-party, support, and conversely is weakened if it does not. But obviously there are arguments against judicial power in the protection of rights. The track-record of British judges in securing appropriate civil rights through the medium of the common law has been criticized, at least until recent years, as being unimpressive, and it might be feared than in interpreting a Bill of Rights the judges might be too quick to find in favour of state power to the detriment of individual liberty. If a new Bill of Rights were (for whatever reason) difficult to amend, the role of the judiciary would clearly be the more important. But British judges do have some experience of applying Bills of Rights. The Judicial Committee of the Privy Council has been the final imperial court of appeal since 1833, and has remained the supreme court for several independent Commonwealth countries. In that capacity the Judicial Committee has had to apply Commonwealth Bills of Rights. In the last 25 years or so the Judicial Committee has tended to a more purposive and generous interpretation of such Bills, rather than a literal and restrictive one. The membership of the Judicial Committee and of the Appellate Committee of the House of Lords is much the same, and so the supreme court within the British legal system has had significant (even though indirect) experience in interpreting and applying Bills of Rights. (The Law Lords will be transfered to be the first Justices of the Supreme Court when it begins work, probably in 2009, but the Judicial Committee's jurisdiction over Commonwealth appeals will continue.[22]) Judges of all ranks have had to consider the terms of a Bill of Rights by having to become used to the provisions of the European Convention on Human Rights, especially since 2000 when the Human Rights Act came into force. Exposure to a new British Bill of Rights would not be as much of a cultural shock as some have suggested.

---

[22] See Ch. 10.

The next steps

It will come as no surprise to the reader who has persevered thus far to learn that I believe the best way forward in the debate on civil rights would be for a wide-ranging review to be conducted of the most appropriate method for further improving Britons' rights. And the reader will expect me to say (as I do) that such a review would most appropriately be carried out by a body such as the Constitutional Commission proposed in Chapter 2, advised by an expert legal committee appointed by the Commission. The political debate on a possible Bill of Rights has revolved around the 'impossibility' of entrenchment, and the inability of the judges (who, in the process, would become politicized) to implement its provisions impartially. In recent years the discussion has been complicated by the so-called war on terrorism, with Ministers objecting to the limits placed on their freedom of action by judicial interpretation of the Human Rights Act. A rational investigation into the underlying issues, including of course a full examination of the desirability and possible means of specially protecting any new Bill, ought to be the necessary precursor of any political decision on whether to seek new arrangements for safeguarding human rights in the United Kingdom. Such an investigation might recommend anything from a range of possibilities—to continue the status quo, or to suggest that a brand-new Bill of Rights be written. There would certainly be difficulties in trying to draft a brand-new Bill of Rights, particularly if it were designed to attract multi-party support. If the parties were to start with a blank sheet of paper, controversy would rage over many possible provisions—those on the method of voting which would be necessary to give effect to a right to fair elections, the right to property, to private health care and to private education, and all the rest. There is also the worry that the new, domestic Bill of Rights might make life rather easier for politicians when invoking anti-terrorism legislation. In the meantime, there is much to commend the Human Rights Act. Britain is bound by the European Convention in any event; the European Convention is enforced by the European Court of Human Rights; the British Government always acquiesces in its findings; and there is no prospect of, or desire to, withdraw from the Convention. Quite apart from any other consideration, the 1998 Act has placed the terms of the Convention into a British statute, and requires that its provisions be applied in all courts in the United Kingdom. Enforcement is no longer entirely a matter for a *European* court and judicial system. Condemnations from abroad should largely be a thing of the past. The law is, once again, in the hands of British judges.

But the Human Rights Act 1998 is not, in my opinion, enough. The European Convention is showing signs of the times in which it was written, particularly in the things which it does not seek to safeguard. An ideal combination, therefore, would be the entrenchment of the Convention and the passage of other specific legislation so as to protect rights that would otherwise be outside its ambit. How might all this be specially protected against the deprivations of elective dictatorship (assuming that that form of Government were to continue)?[23] If the judiciary were to indicate, in reply to my questions suggested earlier, that parliamentary sovereignty is parliamentary sovereignty, was, is, and will be, then I would find the most appealing of all the ways of giving some measure of protection to be a combination of both the interpretative method and a House of Lords veto. So, an Act incorporating the European Convention (and any other Acts setting out additional rights) would require that prior inconsistent legislation be of no effect, and that later legislation be interpreted in a way consistent with those Acts, unless that were impossible or unless the later legislation expressly stated that it was to override the Bill of Rights Act. The Parliament Acts 1911 and 1949 could be amended so as to restore to the House of Lords an absolute veto over any Bill which would amend or repeal anything in the Bill of Rights Act and any Acts forming part of it. Such a mechanism would be completely consistent with even the most orthodox view of parliamentary sovereignty, but would provide a better check than could be imposed through the existing law. Of course, a Government which was determined to amend a Bill of Rights Act *despite* a House of Lords veto could amend the Parliament Acts yet again to remove the newly restored veto, and could force such a Bill through under the Parliament Act itself (that is, after a Lords' delay of about a year). In doing so, the determination of that Government to derogate from civil rights would appear the more stark. Of course, this reliance is placed on the House of Lords before the final shape and powers of that chamber are known,[24] and it could be that a weaker chamber would make the suggested mechanism less attractive.

Against that background Mr Brown's first Green Paper published as Prime Minister reopened the whole debate about a possible new Bill of Rights.[25] The initiative deserves the warmest welcome. Mr Brown is concerned that the notion of 'Britishness' should be better understood, and the Green Paper sketches out some elements of that notion.[26] The paper asks whether there should be a codification of such 'principles and ideas'. The sources of rights in the United Kingdom are enumerated, and the overarching importance of the European Convention on Human Rights—the ultimate effect of which would not be altered by any repeal of the Human Rights Act 1998—is noted. The paper recalls that that statute was 'the first step on a journey'.[27] The paper balances the possible advantages of a new code (for example, that it would give citizens a clearer idea of their rights and obligations) against possible drawbacks (for instance, that it should 'not restrict the ability of the democratically elected Government to decide upon the way resources are to be deployed in the national interest',[28] nor should it prejudice measures necessary

---

[23] See Ch. 4.
[24] See Ch. 5.
[25] *The Governance of Britain*, Cm. 7170 (2007), paras 204–10.
[26] Ibid, para. 204.
[27] Ibid, para. 208.
[28] Ibid, para. 209.

to protect public safety[29]). While there is no explicit reference to the question of entrenchment, drawbacks such as those just enumerated might suggest that any special legal status for such a code might be eschewed. The Green Paper gives no commitment to legislate, but it does reverse ten years of the Labour Government in effect treating the Human Rights Act as the last word on the protection of rights.

The Liberal Democrats have argued consistently for a new Bill of Rights, which would balance the rights of citizens against the requirements of public safety. They want to see such a Bill as part of a new, entrenched and codified constitution.[30]

---

[29] Ibid, para. 210.

[30] Liberal Democrats, *For the People, By the People* (London: Liberal Democrat Policy Paper No. 83, 2007), Ch. 4.

10

Government, law, and the judges

Ministers, the constitution, and the law

In 2003 the old Lord Chancellor's Department (LCD) was replaced by a Department for Constitutional Affairs (DCA), headed by the Secretary of State for Constitutional Affairs and Lord Chancellor. Under the Constitutional Reform Act 2005 radical changes were made to the office of Lord Chancellor and to the way in which judges were henceforth to be appointed; and a new Supreme Court is to be established under that Act in 2009. Moreover, in 2007 a new Ministry of Justice was created, taking over the functions of the DCA (which was abolished) together with important duties from the Home Office. That arrangement, made by Mr Blair near the end of his premiership, was continued under Mr Gordon Brown. In order to understand why those changes were made it helps to recall the previous, centuries-old, dispensations. Doing so should also disclose any remaining defects in vital areas of the constitution.

The United Kingdom did not have a Minister entirely responsible for constitutional affairs. As is so often the case, ad-hockery reigned: whenever a Government decided to embark on a constitutional change it made ministerial dispositions especially for the purpose, and wound them up when that purpose had been achieved (or had failed). The Labour Government that took office in 1997 did so committed to a bigger programme of constitutional reform than any previous Government.[1] But this work was not entrusted to a single Government department which might possess the expertise and resources which such grand schemes deserve. This approach was, of course, typical of what had gone before. The wide-ranging plans of the Liberal Democrats to work towards a written constitution, to introduce proportional representation, to create a Senate in place of the House of Lords, and to adopt a new Bill of Rights, were not, as conceived, to be spearheaded by new constitutional machinery, either. A contributory, although by no means dominant, factor in the United Kingdom's historical failure to reform its constitutional system may well have been the absence of adequate Government machinery which could act as a focal point for ideas, as a catalyst for change, and as a depository of legislative

[1] See Ch. 3.

and administrative expertise.[2] The Conservative Party was able easily to defend its refusal to allocate governmental resources appropriate to the importance of constitutional affairs on the ground that it rejected the case for general constitutional reform.[3] The other political parties had no such defence.

Governments of all colours, however, have had to make ministerial dispositions in relation to the general law. No Government would wish to claim that it had no responsibility for legal affairs. Whether Governments like it or not, important constitutional issues are entwined in that responsibility. They include the independence of the judges, the appropriate training for the judiciary which would not improperly interfere with that independence, ministerial accountability for the law, the administration of justice, and the provision of appropriate legal services for citizens. Yet the ministerial dispositions which developed, mainly as between the Lord Chancellor and the Home Secretary, were such as would not be acceptable in other broadly similar states.[4] No modern state which wished to establish ministerial responsibility for such things as the administration of justice, public order, the treatment of offenders, law reform, and the appointment of the judiciary would follow the historical British pattern and allocate those and related matters almost haphazardly between two Ministers. Nor would it place each of those Ministers in different chambers of the legislature, with one Minister (equivalent to the Lord Chancellor) having for good measure judicial and parliamentary duties as well. Such a state would not charge one of the Ministers (the equivalent of the Home Secretary) with two largely incompatible functions, police and public order on the one hand, and the protection of civil rights on the other. Nor would it be likely to follow the United Kingdom in giving law responsibilities to another five Ministers as well.[5]

Under this chaotic British system the Lord Chancellor was responsible for judicial service matters (that is, judicial appointments, the determination of judicial salaries, and the disciplining of the lower judiciary); judicial administration; the state of the civil law, and legal aid and advice. If that were not enough for any Minister, he could also write chronicles of wasted time while acting as Speaker of the House of Lords—wasted time given that peers keep themselves in order and given that he (always a he to date) was only occasionally present for business in which he had any departmental responsibility. The Lord Chancellor could also sit as a judge in the House of Lords. In all this the Lord Chancellor did not even have a junior

---

[2] These organizational questions are examined in depth in Constitution Unit, *Delivering Constitutional Reform* (London: Constitution Unit, 1996).

[3] See Ch. 3.

[4] On the Lord Chancellorship before the office was reformed in 2003 see D. Woodhouse, *The Office of Lord Chancellor* (Oxford: Hart Publishing, 2001).

[5] The Prime Minister, the Attorney-General, the Solicitor-General, the Chancellor of the Duchy of Lancaster, and the Financial Secretary to the Treasury all had responsibilities for aspects of the law.

Minister to help him until a Parliamentary Secretary was appointed in 1992.[6] That development brought the LCD within the reach of the House of Commons for the first time, and the Select Committee on Home Affairs was also given oversight of the LCD (although—rightly—not of particular court cases or judicial appointments). In his or her turn, the Home Secretary was required to reconcile two inconsistent responsibilities: those relating to civil rights and justice (criminal-law reform, magistrates' courts, race relations legislation, data protection, nationality, and the like), and those concerning public order and security (the police, MI5, and the treatment of offenders). It must be assumed that Home Secretaries could cope with this rather schizophrenic life, or else many would have left office very precipitately. But that is not the point. It is obvious that a Minister with vital public order responsibilities may be unable or unwilling to give enough of his or her energies to issues such as the freedom of the individual or minority rights. Indeed, a Government's commitment to 'law and order' policies might mean that he or she would have no personal political incentive to argue for the enlargement and development of civil rights.

Highly undesirable results flowed from a further division of responsibilities between the Home Office and the LCD. Because the Home Office was in charge of criminal law reform while the LCD was responsible for the state of the civil law, no single Minister had overall responsibility for law reform. If a particular proposed reform concerned the civil law (which quantitatively most will), pressure could not be put by Members of Parliament directly on the Lord Chancellor to accept the need for that reform. Each Government department is fully responsible for promoting changes in the law within its particular field. Such devolution of law reform duties to individual departments is necessary and probably inevitable, given that expertise in particular areas of Government is naturally concentrated in them; but departmental Ministers have many other calls on their time, and what is lacking is a single Minister who could spur ministerial colleagues to action. In establishing the political priorities for Government legislation, interdepartmental claims for resources and parliamentary time are, in short, settled with insufficient ministerial weight behind the case for law reform. Further confusion in law reform responsibilities is caused by the pattern of reform bodies. For example, the Law Commission has undertaken important criminal law work, not least in developing a draft Criminal Code, but it reports to the Lord Chancellor, who until 2007 had no ministerial responsibility for criminal law.

These ministerial dispositions resulted in a complete lack of ministerial responsibility and accountability in a number of areas. The worst example concerned accountability to Parliament for judicial service matters. Lord Hailsham of St Marylebone LC in particular frequently claimed that he was answerable to Parliament for such questions. He often proclaimed the virtue of his position, which

---

[6] The Attorney-General and the Solicitor-General were and are in no sense junior Ministers to the Lord Chancellor.

interposed the Lord Chancellor between the independence of the judiciary and what he considered were improper attacks by Members of Parliament on the judges. That claim of accountability is really bogus—or at any rate is one whose truth has not been tested. From first to last during his Chancellorship no peer called Lord Hailsham to account in these matters. Had the Lord Chancellor been in the House of Commons he would certainly have been challenged on such questions.

Some of the issues touched on so far concern technical legal matters. Others are of significant constitutional importance. The law and the constitution are inseparably mixed. The way in which a Government equips itself to address such interlocking legal and constitutional issues is something which should attract the attention of constitutional reformers. One political party, the Liberal Democrats, has had for a long time plans to recast ministerial responsibility for the law: another, the Labour Party, had such plans, but alas ditched them before coming to power in 1997. The Liberal Democrats proposed the creation of a Ministry of Justice.[7] It would be charged with the protection of human rights, the administration of the legal system, and law reform. The Home Office would retain its 'internal security' functions. It is not clear from the plan whether such a new Minister would sit in the House of Commons: proper accountability would require that he do so, but an earlier paper suggested that the Lord Chancellor might be the Minister of Justice, and that as such he should be enabled to sit in either House.[8] That cannot be right. Nor was it clear whether the new Minister would take responsibility for all law reform. Again, the earlier paper suggested just that, but a degree of devolution of responsibility to individual departments for law reform is unavoidable. But the general idea behind the plan—to rationalize ministerial tasks—was highly desirable. Labour had plans in opposition to abolish the Lord Chancellor's ministerial functions,[9] but abandoned them in 1995.[10] Under its former scheme a Minister of Legal Administration, sitting in the Commons, would have become responsible for all courts and tribunals, court procedure, the organization, training, and appointment of the legal professions, magistracy, and (indirectly) the judiciary, and for legal aid. The Home Secretary would have retained his duties with regard to the police, prisons, penal policy, and the criminal law. Mr Tony Blair on coming to office as Prime Minister continued the traditional arrangements for the Lord Chancellor and his Department, and for the Home Office. The Conservative Party had nothing to contribute to the debate. The late Conservative Government was unconvinced by any of the proposals that had been made for new ministerial arrangements for the law.[11]

---

[7] See *Here We Stand: Proposals for Modernising Britain's Democracy* (London: Liberal Democrats, 1993).

[8] *Government, Justice and Law,* Alliance Paper No. 1 (London, 1985).

[9] See *Meet the Challenge: Make the Change* (London: Labour Party, 1989), 61.

[10] See *Access to Justice* (London: Labour Party, 1995), 7. See further Ch. 3.

[11] See, e.g. the Chancellor of the Duchy of Lancaster at 254 HC Debs. 2 (written answers 6 Feb. 1995).

I want to set out a number of principles upon which reorganization of Government in this area might have been based. First, ministerial responsibility for the law should be fully founded in the House of Commons, and be subject to select committee scrutiny, in the same way as any other Government activity. Secondly, ministerial dispositions should be related entirely to functions and efficiency, so that, for example, one department (the Home Office) should be responsible for matters such as public order and the treatment of offenders, while another department should be charged with responsibilities such as civil rights, the general oversight of the law and law reform, and judicial administration. Thirdly, any major recasting of ministerial responsibilities should have taken advantage of a fresh start, so that rather than trying to reform the office of Lord Chancellor, and trying to graft new and dynamic duties on to the LCD, a new department could have been created and both the office of Lord Chancellor and the LCD could be abolished. Fourthly, judicial service matters (relating principally to judicial appointments, promotions and discipline) should be moved completely away from ministerial authority, and machinery independent of Ministers should be created to discharge responsibilities for them.

How might such principles have been translated into practice?[12] As I argued in the first edition of this book in 1991, at the centre of the reorganized machinery of Government, I believe, should be a Department of Law. Nomenclature is important, if only because some of the reaction against the proposals of the Haldane Committee on the Machinery of Government[13] over eighty years ago was fuelled by the use of the continental title of 'Ministry of Justice'. To avoid stirring up misplaced fears that a new Government department would be intended to interfere in the judicial process, the word 'justice' would be better avoided. Rather, the work of the Department would be accurately summed up in the word 'law'. The principal duties of the Department might include the following: (a) legal services, legal aid, and relations with the professions; (b) the reform of civil and criminal law (although the initial responsibility of other Government departments for this would remain), and responsibility for all law reform agencies; (c) the provision, administration, and procedure of all courts and tribunals; and (d) determination of judicial salaries. If the Department of Law had duties such as those, the Home Office would be left with functions relating to public order, public safety, national security, the treatment of offenders and penal policy, and the enforcement of immigration control. Those are important responsibilities, most of which fit logically within a department such as the Home Office. The Home Secretary's main burden would involve fighting for the public money and parliamentary time necessary to fulfil those functions, without having to seek such money and time for different, and sometimes opposing,

---

[12] More detail is given in my article 'Government and the Law: Ministerial Responsibility for Legal Affairs' [1989] *Public Law* 64.

[13] *Report of the Committee on the Machinery of Government*, Cd. 9230 (1918), Ch. X.

responsibilities as well. As will be seen later, dispositions along those general lines—but with important differences—lay behind the creation in 2007 of the Ministry of Justice, which assumed several important functions from the Home Office. But those changes left an entirely inadequate ministerial responsibility for constitutional affairs.[14]

It was impossible to justify the pre-2003 split of responsibilities between the Home Office and the old LCD for the state of the criminal and civil law, and for their reform. My suggested Department of Law would be responsible for both—but in a way which would maintain the necessary diffusion of some responsibility to individual Government departments. The Law Secretary alone would decide on the importance of particular law reform measures, and would have to argue for parliamentary time in which to enact them. A watching brief would also be kept by the Law Secretary over the fate of reform proposals emanating from bodies such as departmental committees of inquiry, set up by other Ministers and reporting to them. The Department of Law would not, however, attempt to take over the law reform which is now undertaken by individual Government departments: no one central department could match the knowledge and policy expertise which exists in those departments. The Department of Law would not be involved in criminal law enforcement, which would remain with the Home Office; but the Department might take over responsibility for the state of the criminal law. This law reform work would shade into the new Department's general oversight of the form of legislation sponsored by other departments, and into its responsibility for the consolidation programme. One purpose behind giving the Department that oversight would be simple: to ensure that new legislation was as comprehensible as possible. All Government legislation would be tested for comprehensibility and other desirable qualities in the Department of Law, which would have the last word over the form in which it was submitted to Parliament. As an overall consequence the quality of such legislation ought to improve.

The Law Secretary would, of course, be a Member of Parliament, and he or she should have ministerial support appropriate to the size of his or her departmental duties, including one or two junior Ministers. There is no cogent reason why the Law Secretary should necessarily be a lawyer. Ministers are not expected to be professionals in their departmental specialities, and the Law Secretary would be no exception. Parliamentary supervision of the two Ministers who would have responsibility for legal affairs under this scheme, the Home Secretary and the Law Secretary, would be asserted through the House of Commons. A Select Committee on the Department of Law would be established, and no part of the Department's duties would be beyond its reach.

[14] See below.

The Department for Constitutional Affairs; the Ministry of Justice

Some of the arguments just set out were implicitly accepted by Mr Tony Blair as Prime Minister in 2003. In a shock announcement in the context of a Cabinet reshuffle the LCD was abolished and the DCA was set up, using royal prerogative powers to do so. A new way of appointing judges, and a new Supreme Court, were also to be established. The DCA was headed by a new Secretary of State who was also to be the Lord Chancellor until (under the original plan) that office could be abolished. Lord Falconer LC thus became Secretary of State for Constitutional Affairs as well. This was an object lesson in how not to do constitutional reform. There had been no public consultation on such a major constitutional change, not even privately with the judiciary; no mention of it had been made in the Labour Party's general election manifesto or any other policy paper. Not surprisingly, the plan ran into heavy weather. It became clear that legislation would be required to abolish or alter the functions of the Lord Chancellor, because the office was governed by numerous statutory provisions; and many people, including some senior judges, the Conservative Party, and some MPs and peers, were not convinced by the case which had been sketched out to support these plans, especially those involving the abolition of the ancient office of Lord Chancellor. Lord Hailsham, no doubt, would be turning in his grave. Lord Falconer *then* began consultations.[15] A Bill followed, which (oddly for a controversial measure) began its parliamentary journey in the House of Lords, where it faced sustained criticism and reference to a select committee.[16] The Bill was revised by the Government and reintroduced in the following parliamentary session. In the event the Constitutional Reform Act retains the office of Lord Chancellor, but in a reformed guise.[17] In particular, the Lord Chancellor ceased to be, even nominally, head of the judiciary (a role taken over by the Lord Chief Justice); he (or surely one day she) can no longer sit as a judge; a new Lord Speaker of the House of Lords has been elected by peers to take over the Lord Chancellor's duties as presiding officer of that House. The title of Lord Chancellor remains, and Lord Falconer remained Secretary of State for Constitutional Affairs as well. It is in that ministerial role that the Minister's energies were to be concentrated. The Government's single— and cogent—justification for this change rested on the doctrine of the separation of powers. The Secretary of State for Constitutional Affairs and Lord Chancellor became a Minister of the Crown, and a Minister of the Crown alone—not a judge, nor an officer presiding over a House of the legislature. Indeed, under the 2005 Act

---

[15] Department for Constitutional Affairs, *Constitutional Reform: Reforming the Office of Lord Chancellor* (London: DCA, 2003).

[16] Select Committee on the Constitutional Reform Bill, *Report*, HL 125 (2003–4).

[17] Constitutional Reform Act 2005, Pt 2.

the Lord Chancellor is no longer required to be a lawyer: membership of one or other House, along with other specified criteria, are enough.[18] The DCA was to be, unambiguously, *the* Government department responsible for the state of the constitution. It was overseen by the Constitutional Affairs Committee of the House of Commons, and the department had junior Ministers sitting in that House. The new Secretary of State—as will be seen in a moment—had much reduced responsibilities for the choice of new judges.

But in 2007 the DCA disappeared. The then Home Secretary, Mr John Reid, was determined to reduce the burden on the Home Office to that of securing public safety, and wanted, for example, responsibility for convicted people to be some other Minister's problem. The Prime Minister agreed with him. But, rather like the Bourbons, at least according to Talleyrand, Mr Blair had learned nothing and forgotten nothing, in his case from his handling of the creation of the DCA merely four years earlier. True, there was some consultation this time with the judiciary, but the principle of splitting the Home Office, and of transferring many of its responsibilities to a new Ministry of Justice (which would also absorb the DCA), was presented as a fait accompli.[19] No agreement was achieved between the Lord Chancellor (who was to become Secretary of State for Justice, in lieu of Constitutional Affairs) and the judges. Judicial criticism of this was supplemented by the Public Administration Select Committee[20] and the Constitutional Affairs Committee.[21] The Home Office remained in charge of counter-terrorism, crime and policing, immigration, passports, and drugs policy. The Ministry of Justice took over (*a*) all the functions of the young DCA, which was abolished, including the judiciary and the courts, tribunals, legal aid, the voting system, human rights, and freedom of information, together with (*b*) responsibility for prisons, probation, parole, criminal justice reform, and criminal law. The Ministry assumed general responsibility for the state of the civil law, together with numerous other, less important, matters.

The substance of these changes was criticized by, among others, the Lord Chief Justice, the Judges' Council, and the Magistrates' Association. They were worried that funding for courts and legal aid would be vulnerable to cuts in the Ministry's budget which might be necessary to pay, for instance, for more prison places. Judges were also concerned about judicial independence, in that they might face pressure from their own Secretary of State for Justice to send fewer people to grossly overcrowded prisons. In addition, it may be noted that the creation of the Ministry set the clock back in that one Minister, the Secretary of State for Justice, was to be in charge both of human rights and post-sentencing matters, two responsibilities that

---

[18]   2005 Act, s. 2. See generally Lord Windlesham, 'The Constitutional Reform Act 2005' [2005] *Public Law* 806 and [2006] *Public Law* 35.

[19]   458 HC Debs. *133–5* (WS 29 March 2007).

[20]   Public Administration Select Committee, *Machinery of Government Changes*, HC 672 (2006–7), paras 1–3, 25, 27, 41.

[21]   *The Creation of the Ministry of Justice*, HC 466 (2006–7).

can be incompatible. But Mr Brown continued with the arrangement, and indeed on forming his first Cabinet he appointed Mr Jack Straw as the first MP ever to be Lord Chancellor (and Secretary of State for Justice).

In my view it would be much preferable to continue with the slimmed-down Home Office, but to revive a Department for Constitutional Affairs, and to rejig the Ministry of Justice. The Home Office, quite rightly, focuses on national security and public safety. But the loss of the DCA is to be regretted. The United Kingdom should have a Government department wholly and exclusively responsible for constitutional affairs, constitutional reform, human rights, and the judiciary. The rump Scotland Office and the Wales Office could also be merged into it, so that the constitutional structure of Great Britain would be presided over by one Government department. (Northern Ireland remains a special case, requiring its own Secretary of State at least for the time being.) Such a department would be responsible for my suggested Constitutional Commission. Simply put, the British constitution deserves a dedicated Government department to develop the framework through which the United Kingdom is governed—a principle which Mr Blair accepted for what, alas, turned out to be but one brief shining moment (well, for four years). It is unacceptable that the constitution should be but one part of a busy Cabinet Minister's remit, which includes many other very important matters unrelated to constitutional affairs. My proposal would leave the Ministry of Justice to preside over post-sentencing matters (prisons, probation, and so on), criminal justice reform, and the civil and criminal law—in other words, with many of the duties which I originally sketched out for the suggested Department of Law.

I turn next to the judiciary, and especially to how judges are appointed. Once again, it is helpful to begin with a glance back to the old days before the passage of the Constitutional Reform Act 2005.

The judges

The judges play a pivotal part in the British constitution. It is misconceived to propose major reforms to that constitution, many of which would require changes in the law, without addressing the general question of the judiciary. Any suggestion of major reorganization of ministerial responsibility for the law has often been met with the objection that the judges would become subject to ministerial control and dependent on ministerial approval for appointment and promotion. 'Judicial independence' is a phrase which has often in the past been deployed in order to maintain the status quo. Lord Chancellors before Lord Falconer have vigorously asserted that judicial independence required a continuance of the old arrangements. Lord Hailsham asserted this the most vigorously and his successors did nothing until 2003 to dissociate themselves from that view. What does judicial independence, properly defined, entail? In general, the public must feel confident in the integrity and impartiality of the judiciary: judges must therefore be secure from undue influence and be autonomous in their own field. That possibly implies that neither the Government nor Parliament should have any role in the appointment or removal of judges, which has never been the case in this country. More precisely, judicial independence may be said to require: (*a*) that appointments to judicial office, renewal of part-time appointments, and promotions, should not depend on uncontrolled ministerial patronage; (*b*) that judges should be free from improper attempts by Ministers, Members of Parliament, or peers to influence the result of cases still under adjudication; (*c*) that judicial salaries should not be reduced; and (*d*) that judges should not be removed from office unfairly or without reason. Those four precepts should be the bedrock of judicial independence and should find broad acceptance in any western liberal democracy. It was mainly the first of them that caused most difficulty in this country.

Before the enactment of the Constitutional Reform Act 2005, the entire judiciary in England and Wales owed its appointment to one, and occasionally to two, politicians. Anyone wishing to become a judge, however low or however high, had to receive the approval of the Lord Chancellor. Even those aspiring to the highest judicial offices, in the Court of Appeal and the House of Lords, to which appointment is made by the Queen on the Prime Minister's recommendation, must in practice have had the Lord Chancellor's support. He was always consulted by the Prime Minister on such appointments, and it would be most unlikely that anyone would be recommended against his or her wishes.[22] Moreover, since 1980 a career structure has been developed so that no one was appointed to a full-time judicial office without first having proved himself or herself to be up to the mark in a relevant part-time post to which appointment was made by the Lord Chancellor. No one was appointed to the High Court without such a successful apprenticeship. Appointments to the Court of Appeal and to the judicial House of Lords were made exclusively from the High Court, so that the career progression ran from appointment to part-time judicial work, to appointment to the High Court, and beyond. The Lord Chancellor's patronage was thus all-pervasive throughout the judiciary.[23]

Obviously the longer a Prime Minister and Lord Chancellor held office the more judicial appointments would fall to be made. So Mrs Thatcher and her Lord Chancellors between them appointed all the Lords of Appeal in Ordinary, all the Lords Justices of Appeal, and three-quarters of the High Court bench. Such ministerial patronage may reasonably cause concern about the precise role of Ministers— for the Lord Chancellor's former judicial and parliamentary duties must not obscure

---

[22] Indeed, the Select Committee on Home Affairs has recommended that the Prime Minister's formal role in judicial appointments could be ended: 3rd Report from the Home Affairs Committee, *Judicial Appointments Procedures*, HC 52 (1995–6), i, para. 128.

[23] For a thoughtful defence of the old regime by a former Permanent Secretary at the LCD see Sir Thomas Legg, 'Judges for the New Century' [2001] *Public Law* 62.

the simple fact that he was always as much a departmental Minister as any other member of the Cabinet. Indeed, some of the criticisms voiced in the past about a possible Minister of Justice (lawyers' dependence on a party politician for preferment, and so on) could in fact be more appropriately aimed at the Lord Chancellor himself. His former role in judicial appointments may be objected to on a number of grounds. First, the concentration of power in the hands of one person, without the benefit of a structured system of advice, was unsatisfactory. The patronage system at the disposal of Lord Chancellors, to put it bluntly, looked bad. Secondly, the increasing size of both branches of the profession meant that the civil servants in the LCD could not have had adequate knowledge of all potential candidates for judicial posts or of the particular situation in each of the six Circuits. This problem worsened as more solicitors were considered for senior judicial appointments under the Courts and Legal Services Act 1990. Despite the soundings taken from the LCD, the appointments system was too centralized. Lastly, it was notorious that the system produced few women and ethnic-minority judges. In late 1995, for example, all the Lords of Appeal were men, there was only one Lady Justice of Appeal, and seven women High Court judges (alongside eighty-nine male colleagues); some 15 per cent of Recorders and Assistant Recorders (a rank since abolished) were female. Five Circuit judges (out of 517) and twelve Recorders (out of 891) were of ethnic-minority origin.[24] Those figures were depressing, especially given that junior judicial posts constitute the bottom rung of the career progression to the top judicial jobs. There may, of course, be reasons why this was not entirely the fault of the appointments system: if, for example, there is prejudice in the profession against black people, or if women are indirectly penalized for taking career breaks to have children, fewer will be able to enter or stay in it and the pool of potential judges will be smaller. But a different appointments system might bring with it greater enthusiasm to seek out qualified people from groups which remain absurdly under-represented on the bench. Now the last Conservative Lord Chancellor, Lord Mackay of Clashfern, adopted a comprehensive equal opportunities policy designed to increase the appointment of suitably qualified women and ethnic-minority judges,[25] and that policy was being continued by Lord Irvine of Lairg LC and Lord Falconer LC.

The other three components of judicial independence noted earlier were (with one proviso) achieved through the old arrangements. That proviso concerns the tenure position of the lower judiciary, which was conspicuously weak. They were subject to non-renewal of part-time appointments, and to removal, at the hand of the Lord Chancellor, advised by his officials. This was a disturbing accretion of power in a Minister's hands, could be controversial in its use, and may not always have been exercised incontrovertibly within the requirements of natural justice.

---

[24] See 3rd Report from the Home Affairs Committee, paras. 77, 92.
[25] See 555 HL Debs. *28–29* (written answers 23 May 1994).

Reform of the judicial appointments machinery was necessary so as to remove the theoretical threat which is posed to it by ministerial power in judicial service matters. Indeed, the Liberal Democrats had long advocated the setting up of a Judicial Service Commission which would nominate all the senior judges to office, and consist of a President, five judges, four barristers or advocates, four solicitors, and four lay members.[26] In opposition, Labour wished to establish an independent commission, responsible to the Lord Chancellor, to recommend the appointment of judges.[27] The precise relationship between that commission and the Lord Chancellor would clearly be of great constitutional significance. An improved appointments system for magistrates, designed to ensure that benches reflected the communities which they served, would also be put in place.

After his appointment in 2003 Lord Falconer initiated a consultation on how judges could be appointed in a fresh way.[28] This came to fruition in the Constitutional Reform Act 2005.[29] The Judicial Appointments Commission which resulted has been operating since 2006. In essence, it is an independent, advisory body which makes recommendations to the Lord Chancellor about the filling of judicial vacancies. It does not make appointments: responsibility for that remains formally with the Queen on the advice of the Minister. The Commission is made up of fifteen people, five judges, five lawyers, and five non-lawyers. A former First Civil Service Commissioner was appointed as the first chairman. The Commission advertises for applications to fill specific judicial vacancies, and issues job descriptions. It seeks written references for candidates, and interviews them. The Commission then recommends one name to the Lord Chancellor for the vacant post. The Lord Chancellor can accept that nomination, or ask the Commission to reconsider, or reject the recommendation out of hand. Unsurprisingly, the Lord Chancellor has so far accepted every nomination. The Judicial Appointments Commission certainly enhances the doctrine of the separation of powers. The Lord Chancellor's previous unfettered choice of judges has gone. It is a clearer and defensible way of appointing the judiciary. As confidence in the Commission grows, however, it would be good to see the law changed so that recommendations would go straight from the Commission to the Queen, for it is difficult to justify retaining any ministerial role in this task. Indeed, Mr Gordon Brown has expressed his willingness to look at the future of the ministerial role in judicial appointments.[30]

---

[26] *Here We Stand: Proposals for Modernising Britain's Democracy* (London: Liberal Democrats, 1993), 49.

[27] *Access to Justice,* 12–14.

[28] Department for Constitutional Affairs, *Constitutional Reform: A New Way of Appointing Judges* (London: DCA, 2003). See also Constitutional Affairs Committee, *Judicial Appointments,* HC 48 (2003–4).

[29] 2005 Act, Pt 4.

[30] *The Governance of Britain,* Cm. 7170 (2007), paras 69–71.

A new Supreme Court

England has had a Supreme Court for a long time, although I doubt whether many non-lawyers (and even some lawyers) know what it is. The Court of Appeal, the High Court, and the Crown Court all make up the Supreme Court—not for the United Kingdom, but for England and Wales only.[31] The jurisdiction of the judicial House of Lords would have been abolished in 1874, had not Mr Disraeli displaced Mr Gladstone in the nick of time. A retentionist movement gathered sufficient strength to ensure that, under the Appellate Jurisdiction Act 1876, the House of Lords remained at the apex of the judicial system, alongside the Judicial Committee of the Privy Council for imperial appeals. The title of Supreme Court was designated by the Liberal Government for the new Court of Appeal and High Court: when the judicial House of Lords was confirmed in 1876 it remained supreme in the hierarchy but was not included in that name.

There was a strong case for establishing a new Supreme Court, entirely separate from the legislative House of Lords. It is wrong in principle that senior judges should also be legislators. This is not so much because the participation in debates by the Law Lords and other peers who are judges offends the principle of the separation of powers (although it certainly does that): rather, it is objectionable because interventions by the judges in the House of Lords occasionally put them in the front line of political controversy. Professor Griffith has catalogued those interventions.[32] Notable interventions in the last decade have included speeches during the debates on the Government's Green Papers on the reform of the legal professions and on the Courts and Legal Services Bill in 1990. Six Lords of Appeal joined the debate on the Green Papers, along with the Lord Chief Justice and the Master of the Rolls. All were highly critical of the policies behind the changes: the language used to oppose Government policy by the Master of the Rolls in particular was perhaps the most trenchant ever uttered by a serving judge. Senior judges in the House of Lords were also bitterly critical of the late Conservative Government's criminal justice legislation, criticisms which often put the Home Secretary and (in particular) the Lord Chief Justice at public loggerheads. Such judges also clashed with Labour Ministers after 1997. These interventions went way beyond any comfortable notion that Law Lords and other peer-judges merely assist the House on the technical details of legislation (although they do that as well). And so the Lords of Appeal in Ordinary adopted a Practice Statement in 2000 which embodied a self-denying ordinance not to intervene legislatively in political matters. Given that these senior judges are able to communicate their views on policy questions directly to the Government, through, for example, the Judges' Council, Ministers would still have the benefit of their advice if they were excluded from membership of the House of Lords. The

---

[31] Supreme Court Act 1981, s. 1.

[32] J. A. G. Griffith, *The Politics of the Judiciary* (London: Fontana, 5th edn., 1997), 42–5.

House as a legislative body would lose highly experienced lawyers, but a sizeable percentage of other peers have legal qualifications.

The simplest way to have effected the creation of a new Supreme Court would be through the abolition of the judicial House of Lords, and by the transfer of its functions, together with those of the Judicial Committee of the Privy Council, to a new Supreme Court. If Commonwealth states which retain appeals to the Judicial Committee objected to that on the ground that the Judicial Committee is perceived as being a Commonwealth court set apart from the British court system, the Judicial Committee could have been kept as a separate body for such appeals. So the new Supreme Court might have a Commonwealth jurisdiction; its United Kingdom jurisdiction might have consisted of two main elements. First, it could keep the civil jurisdiction now exercised by the House of Lords, but it should not succeed to that House's criminal jurisdiction. The decisions of the House of Lords in criminal appeals have had lamentable effects on criminal law which have often had to be corrected by legislation, and that jurisdiction should not be continued. Secondly, the new Supreme Court might also have had a special part to play in constitutional matters. Appeals on matters under the Human Rights Act 1998, for example, might have leapfrogged from the court of first instance straight to the Supreme Court. This would shorten proceedings, and would allow authoritative rulings to be given on civil rights questions. It could also have been given jurisdiction over disputed questions about the powers of the Scottish Parliament, the Welsh Assembly, and the Northern Ireland Assembly. In that way, the Court would ensure that the con- stitutional balance between the nations and regions of the United Kingdom set by Parliament was maintained, and that the general civil and constitutional law in England, Scotland, Wales, and Northern Ireland was developed in a unified way.

Given the importance of any such Court and the political context of part of its proposed jurisdiction, I think it would be right that the members of the Court should be subject to a new selection procedure. The basic qualification might be the same as for a Lord of Appeal in Ordinary, but candidates could be named by the new Judicial Appointments Commission, and could then be examined by a joint select committee of both Houses. Its task would be to satisfy itself that can- didates were fit and proper people to be appointed to the apex of the legal system. Part of the inquiry would be directed to the political, philosophical, and social views and attitudes of candidates. If the Supreme Court had functions in relation to civil rights, the judges would necessarily have to adjudicate from time to time on controversial matters, and it would be important that candidates' views were publicly known and their acceptability tested. There is currently no mechanism in the United Kingdom through which suitability for high judicial office can be investigated in detail and, at least in part, in public, and if necessary at length; there is no means through which the weaknesses of a British equivalent of, for example, Mr Robert Bork[33] could be brought out so as to bar his appointment.

---

[33] Mr Bork's nomination to the Supreme Court was rejected by the United States Senate on the grounds of his unsuitability.

Traditionalists may well view this proposal with horror: what price judicial independence in such a scheme, with political interference in the judicial selection process? But it would have nothing to do with judicial independence, and of course once appointed Supreme Court judges would have a very high degree of security of tenure. Indeed, as some appointments to the United States Supreme Court have shown, attempts to make partisan appointments to uphold the philosophy of the appointing President have often backfired. There would be a political intervention in the appointment process, but in my opinion that would be an advantage if it fully brought out into the public domain the political and social beliefs and attitudes of those who would have such an important part in the governance of the United Kingdom. A Court which would hold sway in constitutional and civil rights issues must not be composed only of men, drawn from a small pool, unrepresentative of the general population.

But the Labour Government opted for a much more conservative change than all that.[34] The Constitutional Reform Act 2005 establishes a new Supreme Court.[35] It will start work in 2009 when the Middlesex Guildhall building in Parliament Square has been converted for the purpose. The first Justices of the Supreme Court will be the twelve Lords of Appeal in Ordinary then in office, who will be moved from their accommodation in the House of Lords to the refurbished building. They will take with them their existing jurisdiction, although they will gain the jurisdiction of the Judicial Committee of the Privy Council on devolution matters. (That had rightly been denied to the Law Lords on the ground that, as members of a House of Parliament, they could have appeared to have been a party to such proceedings.) The Judicial Committee will keep the rest of its jurisdiction. Vacancies in the office of Justice of the Supreme Court after the transition in 2009 will be filled by the Queen on the recommendation of the Prime Minister, on advice from the Judicial Appointments Commission. Again, the justification for keeping the Prime Minister as part of the appointments process is very hard to see. Indeed, there is not even the excuse that the appointment of a new Justice would involve conferment of a peerage, or a Privy Counsellorship—conferments which justified the Prime Minister's role in making formal recommendations to the Queen for Lords of Appeal in Ordinary and Lords Justices of Appeal. (True, new Supreme Court Justices might receive either or both such marks of esteem, but neither is a qualification for the office.) As already noted, it is gratifying to record that Mr Gordon Brown intends to examine whether Ministers should continue to have a role in judicial appointments. Moreover, the Supreme Court in essence will be the same as the Appellate Committee of the House of Lords in that (apart from devolution disputes) it will have no additional constitutional powers. It will remain

---

[34] Department for Constitutional Affairs, *A Supreme Court for the United Kingdom* (London: DCA, 2003).

[35] 2005 Act, Pt 3.

quite unlike constitutional courts around the world which have power to rule on the constitutionality of Acts and actions and to strike down that which is unconstitutional. So what is the point of the upset and expense of this change? It comes down, once again, to the separation of powers. It was in order to give a physical and juridical manifestation of that doctrine that the new Supreme Court will soon exist. Perhaps that is justification enough for its existence, but its limited powers will be disappointing.

11

Codifying the constitution

In this chapter a number of themes that have been developed and several matters that have been examined earlier will be considered in the rather different light of the question of whether, and if so how, a codified constitution might be adopted for the United Kingdom.[1]

Reforming the form of the constitution

One of the lasting achievements of the 1997 Labour Government will be its constitution-making, primarily of course in the sense of giving effect to new constitutional dispensations, but also in the narrow, technical sense of producing new legal rules which prescribe how the state is to be governed. The former is more important in practical and political terms than the latter, but the effect of the latter on the form of the British constitution is centrally relevant to the question of writing a codified constitution.

As every schoolchild is supposed to know, the United Kingdom does not have a written constitution. A British citizen has to seek the rules of the constitution in a daunting number of places—legislation, judicial decisions, statements about constitutional conventions, the law and practice of Parliament, European Community law, and so on. It is hardly surprising that the interested citizen will normally leave those sources to one side and, if still inquisitive, will rely instead on books written by authoritative writers. But just listing the primary materials which form the constitution demonstrates the extent to which the British constitution is largely a written one. Indeed, all the sources exist as official statements made by organs of the state, except for conventions, most of which have been reduced to writing only by the unofficial efforts of constitutional commentators.[2] The British constitution is written, but it is not codified into a single official document, or a limited number

---

[1] I examined such possible codification in more detail in 'How Near is a Written Constitution?' (2001) 52 *Northern Ireland Legal Quarterly* 1.

[2] For an overview see J. Jaconelli, 'The Nature of Constitutional Convention' (1999) 19 *Legal Studies* 24.

of such documents, setting out the legal rules which prescribe how the state is to be governed.

In implementing its range of reforms the Labour Government has caused Parliament to enact an additional and substantial corpus of statute law of a constitutional character. While, therefore, the United Kingdom still lacks a codified constitution, it has been given rather more of a written constitution by the addition of over twenty Acts of Parliament which, in whole or in part, add to the British constitution. Perhaps most importantly towards that end, the United Kingdom now has the kind of Bill of Rights which features prominently in so many national constitutions, supplied by the Human Rights Act 1998. The lacuna which had existed in the enforcement of civil rights has now been filled, although whether by the best method remains a moot point.[3] The devolution statutes have answered—at least for the time being—many long-standing queries about the appropriate relationships between the various parts of Great Britain, and with luck of the United Kingdom, and have redefined the juridical balance between them;[4] the composition of the national legislature has been radically altered by the House of Lords Act 1999[5]; and so on. There has been an exponential growth in the body of constitutional statute law since 1997, and because statute overrides both case law and convention in the constitutional order the new laws represent some of the ground work which would be required for the production of a codified constitution. When it was still in opposition the Labour Party recognized that its legislative programme would have that effect in the narrower sense of the phrase constitution-making. In what was then its main constitutional policy document, *A New Agenda for Democracy*, adopted four years before coming to power, the party claimed that its changes would be a significant step in the direction of a written constitution, and the paper stated that the party would leave open the question of whether at a later stage progress should be made towards formal codification.[6] Now that statement needs to be put into context. On the one hand, it was the first move—however tentative—by either of the two big political parties towards the idea of constitutional codification.[7] On the other hand the statement did not really take account of all the other areas of the constitution which Labour's proposed changes would not affect, but which would have to be reassessed and considered for inclusion in any constitutional code. For even after Labour's current reform programme has been fully implemented, vital matters would remain untouched, such as the monarchy, the voting system, and the

---

[3] See Ch. 9.

[4] Notoriously, the West Lothian question remains just that. See Ch. 8.

[5] See Ch. 5.

[6] *A New Agenda for Democracy* (London: Labour Party, 1993), 44.

[7] The Liberal Democrats, like their predecessors, want to see a written United Kingdom constitution: *Reforming Governance in the UK: Policies for Constitutional Reform* (London: Liberal Democrats, 2000); 'Constitutional Reform' (London: Liberal Democrats Briefing Paper No. 22, 2005); *For the People, By the People* (London: Liberal Democrat Policy Paper No. 83, 2007), Ch. 2. See also Charter 88, *Unlocking Democracy* (London: Charter 88, 2000).

powers of the House of Commons. Clearly, too, that statement in the policy paper was over-terse, in that it ignored other important matters which would be crucial in any codification exercise, such as how and by whom it would be undertaken. Nor did the comments about codification find any place in Labour's 1997, 2001, or 2005 general election manifestos. Lord Falconer LC was to rule out any move towards such a constitution. But in his important Green Paper on constitutional reform, *The Governance of Britain*,[8] Mr Gordon Brown acknowledged that the constitutional changes since 1997, and those envisaged in the route-map set out in the Paper, meant that the United Kingdom might be heading towards 'a concordat between the executive and Parliament or a written constitution.' And he promised that a national debate on the matter would begin.[9] That statement is to be welcomed wholeheartedly. Whatever the Labour Party had in mind about revising the formal state of the constitution in 1993, the question which should be addressed now that so much of the party's constitution-making is in place is what could be done with the legal form of the United Kingdom constitution.

In considering that question four options emerge. The most conservative course—and the one which has been followed for the whole of English and British constitutional history—would be to continue to build on the laws and conventions already in place, altering them only as and when required. Constitutional change has happened in fits and starts, with occasional bursts of legislative activity which has usually been caused by events which forced Governments to act.[10] It would be perfectly possible for that reactive method to continue to be followed so as to leave the British constitution in an uncodified state. A second option, however, would be built on the Labour Government's constitution-making through a programme of consolidation. That could be a traditional exercise in statutory consolidation, that is, bringing all related statutory rules together in one statute (or, more likely, a series of statutes). Such consolidation might be the first step towards the apparent aspiration indicated in Labour's 1993 policy document of working towards a written constitution. There has been little attempt to consolidate constitutional statutes, the main fairly recent examples being the Representation of the People Act 1983, the Parliamentary Constituencies Act 1986, and the European Parliamentary Elections Act 2002. Consolidation work is usually carried out by the Law Commission, with parliamentary time being found for consolidation Bills only where there is a clear need to help the user of the statutes affected.[11] It is hard to make a particularly strong case for constitutional consolidation on that ground alone. Indeed, depending on how extensive the consolidations were to be,[12] issues of principle would be

---

[8] Cm. 7071 (2007), paras 211–15.

[9] Ibid, paras 212, 213.

[10] See Ch. 2.

[11] This process could be speeded up under the Legislative and Regulatory Reform Act 2006.

[12] There are, e.g. about twenty principal Acts relating to Parliament, twelve concerning the Crown, and seven dealing with ministerial offices, which would all be candidates for consolidation.

thrown up which went way beyond a technical improvement exercise. For instance, would the present controversial religious tests for accession to the Crown be consolidated when there is a principled case for abolition?[13] Consolidation of constitutional law would disclose many similar problems. Overall, the case for simple consolidation is weak.

A third possibility would be codification, not of the whole constitution, but of suitable or desirable areas. By codification is meant the reduction to coherent legal rules, in a logical and structured form, of all the source material on a given topic, changing the substance where necessary to meet contemporary requirements. In that sense, constitutional codification would be similar to such law reform exercises in other areas, but there would be significant differences. One would be that—unlike all other areas of law—the question would have to be addressed of what to do with relevant and important non-legal rules. No other area of law in the United Kingdom has such a rich gloss of non-legal rules which in practice modify the operation of those rules. In a limited codification, it is true, the problem of how to codify conventions could be avoided by starting the exercise in areas untouched by convention. Another factor which would distinguish constitutional codification from others is the deeply political and sometimes controversial nature of parts of constitutional law. For that reason the task could not be the equivalent of a Law Commission exercise.[14] Yet another distinction is that, for codification to be a worthwhile task, the subject-matter needs to be fairly well settled. If there is a prospect of significant subsequent change to a proposed code the later statutory accretions would spoil the elegance of the code. It might be said that the British constitution is in a state of flux at present for even limited codification to be embarked on now, especially because there are too many key areas (such as the form of the second chamber, and voting reform) which remain in a state of uncertainty.

The fourth and final and the boldest option for the reform of the technical form of the constitution would be to achieve *complete* codification, that is, a written constitution properly so-called.[15] Were that to be done the United Kingdom would leave that very exclusive club whose members are the developed states which lack a codified national constitution. I want now to examine in some detail the issues involved in producing a constitutional code for the United Kingdom.

[13] See e.g. V. Bogdanor, *The Monarchy and the Constitution* (Oxford: Clarendon Press, 1995), Ch. 2.

[14] For an analysis of the advantages and drawbacks of codification of criminal law (which has resonances with constitutional law in this context), see the Law Commission, *A Criminal Code for England and Wales*, HC 299 (1988–89), paras 2.1–2.28.

[15] I have examined at length the technical legislative techniques which would be relevant to the enactment of a codified constitution for the United Kingdom in 'Enacting a Constitution' [1992] *Statute Law Review* 104.

A constitutional code?

Constitutions have been granted or adopted for many different reasons. New constitutions have marked stages in a progression towards self-government (as in most British colonies before independence); they have established a system of Government in a newly independent state (as in the United States of America in 1787), or in a reconstituted state (such as Malaysia in 1963 or Tanzania in 1964 or in Germany on reunification in 1990); they have marked a major change in the system of Government (as in Spain in 1978); they have been adopted in order to rebuild the machinery of Government following defeat in war (as in the Federal Republic of Germany in 1949); and they have declared a new beginning after a revolution, or after the collapse of a regime (as in France in 1789 and in 1958). None of these factors has operated in Britain. There has been no successful military invasion since 1066. True, there were two revolutions in the seventeenth century, but their effects were limited. The English Civil War of 1642–8 led to the execution of the King and to a republican Commonwealth and then Protectorate—but it was followed by the restoration of the monarchy in 1660. The second revolution, of 1688–9, forced the abdication of James II, gave the Crown jointly to usurpers, William and Mary, changed the line of succession to the throne and, through the Bill of Rights of 1689, restricted the royal prerogative in important respects—but Parliament made no greater attempts than that to restate the constitution. The union of England and Scotland in 1707, and of Great Britain and Ireland in 1800, produced rudimentary frameworks of a written constitution, but nothing more sophisticated.

The advantages for a state having a fixed, though amendable, constitution are well-known and need not be rehearsed in any detail.[16] They include the fulfilment of a natural expectation that the main rules which regulate the governance of a state should be knowable to any citizen, the certainty which flows from having formally-stated and binding rules of constitutional law, the ability to see the importance of constitutional rules over other rules in a legal system, and usually the protection of those rules, by entrenchment, from what would otherwise be the effective control of the Government of the day through the passage of ordinary legislation. But so far those attributes have not been sufficiently attractive to either of the two main political parties to persuade them to embark on such a momentous reform of the British

---

[16] The case for a new written constitution for the United Kingdom has been argued, among others, by Lord Hailsham, *Elective Dictatorship* (London: BBC, 1976) and *The Dilemma of Democracy* (London: Collins, 1978)—although he was less sure by the time he published *On The Constitution* (London: Collins, 1992); Lord Scarman, 'Bill of Rights and Law Reform' in R. Holme and M. Elliott, *1688–1988: Time for a New Constitution* (London: Macmillan, 1988); the Liberal Democrats, 'We the People ...'—Towards a Written Constitution (London: Liberal Democrats, 1990), and *Reforming Governance in the UK*, para. 2.2.2; Institute for Public Policy Research, *A Written Constitution for the United Kingdom* (London: Mansell, 1993).

constitution—subject to Mr Brown's promise, made at the start of his premiership, of a national debate on the matter. Why is that?

Like everyone else the political parties are products of their country's past. English and British constitutional history has brought heavy baggage to be borne by policy-makers and citizens alike. Obviously, no events in that historical sweep have unavoidably required the adoption of a written constitution. Equally obviously, cataclysmic episodes have certainly occurred, such as the triumph of Parliament in the English Civil War, and the later crowning of parliamentary sovereignty in 1688; and the state itself has been radically altered by the merger of England and Scotland, and Great Britain with Ireland. But looked at from the limited perspective of forces which might have produced a written constitution, England and Britain went through such tremors as much as a century too soon. The idea that a state should possess a document containing its basic constitutional rules did not form until the late eighteenth century. France and the American colonies underwent their constitutional upheavals as statesmen (all men at the time, of course) came to recognize that such events required the adoption of written statements about a country's constitution, often to be drafted in order to prevent the kind of abuses which had precipitated revolution. Had the seventeenth-century English Civil War and revolution occurred a hundred years later, England just might have been swayed by the intellectual movement which saw the necessity for constitutional codes, and she might have resorted to a similar constitutional prescription. But by (say) 1700 the main constitutional arrangements in England had been settled, albeit that royal power remained significant and parliamentary democracy was very limited. The formal constitutional instruments adopted abroad later that century were viewed by the English elite as the work of revolutionaries—and England had done with revolutions.[17] Subsequent constitutional change, including the creation of Great Britain and later of the United Kingdom, and the extension of parliamentary democracy, were achieved through ordinary exercises of parliamentary sovereignty, that is through the passage of ordinary legislation.

Yet what may be seen now as a misalignment between, on the one hand, seventeenth and eighteenth century English political history and, on the other, the development of ideas about constitution-making was to be exacerbated by parliamentary developments in the nineteenth century. The party whip system ensured with increasing effectiveness that each political party in the House of Commons was loyal to its leaders and malleable. The absence of restraining constitutional rules was highly convenient for successive British Governments, which knew that they were able to deliver whatever they had promised in their election manifestos (and more) without having to make sure that their commitments were consistent with superior legal rules, and having to abandon any which were not. It is not too cynical to say that the absence of a codified constitution—which would be likely to limit

---

[17] See generally L. Colley, *Britons: Forging the Nation 1707–1837* (London: Pimlico, 2003), Ch. 4.

the powers of Ministers and Parliament—came to be seen as agreeable to modern Governments: why should they risk that power by embarking on the search for a limiting constitution? Now politicians might find the argument a touch embarrassing expressed in that way, and it can be cast very differently. A codified constitution, it can be asserted, can be undemocratic, unlike the British arrangement which is wholly democratic. A political party can present its wares to the electorate at a general election: if sufficient voters buy them, the resulting Government can cause Parliament to give legal force to them. This is the majoritarian argument writ large: that which most voters want they must be given, and no constitution must prevent it. By contrast, if the United Kingdom were to have a constitutional code which restricted the ability of the parties to offer exactly what they wished, then some policies might only be brought about if a constitutional amendment could be carried—a process which in most constitutions is notoriously hard to achieve. For instance, it might have been that some of the 1979 Conservative Government's policies could not, through ordinary legislation, have been implemented, such as the abolition of tiers of local Government, or the reduction of trade union rights; nor might the 1997 Labour Government have been able, by ordinary legislation, to have put into place most of its great constitutional reform programme. In that theoretical and alternative constitutional world those Governments might well have had to crank into operation the amendment mechanism provided, whether referendums, or special parliamentary majorities, or whatever it might have been. Such a required majority is often at least a two-thirds vote in the legislature: no British Government in ordinary peacetime circumstances has had such a majority in the House of Commons in modern times.

Now that defence of the status quo is based on the assumption that a codified United Kingdom constitution would *necessarily* involve significant limitations on Government. Such limitations are generally considered to be desirable. But it would be possible to write a constitution for the United Kingdom which broadly preserved the balance of powers obtaining before its adoption. As such it would be conservative codification, a legal restatement of the constitutional status quo ante which did not alter its main provisions. The same point applies in relation to concerns about entrenchment. There is no ineluctable reason why a constitution must be entrenched against easy amendment or repeal, although again normally it is. It all depends on what decisions in principle are taken and what the resulting constitution prescribes: there is, of course, no template of a model constitution which must be followed slavishly. Once that fairly obvious fact has been asserted opponents of codification of the British constitution sometimes then switch the argument about entrenchment. They say that a written constitution is only worth having if it is entrenched, and then they assert the old point that it would be legally impossible to entrench a British constitution, given the unique nature of parliamentary sovereignty in the United Kingdom. In that case (the argument runs) what would be the point of subjecting the political process to the great effort of codifying an ancient constitutional settlement when the result could be altered by any Parliament through ordinary legislation at the behest of a subsequent Government? Attempts have been made to counter this canard: there are at least five ways through the constitutional conundrum.[18] Indeed, in the contemporary political context the Labour Government's principal constitutional measures enjoy a form of protection, at least from possible assault by a non-Labour Government. No political party is likely to appeal to the voters with the battle-cries of 'Abolish the Scottish Parliament and the Welsh Assembly, repeal, and don't replace, the Human Rights Act, and restore the hereditary peers!'. Those, and other, measures enjoy the sanctity of the populist appeal represented by such things as the extension of national aspirations, or the protection of civil liberties, or the abolition of privilege.

The reluctance of the Labour and Conservative Parties to embrace full-blown constitutional codification does not seem to be based on concerns about the methodology which would be appropriate to the enterprise. The present Prime Minister, it is true, is committed to a wide consultation and national debate about whether there should be some kind of formal written statement. The Liberal Democrats think that a constituent convention or assembly would be the only way to carry out such an important enterprise. But the two big parties have not considered how a code might be produced. This is, however, a vitally-important question which must be considered in this context. In part this is an issue of mechanics: how would a draft be arrived at, and how would it be approved? Resort could be had to an independent body which could prepare a text—the Constitutional Commission suggested in Chapter 2 would be ideal for the purpose—or to a specially-elected constituent assembly of some kind, or the task could even be done within Government. Once a text had been produced it could then be adopted by Parliament alone, although there would be a natural expectation (given in particular the use of referendums since 1997) that a national referendum would be held. While that mechanical question is very important, the more significant issue is rather different. Ideally a national constitution should be brought forth by national consensus, itself forged by a national purpose resulting from, for instance, the recognition that fundamental constitutional change is necessary, or the adoption of a new settlement on gaining independence, or the renewal of a state after collapse, or the confirmation of a fundamental change in the basis of the state. Through broad consensus among the people and political parties in a state the text should achieve a legitimacy which is denied to legislation passed by any transient parliamentary majority, and it should have greater durability, too. Similarly, the new constitution should achieve a special place in the legal system, marked out from other laws; any proposed changes to it would be recognized as raising constitutional, and not just political, issues; and, through entrenchment, it may be made legally more difficult to alter it. The

---

[18] See Ch. 9.

paradigm case is that of the Constitution of the United States of America.[19] It is my view that constitution-making *ought* to proceed by consensus if possible. But I am forced to acknowledge that no such national consensus or national purpose is likely to emerge in foreseeable circumstances in the United Kingdom. The political parties disagree on matters which would be the bases for crucial parts of the text. The Conservative, Labour, and Liberal Democrat Parties disagree, for example, on the appropriate voting system for the House of Commons. The Conservatives opposed reform of the House of Lords, and now that the first stage of it has been completed all the parties (and members of the same party) have rather different views on what proportion of the replacement body should be elected, and to some extent on its powers. The Conservatives oppose further devolution to England, whereas the Labour Government has tried to take it forward, but with its dreams of elected Regional Assemblies ending in tears; the Liberal Democrats cherish the ideal of a federal United Kingdom. The Liberal Democrats want a reduction in the constitutional power of the Sovereign, but the other two parties do not; and so on. It is of course true that there has been much common ground between Labour and the Liberal Democrats since the mid-1990s on constitutional reform, and that their co-operation carried over into the new Labour Government in 1997 in the unprecedented Joint Consultative Committee of the Cabinet on which Liberal Democrat parliamentarians sat with senior Ministers.[20] That which still divides the three main political parties would make the sort of political consensus that I have described unachievable.

But might there be a fall-back, or second-best, position? Could the ideal of a broadly-based acceptance of a text be brought about despite the divergence of views between the main political strands in the United Kingdom? The manner of adoption of the Constitution of the Fifth French Republic is instructive in this context.[21] That Constitution was drafted—as Charles de Gaulle demanded—so as to give France a strong executive following the weak Governments of the Fourth Republic. The body which drafted it was dominated by representatives of the parties of the right. The draft Constitution was opposed by the Communists and by some Socialists, particularly on the ground that, unlike the Constitution of the Fourth Republic, the balance of power would be struck too much in favour of the President of the Republic and the Government at the expense of a weaker legislature. In the subsequent national referendum held on the text some 79 per cent of the French people

---

[19] Indeed, in the United States respect for the Constitution has, for many, become reverence, which makes constitutional amendment even more difficult to achieve than the formal amendment mechanisms imply.

[20] See Ch. 3.

[21] See J. Bell, *French Constitutional Law* (Oxford: Clarendon Press, 1992), Ch. 1. For the political context see J. Lacouture, *De Gaulle: The Ruler* (London: Collins Harvill, 1991), 193–206, and for the General's own account see C. de Gaulle, *Memoirs of Hope* (London: Weidenfeld and Nicolson, 1971, trs. by T. Kilmartin), 3–36.

who voted approved it. The Constitution of the Fifth French Republic survived its first Socialist President, François Mitterrand, elected in 1981 (and who was to hold office for 14 years): the fundamentals of the Gaullist Constitution all remain in their essentials as they were set in 1958. It could be argued that that Constitution had achieved the consensus in the referendum which politicians had failed to secure during the writing of it. That is a possible model for the adoption of a new Constitution of the United Kingdom. Those who opposed the draft might accept the verdict of the voters, as happened in France.[22] Indeed, there is a modern British analogy for such acquiescence: this is what the Conservative Party has done since 1997, accepting not only most of the Labour Government's constitutional changes which had been approved at referendums but also those that had not been. The Conservatives fought that election as determined champions of the then status quo, which was a principled stance which had been taken by the party since it took its modern form in the nineteenth century. But they recognized after the election that they had lost the argument.

Such a neat solution to the search for consensus, however, omits a possible prior political decision by the main opposition party. Might it not so oppose the codification exercise that it would refuse to take any part in the process? Might it boycott the search for a text, whether that quest was to be conducted through Parliament itself or through a specially-convened commission or elected constituent assembly? After all, that is precisely what the Conservative Party, together with the Scottish Nationalists, did when they were invited to join the Scottish Constitutional Convention which went on to write detailed plans for what became the Scottish Parliament.[23] Indeed, successful Conservative–Labour co-operation on constitutional matters has not been seen since 1936, when Stanley Baldwin ensured that all the party leaders took the same approach towards the abdication crisis—although wherever possible all Prime Ministers have tried to ensure that the constitutional problems of Northern Ireland have been approached on an all-party basis within Britain. A refusal to join a codification exercise would preserve the party's ability to fight the text in the last ditch, if necessary, but whether to do so would be a matter of political judgement. It would retain the purity of its opposition: but it would lose any ability to influence the resulting text, which for all the party could know might prove acceptable to voters.

The issue of whether to codify the United Kingdom constitution inevitably raises the question of what would be done in that process with constitutional conventions. This is a particular problem for the United Kingdom because of the heavy reliance which is placed on those non-legal rules, although even written constitutions attract conventions to them. If a codified constitution for the United Kingdom

[22] But it has been said that the 1975 UK referendum on continued membership of the European Community did not cause all those on the losing side to accept the result with good grace: D. Oliver, *Constitutional Reform in the United Kingdom* (Oxford: Oxford University Press, 2003), 155.

[23] J. McFadden, 'The Scottish Constitutional Convention' [1995] *Public Law* 215.

were to be embarked on a number of possibilities would present themselves to deal with the conventions.[24] The easiest by far would be to leave them (or at least most of them) outside the code, so that they would continue to enjoy the same status and functions as now. To the extent that any existing convention was later discovered through experience to be incompatible with the new constitution, it would disappear just as any redundant convention disappears. The principal drawback with such a solution, however, is that the present disadvantages of constitutional conventions—imprecision, the room for disagreement whether a convention exists and if so what it ordains, and inaccessibility—would remain. Alternatively, some of the most important conventional rules could be incorporated into the constitutional code, leaving others outside it. Again, in theory all the principal conventional rules could be reduced to rules of law (whether in the constitutional code itself or in statute). But that would be unwise: it would introduce certainty while sacrificing the flexibility which is rightly claimed as an advantage of constitutional conventions, and it would also open the door to justiciability of issues many of which are overwhelmingly political and not suited to judicial intervention. Lastly, therefore, some other authoritative, but non-legal, statement might be made of the major United Kingdom constitutional conventions. That would be my preferred option.[25] This is what was done in Australia, which has a formal but non-justiciable statement of most of the main constitutional conventions concerning federal Government.[26] There is no dearth of answers to the question of what to do with conventional rules in any constitutional codification process, and the conventions do not erect an insurmountable barrier to such an enterprise.

It needs to be remembered that a complete grasp of any state's constitution will entail more than reading the formal text. In the United States, for instance, a citizen can read the Constitution in less than half an hour, but he or she would then have to get to grips with decisions of the Supreme Court to apply its authoritative rulings on the meaning of that text, as well as watching out for any constitutional conventions. Even so, that is an easier task than one which faces the scholar of the British constitution.

Prospects for a new code

Any likely codified constitution would probably contain provisions which would be inconvenient for any Government. Of course, this point is wholly dependent on what went into the text, but it seems more likely that if the United Kingdom went

---

[24] See Brazier, 'Enacting a Constitution' [1992] *Statute Law Review* 112–13.
[25] See Ch. 2.
[26] Ibid.

back to first principles (or, more accurately, visited them for the first time), there would be some transfer of power away from the central executive.

Over any suggestion of a full-blown codification would be cast the prudent eyes of the Treasury. Accurate costings are impossible to suggest, for they would depend on exactly how the process was to be conducted. If, for example, something along the lines of the work of the Australian Constitutional Commission[27] were to be employed to do the detailed work on a possible draft, involving the appointment of an independent body, consulting widely, the use of expert committees, publication of consultation documents, and consequent referendums, then millions of pounds would be needed.

It is easy to see why some commentators have viewed the adoption of a codified United Kingdom constitution as unlikely.[28] Some people have argued against trying to achieve it because doing so would divert energies from the reform of particular constitutional rules, which they say is a more urgent cause. That point—quite right when deployed even a few years ago—has been weakened by Labour's constitution-making since 1997. The Labour Government *has* devoted energy to specific projects of constitutional change where it judged the most necessary work was needed. As noted, *The Governance of Britain* has opened the door to possible codification. And so how, in today's circumstances, can the argument for a codified constitution be expressed?

It makes the most practical sense to consider that question primarily from the perspective of the two main parties: what, politically, might either have to gain from a commitment to such a grand project? First, such an initiative would be an historic one, confirming that party's modernizing credentials. For the first time a major political party would promise a fundamental review of the historic constitution, free from the exigencies of awkward political events that heretofore have forced piecemeal changes. In the process some of the Liberal Democrats' clothes would be stolen. Secondly, such a policy would not in fact commit a party to very much in practical terms when it was in power. It would be a long time before Ministers had to react to any result of a comprehensive review. Because of the scale of the enterprise no action would be required to give effect to any recommendations for a number of years. And it must always be kept in mind that very few advisory inquiries bind a Government for political reasons to act on their recommendations. Depending on the methodology, no text might be ready for public or parliamentary consideration even in the following Parliament; if the drafting were to be conducted outside Parliament the result would have to be assessed by Parliament, whether by a joint select committee of both Houses or otherwise. Then there might be a referendum on the text, but even that might be made conditional on the Government feeling

27 See Ch. 2.

28 For instance, D. Oliver (see note 22 above), op. cit., 387–8; R. Hazell, 'The New Constitutional Settlement' in R. Hazell (ed.), *Constitutional Futures: The History of the Next Ten Years* (Oxford: Oxford University Press, 1999), 239–40.

able to commend the draft to the nation, rather like Ministers' attitude to the possible adoption of the euro.[29] A referendum would require legislation to permit it. In short, a commitment to see what a codified United Kingdom constitution might look like would require the Conservative or Labour Parties to agree to little more in practical terms than to initiate an inquiry and to find out; if the result were not to a party's taste it could decline to take the matter any further. A third party-political point for the Labour Party to consider is that Labour Ministers would avert any danger that the Conservative Party might outflank the Government and make such a project its own. While such a move by the Conservatives might seem unlikely, it could be adopted in part as a desire to limit the power of Government—a policy that has appeared increasingly attractive the longer the Labour Government has been in power.[30] A final party point is that, while the Labour Party is presently victorious, support from the Liberal Democrats might be desirable or even essential if there were to be a close result in a general election or even a hung Parliament after it. The Liberal Democrats have already embraced the codification ideal, and they would find such a commitment by Labour attractive, although admittedly not as tantalizing as moves towards a more proportional voting system for Parliament.

For the sake of completeness, it can be noted that membership of the European Union is unlikely to affect the prospects for a codified United Kingdom constitution. In making up its mind whether to take such a project further, the EU should be a neutral factor for the Government. That membership has not required, and will not require, member states to do things to the *form* of their national constitutions that they would not otherwise have done. Of course, making European Community law sovereign over national law was a supremely important matter, in the United Kingdom as elsewhere throughout the EU. Other laws have been given force in member states as a consequence of membership, but by and large they are not of a constitutional character.[31] The adoption of the euro, too, has been a major constitutional matter—and an unprecedented one, given that sovereign states who have adopted it have harmonized their money before they have adopted a common constitution, thus almost unprecedentedly putting economics before politics. But membership of the EU is unlikely to require any state to alter the format of its national constitution: the United Kingdom is not likely to move towards a codified constitution solely or even primarily as a result of that membership. Even a future Eurosceptic Conservative Government could seek to restrict the perceived encroachments of the EU by amending the European Communities Act 1972, which would have nothing to do with codifying the British constitution.

---

[29] The Labour Government describes the adoption of the Euro as being subject to triple approval, of the Government, Parliament, and the people (through a referendum).

[30] This desire was one of the reasons why Mr David Cameron as Conservative leader appointed his Democracy Task Force in 2006 under the chairmanship of Mr Kenneth Clarke.

[31] There are examples of new constitutional laws which have been adopted to reflect the obligations of membership, such as providing for a common system to elect Members of the European Parliament.

The old arguments about whether the British constitution should be codified, or whether its sources should be left just as history has made them, are well-known, and they remain. But those arguments had been rebalanced somewhat by the turn of the last century. A reforming Government altered many constitutional rules, and thereby added to the statute-base of the British constitution. In doing that significant parts of any constitution—such as a Bill of Rights, and the legal delineation of power between different geographic parts of the state—were added to the constitution of the United Kingdom. In doing all that the apparent taboo which had seemed to prevent British Governments from making planned changes to the constitution was broken. Someone contemplating a wager on whether the United Kingdom might give itself a codified constitution in the foreseeable future would have to weigh the historical evidence against recent developments such as those before deciding whether to risk a bet. The odds are still against a new constitutional code, but perhaps it can be said that they have shortened. Mr Brown has helped that to happen by his commitment to a national debate on the issue.[32] He is concerned that there should be a clearer understanding of what is involved in being British, and a statement of values, or a declaration of rights and responsibilities, or a codified constitution—or all of those things—obviously matters towards which he is much more receptive than any of his predecessors in 10 Downing Street.

[32] *The Governance of Britain*, Cm. 7170 (2007), paras 213, 215.

Bibliography

Chapter 1: The story so far

BAGEHOT, W., *The English Constitution* (first pub., 1867; London: Fontana, 1963)

CHARTER 88, *Unlocking Democracy* (London: Charter 88, 2000)

DICKENS, C., *Our Mutual Friend* (London, 1865)

EWING, K., and GEARTY, C., *Freedom under Thatcher: Civil Liberties in Modern Britain* (Oxford: Clarendon Press, 1990)

HAILSHAM, LORD, *The Dilemma of Democracy: Diagnosis and Prescription* (London: Collins, 1978)

MCAUSLAN, P., and MCELDOWNEY, J. F. (eds.), *Law, Legitimacy and the Constitution* (London: Sweet & Maxwell, 1985)

Chapter 2: Constitution-making

BOGDANOR, V., *The People and the Party System* (Cambridge: Cambridge University Press, 1981)

COMMITTEE ON STANDARDS IN PUBLIC LIFE, *The Funding of Political Parties*, Cm. 4057 (1998), Ch. 12

CONSTITUTION UNIT, *Delivering Constitutional Reform* (London: Constitution Unit, 1996)

ELECTORAL REFORM SOCIETY and the CONSTITUTION UNIT, *Report of the Commission on the Conduct of Referendums* (London: Constitution Unit, 1996)

Final Report of the Constitutional Commission (Canberra: Australian Government Printing Service, 1988)

FINER, S. E., BOGDANOR, V., and RUDDEN, B., *Comparing Constitutions* (Oxford: Clarendon Press, 1995)

GORNIG, G. and RECKEWERTH, S., 'The Revision of the German Basic Law' [1977] *Public Law* 55 and 137

Governance of Britain, The, Cm. 7170 (2007)

LEE, H.P., 'Reforming the Australian Constitution' [1988] *Public Law* 535

LIBERAL DEMOCRATS, *For the People, By the People* (London: Liberal Democrat Policy Paper No. 83, 2007)

MORISON, J., 'The Report of the Constitution Review Group in the Republic of Ireland' [1977] *Public Law* 55

SAMPFORD, C., ' "Recognize and Declare": An Australian Experiment in Codifying Conventions' (1987) 7 *Oxford Journal of Legal Studies* 369

SELECT COMMITTEE ON THE CONSTITUTION, *Changing the Constitution*, HL 69 (2001–2)

—— *Reviewing the Constitution*, HL 11 (2001–2)

STATUTES

Constitutional Reform Act 2005

Law Commissions Act 1965
  s. 3

Official Secrets Act 1911
  s. 2

Political Parties, Elections and Referendums Act 2000
  Pt VII

Chapter 3: The parties and the constitution

ASHDOWN, P., *The Ashdown Diaries* (London: Allen Lane, 2000)

BLACKBURN, R., and PLANT, R. (eds.), *Constitutional Reform: The Labour*

Government's   Agenda   (London: Longman, 1999)

CAMERON, D., 'Balancing Freedom and Security: A Modern British Bill of Rights' (London: Conservative Party, 2006)

CONSERVATIVE PARTY, *An End to Sofa Government* (London: Conservative Party, 2007)

—— *Power to the People* (London: Conservative Party, 2007)

CONSTITUTION UNIT, *Delivering Constitutional Reform* (London: Constitution Unit, 1996)

FALKLAND, VISCOUNT, *A Discussion on Infallibility* (1660)

Governance of Britain, The, Cm. 7170 (2007)

HAGUE, W., 'A Conservative View of Constitutional Change' (London: Conservative Party, 2000)

INSTITUTE FOR PUBLIC POLICY RESEARCH, *A Written Constitution for the United Kingdom* (London: Mansell, 1993)

LABOUR PARTY, *A New Agenda for Democracy* (London: Labour Party, 1993)

—— *Democracy and Citizenship* (London: Labour Party, 2000)

—— *Meet the Challenge: Make the Change* (London: Labour Party, 1989)

—— *New Labour: Because Britain Deserves Better* (London: Labour Party, 1997)

LABOUR PARTY and the LIBERAL DEMOCRATS, *Report of the Joint Consultative Committee on Constitutional Reform* (London: Labour Party and the Liberal Democrats, 1997)

LIBERAL DEMOCRATS, *For the People, By the People* (London: Liberal Democrat Policy Paper No. 83, 2007)

McFADDEN, J., 'The Scottish Constitutional Convention' [1995] *Public Law* 215

OLIVER, D., 'Constitutional Reform Moves Up the Agenda' [1995] *Public Law* 193

Scotland's Parliament: Scotland's Right (Edinburgh: Scottish Constitutional Convention, 1995)

STATUTES

Greater London Authority Act 1999

House of Lords Act 1999

Human Rights Act 1998

Life Peerages Act 1958

Northern Ireland Act 1998

Peerage Act 1963

Political Parties, Elections and Referendums Act 2000

Referendums (Scotland and Wales) Act 1997

Reform Act 1832

Chapter 4: Voting reform

BOGDANOR, V., *Multi-Party Politics and the Constitution* (Cambridge: Cambridge University Press, 1983)

BRAZIER, R., *Constitutional Practice* (Oxford: Oxford University Press, 3rd edn., 1999)

BUTLER, D., 'Electoral Reform' in J. Jowell and D. Oliver (eds.), *The Changing Constitution* (Oxford: Oxford University Press, 3rd edn., 1994)

DICEY, A. V., *Introduction to the Study of the Law of the Constitution* (London: Macmillan, 10th edn., 1962, E. C. S. Wade)

DUMMETT, M., *Principles of Electoral Reform* (Oxford: Clarendon Press, 1997)

ELECTORAL COMMISSION, *Age of Electoral Majority* (London: Electoral Commission, 2004)

—— *Postal Voting Statement* (London: Electoral Commission, 2005)

—— *The Funding of Political Parties* (London: Electoral Commission, 2004)

ELECTORAL COMMISSION, *Voting for Change: An Electoral Law Modernisation Programme* (London: Electoral Commission, 2003)

GANZ, G., *Understanding Public Law* (London: Sweet & Maxwell, 2nd edn., 1994)

Governance of Britain, The, Cm. 7170 (2007)

HARLOW, C., 'Power from the People? Representation and Constitutional Theory' in P. McAuslan and J. F. McEldowney (eds.), *Law, Legitimacy and the Constitution* (London: Sweet & Maxwell, 1985)

LABOUR PARTY, *Ambitions for Britain* (London: Labour Party, 2001)

—— *Report of the Working Party on Electoral Systems* (London: Labour Party, 1993) (the Plant Report)

LAKEMAN, E., *How Democracies Vote* (London: Faber, 3rd edn., 1970)

LIBERAL DEMOCRATS, *A Parliament for the People* (London: Liberal Democrats, 1996)

—— *For the People, By the People* (London: Liberal Democrat Policy Paper No. 83, 2007)

OLIVER, D., *Constitutional Reform in the UK* (Oxford: Oxford University Press, 2003)

Report of the Independent Commission on the Voting System, Cm. 4090 (1998) (the Jenkins Report)

ROUSSEAU, J.-J., *Social Contract* (London: Dent, ed. by G. D. H. Cole, 1973)

STATUTES

Electoral Administration Act 2006, Part 7

European Parliamentary and Local Elections (Pilots) Act 2004

Greater London Authority Act 1999

Political Parties, Elections and Referendums Act 2000

WADE, Sir William, *Constitutional Fundamentals* (London: Stevens & Sons, 1980)

Chapter 5: The second-chamber paradox

Agreed Statement on the Conclusion of the Conference on the Parliament Bill 1947, Cmd. 7380 (1948)

BRAZIER, R., *Constitutional Texts* (Oxford: Clarendon Press, 1990), pp 529–40

CONSTITUTION UNIT, *Reform of the House of Lords* (London, 1996)

Governance of Britain, The, Cm. 7170 (2007)

HOOD PHILLIPS, O., *Constitutional and Administrative Law* (London: Sweet & Maxwell, 7th edn., 1987)

House of Lords: Completing the Reform, The, Cm. 5291 (2001)

House of Lords Reform, Cmnd. 3799 (1968)

House of Lords: Reform, The, Cm. 7027 (2007)

JOINT COMMITTEE ON CONVENTIONS, *Conventions of the UK Parliament*, HL 265 (2005–6)

JOINT COMMITTEE ON HOUSE OF LORDS REFORM, *First Report*, HC 17 (2002–3)

LABOUR PARTY, *Ambitions for Britain* (London: Labour Party, 2001), p. 35

—— *New Labour: Because Britain Deserves Better* (London, 1997)

LABOUR PARTY and the LIBERAL DEMOCRATS, *Report of the Joint Consultative Committee on Constitutional Reform* (London, 1997)

LIBERAL DEMOCRATS, *Here We Stand: Proposals for Modernizing Britain's Democracy* (London: Liberal Democrats, 1993)

—— *For the People, By the People* (London: Liberal Democrat Policy Paper No. 83, 2007)

Modernising Parliament: Reforming the House of Lords, Cm. 4183 (1999)

OLIVER, D., *Constitutional Reform in the United Kingdom* (Oxford: Oxford University Press, 2003), Ch. 10

Report of the Conference on the Reform of the Second Chamber, Cd. 9038 (1918)

Report of the Royal Commission on the Reform of the House of Lords, Cm. 4534 (2000)

RUSSELL, M., *Reforming the House of Lords: Lessons from Overseas* (Oxford: Oxford University Press, 2000)

SHELL, D., *The House of Lords* (Hemel Hempstead: Philip Alan, 1988)

TROLLOPE, A., *Phineas Redux* (London: 1874)

STATUTES

Constitutional Reform Act 2005 Pt 3

House of Lords Act 1999

Life Peerages Act 1958

Parliament Act 1911

Peerage Act 1963

Chapter 6: Ministers' powers

BENN, T., *Arguments for Socialism* (London: Cape, 1979)

BRAZIER, R., *Constitutional Practice* (Oxford: Oxford University Press, 3rd edn., 1999)

BUTLER OF BROCKWELL, Lord, *Review of Intelligence on Weapons of Mass Destruction*, HC 898 (2003–4)

COMMITTEE ON STANDARDS IN PUBLIC LIFE, *First Report*, Cm. 2850 (1995)

DE SMITH, S.A., and BRAZIER, R., *Constitutional and Administrative Law* (Harmondsworth: Penguin Books, 8th edn., 1998)

Government Response to the Public Administration Select Committee Report, 'Taming the Prerogative', Cm. 6187 (2003)

Governance of Britain, The, Cm. 7170 (2007)

HEWART, LORD, *The New Despotism* (London: Ernest Benn, 1929)

LABOUR PARTY, *A New Agenda for Democracy* (London: Labour Party, 1993)

—— *Meet the Challenge: Make the Change* (London: Labour Party, 1989)

—— *Standing Orders of the Labour Party* (London: Labour Party (annually))

LIBERAL DEMOCRATS, *For the People, By the People* (London: Liberal Democrat Policy Paper No. 83, 2007)

MACKINTOSH, J., *The British Cabinet* (London: Stevens & Sons, 3rd edn., 1977)

MARSHALL, G., *Constitutional Conventions* (Oxford: Clarendon Press, 1984)

OLIVER, D., *Constitutional Reform in the UK* (Oxford: Oxford University Press, 2003)

PUBLIC ADMINISTRATION SELECT COMMITTEE, *Taming the Prerogative*, HC 422 (2003–4)

SELECT COMMITTEE ON THE CONSTITUTION, *Waging War: Parliament's Role and Responsibility*, HL 236 (2005–6)

STATUTES

Human Rights Act 1998

Intelligence Services Act 1994

Interception of Communications Act 1985

Security Service Act 1989

SUNKIN, M., and PAYNE, S., *The Nature of the Crown* (Oxford: Clarendon Press, 1999)

Chapter 7: A constitutional guiding light

ASHDOWN, P., *The Ashdown Diaries: vol 1: 1988–1997* (London, Allen Lane, 2001)

BARNETT, A. (ed.), *Power and the Throne* (London: Vintage Press, 1994)

BLACKBURN, R., and PLANT, R., 'Monarchy and the Royal Prerogative' in R. Blackburn and R. Plant (eds.), *Constitutional Reform: The Labour Government's Agenda* (Harlow: Longman, 1999)

BOGDANOR, V., *Multi-Party Politics and the Constitution* (Cambridge: Cambridge University Press, 1983)

—— *The Monarchy and the Constitution* (Oxford: Clarendon Press, 1995)

BRAZIER, R., 'A British Republic' [2002] *Cambridge Law Journal* 351

—— *Constitutional Practice* (Oxford: Oxford University Press, 3rd edn., 1999)

—— 'Royal Incapacity and Constitutional Continuity: The Regent and Counsellors of State' [2005] *Cambridge Law Journal* 352

FABIAN SOCIETY, *The Future of the Monarchy* (London: Fabian Society, 2003)

FREEDLAND, J., *Bring Home the Revolution: The Case for a British Republic* (London: Fourth Estate, 1999)

Governance of Britain, The, Cm. 7170 (2007)

HASELER, S., *Britain's Ancien Regime* (London: Cape, 1991)

HEATH, E., *The Course of My Life* (London: Hodder & Stoughton, 1998), Ch. 18

HORNE, A., *Macmillan 1957–1986* (London: Macmillan, 1989)

LIBERAL DEMOCRATS, *For the People, By the People* (London: Liberal Democrat Policy Paper No. 83, 2007)

MARSHALL, G., *Constitutional Conventions* (Oxford: Clarendon Press, 1984)

PETTIT, P. *Republicanism: A Theory of Freedom and Government* (Oxford: Oxford University Press, 1997)

PROCHASKA, F., *The Republic of Britain* (London: Allen Lane, 2000)

STATUTES

Act of Settlement 1701

Bill of Rights 1689

Parliament Act 1911
s. 2(1)

Regency Acts 1937–53

Royal Marriages Act 1772

Chapter 8: Union, dissolution, or federation?

A Mayor and Assembly for London, Cm. 3897 (1998).

A Voice for Wales, Cm. 3718 (1997)

BARENDT, E., *An Introduction to Constitutional Law* (Oxford: Oxford University Press, 1998)

BOGDANOR, V., *Devolution in the United Kingdom* (Oxford: Oxford University Press, 1999)

BRAZIER, R., 'The Constitution of the United Kingdom' [1999] *Cambridge Law Journal* 96

—— 'The Scottish Government' [1998] *Public Law* 212

Choosing Scotland's Future (Edinburgh: Scottish Executive, 2007)

Governance of Britain, The, Cm. 7170 (2007)

HADFIELD, B., 'Devolution, Westminster and the English Question' [2005] *Public Law* 286

—— 'The Belfast Agreement, Sovereignty and the State of the Union' [1998] *Public Law* 599

HAZELL, R., *The English Question* (Manchester: Manchester University Press, 2006)

JOWELL, J. & OLIVER, D., *The Changing Constitution* (Oxford: Oxford University Press, 6th edn., 2007), Chs. 9–11

LIBERAL DEMOCRATS, *For the People, By the People* (London: Liberal Democrat Policy Paper No. 83, 2007)

MAITLAND, F. W., *Constitutional History of England* (Cambridge: Cambridge University Press, 1908)

MCCRUDDEN, C., 'Northern Ireland and the British Constitution since the Belfast Agreement' in J. Jowell and D. Oliver, *The Changing Constitution* (Oxford: Oxford University Press, 6th edn., 2007)

OLIVER, D., *Constitutional Reform in the UK* (Oxford: Oxford University Press, 2003), Chs. 13–15

SAWER, G., *Modern Federalism* (London: Watts, 1976)

Scotland's Parliament, Cm. 3658 (1997)

STATUTES

Government of Ireland Act 1920

Government of Wales Act 1998
   s. 1(1)
   s. 21
   s. 66

Government of Wales Act 2006

Greater London Authority Act 1999

Greater London Authority (Referendum) Act 1997

Interpretation Act 1978
   s. 5
   Sched. 1

Ireland Act 1949
   s. 1(2)

Laws in Wales Act 1535

Northern Ireland Act 1998
   s. 1
   s. 1(2)
   s. 6
   Sched. 2
   Sched. 3

Northern Ireland Constitution Act 1973
   s. 1

Referendums (Scotland and Wales) Act 1997

Regional Assemblies (Preparations) Act 2003

Regional Development Agencies Act 1998

Scotland Act 1998
   s. 28
   s. 28(7)
   s. 29
   s. 30
   s. 63
   Sched. 5, para. 1

Union with England Act 1707

Union with Scotland Act 1706

The Good Friday Agreement, Cm. 3883 (1998)

WELSH ASSEMBLY, *Report of the Independent Commission on the Welsh Assembly* (Cardiff: Welsh Assembly, 2004)

WHEARE, SIR K., *Federal Government* (Oxford: Oxford University Press, 3rd edn., 1953)

Your Region, Your Choice, Cm. 5511 (2002)

Chapter 9: Defending rights

BRADLEY, A. W., 'The Sovereignty of Parliament—Form or Substance?' in J. Jowell and D. Oliver (eds.), *The Changing Constitution* (Oxford: Oxford University Press, 5th edn., 2004)

CAMERON, D., 'Balancing Freedom and Security: A Modern British Bill of Rights' (London: Conservative Party, 2006)

CONSTITUTION UNIT, *Human Rights Legislation* (London: Constitution Unit, 1996)

DE SMITH, S. A., and BRAZIER, R., *Constitutional and Administrative Law* (Harmondsworth: Penguin Books, 8th edn., 1998)

DICEY, A. V., *Introduction to the Study of the Law of the Constitution* (London: Macmillan, 1959)

Governance of Britain, The, Cm. 7170 (2007)

HOOD PHILLIPS, O., *Constitutional and Administrative Law* (London: Sweet & Maxwell, 7th edn., 1987)

IRVINE OF LAIRG, LORD, 'The Development of Human Rights in Britain' [1998] *Public Law* 221

—— 'The Impact of the Human Rights Act: Parliament, the Courts and the Executive' [2003] *Public Law* 308

JACONELLI, J., *Enacting a Bill of Rights: The Legal Issues* (Oxford: Clarendon Press, 1980)

KLUG, F., and STARMER, K., 'Standing Back from the Human Rights Act' [2005] *Public Law* 716

LIBERAL DEMOCRATS, *For the People, By the People* (London: Liberal Democrat Policy Paper No. 83, 2007)

MCAUSLAN, P., and MCELDOWNEY, J. F., 'Legitimacy and the Constitution: The Dissonance between Theory and Practice' in P. McAuslan and J. F. McEldowney (eds.), *Law, Legitimacy and the Constitution* (London: Sweet & Maxwell, 1985)

OLIVER, D., *Constitutional Reform in the UK* (Oxford: Oxford University Press, 2003)

Rights Brought Home: The Human Rights Bill, Cm. 3782 (1997)

SCARMAN, LORD, 'Bill of Rights and Law Reform' in R. Holme and M. Elliott (eds.), *1688–1988: Time for a New Constitution* (London: Macmillan, 1988)

STATUTES

Anti-Terrorism, Crime and Security Act 2001
  s. 23

Human Rights Act 1998

Prevention of Terrorism Act 2005

WADE, SIR WILLIAM, *Constitutional Fundamentals* (London: Stevens & Sons, 1989), Ch. 3

Chapter 10: Government, law, and the judges

BRAZIER, R., 'Government and the Law: Ministerial Responsibility for Legal Affairs' [1989] *Public Law* 64

CONSTITUTION UNIT, *Delivering Constitutional Reform* (London: Constitution Unit, 1996)

CONSTITUTIONAL AFFAIRS COMMITTEE, *Judicial Appointments*, HC 48 (2003–4)

—— *The Creation of the Ministry of Justice*, HC 466 (2006–7)

DEPARTMENT FOR CONSTITUTIONAL AFFAIRS, *Constitutional Reform: A New Way of Appointing Judges* (London: Department for Constitutional Affairs, 2003)

—— *Constitutional Reform: A Supreme Court for the United Kingdom* (London: Department for Constitutional Affairs, 2003)

—— *Constitutional Reform: Reforming the Office of Lord Chancellor* (London: Department for Constitutional Affairs, 2003)

Governance of Britain, The, Cm. 7170 (2007)

Government, Justice and Law, Alliance Paper No. 1 (London, 1985)

GRIFFITH, J. A. G., *The Politics of the Judiciary* (London: Fontana, 5th edn., 1997)

HOME AFFAIRS SELECT COMMITTEE, *Judicial Appointments Procedures*, HC 52 (1995–6)

LABOUR PARTY, *Access to Justice* (London: Labour Party, 1995)

—— *Meet the Challenge: Make the Change* (London: Labour Party, 1989)

LEGG, SIR THOMAS, 'Judges for the New Century' [2001] *Public Law* 62

LIBERAL DEMOCRATS, *Here We Stand: Proposals for Modernising Britain's Democracy* (London: Liberal Democrats, 1993)

PUBLIC ADMINISTRATION SELECT COMMITTEE, *Machinery of Government Changes*, HC 672 (2006–7)

Report of the Committee on the Machinery of Government, Cd. 9230 (1918), Ch. X

Report of the Select Committee on the Constitutional Reform Bill, HL 125 (2003–4)

STATUTES

Constitutional Reform Act 2005
  s. 2
  Pt 2
  Pt 3
  Pt 4

Human Rights Act 1998

Supreme Court Act 1981
  s. 1

WINDLESHAM, LORD, 'The Constitutional Reform Act 2005' [2005] *Public Law* 806 and [2006] *Public Law* 35

WOODHOUSE, D., *The Office of Lord Chancellor* (Oxford: Hart Publishing, 2001)

Chapter 11: Codifying the constitution

BELL, J., *French Constitutional Law* (Oxford: Clarendon Press, 1992), Ch. 1

BENN, T., Commonwealth of Britain Bill (H.C. Bill 161 (1990–91))

BOGDANOR, V., *The Monarchy and the Constitution* (Oxford: Clarendon Press, 1995)

BRAZIER, R., 'Enacting a Constitution' [1992] *Statute Law Review* 104

—— 'How Near is a Written Constitution?' (2001) 52 *Northern Ireland Legal Quarterly* 1

CHARTER 88, *Unlocking Democracy* (London: Charter 88, 2000)

COLLEY, L., *Britons: Forging the Nation* (London: Pimlico, 2003), Ch. 4

DE GAULLE, C., *Memoirs of Hope* (London: Weidenfeld and Nicolson, 1971, trs. T. Kilmartin)

FINER, S. E. et al. (eds.), *Comparing Constitutions* (Oxford: Clarendon Press, 1995)

Governance of Britain, The, Cm. 7170 (2007)

HAILSHAM, LORD, *The Dilemma of Democracy* (London: Collins, 1978)

—— *Elective Dictatorship* (London: BBC, 1976)

—— *On the Constitution* (London: Collins, 1992)

HAZELL, R., (ed.), *Constitutional Futures: The History of the Next Ten Years* (Oxford: Oxford University Press, 1999)

INSTITUTE FOR PUBLIC POLICY RESEARCH, *A Written Constitution for the United Kingdom* (London: Mansell, 1993)

JACONELLI, J., 'The Nature of Constitutional Convention' (1999) *Legal Studies* 24

LABOUR PARTY, *A New Agenda for Democracy* (London: Labour Party, 1993)

LACOUTURE, J., *De Gaulle: The Ruler* (London: Collins Harvill, 1991)

LAW COMMISSION, *A Criminal Code for England and Wales*, HC 299 (1988–89)

LIBERAL DEMOCRATS, 'Constitutional Reform' (London: Liberal Democrats Briefing Paper No. 22, 2005)

—— *For the People, By the People* (London: Liberal Democrat Policy Paper No. 83, 2007)

—— 'We the People ...'—Towards a Written Constitution (London: Liberal Democrats, 1990)

—— *Reforming Governance in the UK: Policies for Constitutional Reform* (London: Liberal Democrats, 2000)

McFADDEN, J., 'The Scottish Constitutional Convention' [1995] *Public Law* 215

OLIVER, D., *Constitutional Reform in the United Kingdom* (Oxford: Oxford University Press, 2003)

SCARMAN, LORD, 'Bill of Rights and Law Reform' in R. Holme and M. Elliott (eds.), *1688–1988: Time for a New Constitution* (London: Macmillan, 1988)

STATUTES

European Communities Act 1972

European Parliamentary Elections Act 2002

House of Lords Act 1999

Human Rights Act 1998

Legislative and Regulatory Reform Act 2006

Parliamentary Constituencies Act 1986

Representation of the People Act 1983

Index

All-party talks
Charter 88 5
methods of consultation and
investigation 9–16
preparations for reform 2

Bill of Rights *see* **Human
rights**

Cabinet *see* **Ministers**
Charter 88 5
Civil rights *see* **Human rights**
Codification
advantages 158–9
alternative
approaches 156–7
conventions 72, 95
emergence of existing
system 159
fall-back solution 162–4
future prospects 164–7
legislative powers 155–6
limitations on
government 160–1
parliamentary
developments 159–60
rationale 158
reluctance of political
parties 161–2
scope 154–5
Consensus
basis for reform 6–7
encouraging signs 39
Conservative Party
effect on balance of
powers 3
freedom under Thatcher 26
House of Lords reform
current position 71
history and
background 64–5
reaction to Labour
reforms 39–41
refusal to embrace
reform 6
reluctance to embrace
codification 161–2
**Constituency
representation** 46–7

Constitutional Commission
Australian experiences
17–18
codification 161
conventions 105
human rights 135–7
original idea 2
overview 16–17
prerogative powers 80–1
proportional
representation 62
referendums 21–4
role 18–20
status 20–1
Constitutional propriety 7
Conventions
appointment of Prime
Minister 44, 94,
98–100
Australian model 17–20
codification 72, 95,
157, 164
Constitutional
Commission 105
control of elected
dictatorship 5
current status 5
dissolution of
Parliament 98–100
majority government 58
ministerial advice 79–81, 97
overridden by statute 155
Prime Minister's powers 82,
87–91
Scotland 30, 35, 39, 163
Scottish devolved
matters 112
sovereignty 115
subordination of House of
Lords 43
unwritten form 154
Court reform 150–3

Democracy
basis for reform 7
Conservative Party Task
Force 40–1
disadvantages of House of
Lords 68–9

failings of House of
Commons 42–51
new approaches
Members of
Parliament 51–5
reduction of monarchy's
powers
hung Parliaments
99–102
national emergencies
103–4
party leadership 98–9
republicanism v monarchy
case for reform 95–6
compromise
solution 96–7
need for constitutional
umpire 94–5
no automatic rights for
monarchy 93–4
transcendent importance of
constitution 15
**Department for
Constitutional Affairs
(DCA)**
creation 16
disappearance 145–6
enhanced Labour
commitment to
reform 37–8
new role 144–5
replacement of LCD 138
Devolution of power
demands for radical
change 14
demands for reform 5–6
enhanced Labour
commitment 36–9
future of UK 119–23
history of the Union 108–10
influences on New
Labour 29–30
Labour Party promise
8–9, 23
legislative powers 110–15
London 117
ministers 118–19
Northern Ireland 22, 115–16
Scotland 116–17

Elections
  advantages and
      disadvantages of House
      of Lords 67–74
  dissolution of Parliament by
      PM 86–7
  failure to indicate
      proposals 8–9
  proportional
      representation 5
  reduction of monarchy's
      powers
      hung Parliaments
          99–102
      party leadership 98–9
  voting
      disadvantages of House of
          Lords 68–9
      failings of House of
          Commons 42–51
      new approaches to
          MPs 51–5
Elective dictatorship
  no basis for reform 7
  origins and effect 3–5
  restoration of cabinet
      government
      committee system 88–9
      dissolution of
          Parliament 86–7
      economic policy 87–8
      international
          relations 91–2
      patronage 83–4
      public appointments
          84–6

Federalism 121–2

Government
  consultation and
      investigation 9–16
  devolution of power
      118–19
  limitations imposed by
      codification 160–1
  ministers
      role of DCA 138–46
      role of LCD 135–7
  prerogative powers
      effect of Margaret
          Thatcher 3
      meaning and
          importance 77–8

Hereditary peerages
  disadvantages of House of
      Lords 68–70
  reductions in
      imbalance 74–6
House of Commons
  democratic failings 42–51
  new approaches 51–5
  report on prerogative
      powers 79
House of Lords
  advantages and
      disadvantages of
      bicameral system 67–74
  case for new Supreme
      Court 151
  history and
      background 64–7
  inability to challenge
      government 5
  reduction of powers in 1911 1
  reductions in
      imbalance 74–6
Human rights
  advantages and
      disadvantages 124–9
  case for referendums 24
  Conservative Party
      approach 41
  Constitutional
      Commission 135–7
  entrenchment
      arguments 129–35
  incorporation into domestic
      law 26
  Labour Party support 14,
      28, 36
  limited powers 5–6
  ratification by political
      parties 33–4

Institute of Public Policy
  Research 5

Joint Consultative Committee
  creation 37
  House of Lords reform 71–3
  methods of consultation and
      investigation 10–11
  party cooperation 31–5
Judiciary
  appointments 147–8
  case for new Supreme
      Court 150–3

control prerogative
      powers 78–9
  entrenchment of human
      rights 129–35
  inability to challenge
      government 5
  independence 146–7
  independence the basis for
      reform 7
  New Labour approach 149
  responsibility of LCD 139
  role of DCA 144–5
  tenure 148–9

Labour Party
  abandonment of cautious
      approach 27–9
  approach to judiciary 149
  case for new Supreme
      Court 152
  continuing demands for
      reform 6
  enhanced commitment to
      reform 36–9
  House of Lords reform
      current position 71–4
      history and
          background 64–5
  Joint Consultative Cabinet
      Committee 10–11
  Joint Consultative
      Committee with Lib
      Dems 31–5
  major reform programme 2
  outside influences 29–30
  radical change towards
      human rights 127–8
  reluctance to embrace
      codification 161–2
Law Commission 11–12
Legislative powers
  codification 155–6
  entrenchment of human
      rights 129–35
  failure to control prerogative
      powers 77–8
  incorporation of human
      rights 26
  Northern Ireland
      110–11
  overriding conventions 155
  role 11–12
  Scotland 111–13
  Wales 113–15

Liberal Democrats
approach to monarchy 96
continuing demands for
reform 5–6
early voice for change 1
House of Lords reform 71–3
Joint Consultative
Committee with
Labour 10–11, 31–5
Limited powers *see*
**Constitutional
propriety**
London Assembly 117
Lord Chancellor
abolition 16
enhanced Labour commitment
to reform 37
former responsibilities
139–41
replacement by DCA 138

*Meet the Challenge: Make the
Change* 26–8
Members of Parliament
failings of House of
Commons 42–51
proportional representation
alternative methods 55–7
disadvantages 57–9
failings of House of
Commons 45–9
second-ballot system
59–61
recall powers 52–5
selection 51–2
Methods of reform
conclusions 24–5
Constitutional
Commission 16–24
government consultation
and investigation 9–16
Ministers
devolution of power 118–19
effect of Margaret
Thatcher 3
prerogative powers
meaning and
importance 77–82
Prime Minister 81–3
restoration of cabinet
government 83–92
committee system 88–9
dissolution of
Parliament 86–7

economic policy 87–8
international
relations 91–2
patronage 83–4
public appointments 84–6
role of DCA 138–46
role of LCD 135–7
Monarchy
case for reform 95–6
compromise solution 96–7
continuity and transfer of
power 105–7
need for constitutional
umpire 94–5
no automatic rights for
monarchy 93–4
reduction of powers
hung Parliaments 99–102
national
emergencies 103–4
party leadership 98–9

New Labour *see* **Labour Party**
Northern Ireland
consultation and
investigation 11
devolution of power 22,
115–16
future of UK 120
history of the Union 108–10
legislative powers 110–11

Parties *see* **Political parties**
Parliament
dissolution by PM 86–7
House of Commons
democratic failings 42–51
new approaches 51–5
report on prerogative
powers 79
House of Lords
advantages and
disadvantages of
bicameral system 67–74
case for new Supreme
Court 151
history and
background 64–7
inability to challenge
government 5
reduction of powers in
1911 1
reductions in imbalance
hung Parliaments 99–102

report on prerogative
powers 79–80
Political parties
approach to monarchy 96
Conservative Party
effect on balance of
powers 3
freedom under
Thatcher 26
reaction to Labour
reforms 39–41
refusal to embrace
reform 6, 26
election manifestos 8–9
House of Lords reform
current position 71–4
history and
background 64–5
Labour Party
abandonment of cautious
approach 27–9
approach to judiciary 149
case for new Supreme
Court 152
enhanced commitment to
reform 36–9
Joint Consultative
Committee with Lib
Dems 31–5
outside influences
29–30
leadership elections
Liberal Democrats
continuing demands for
reform 5–6
early voice for change 1
Joint Consultative
Committee with
Labour 10–11, 31–5
reluctance to embrace
codification 161–2
response to proportional
representation 59–61
Prerogative powers
Constitutional
Commission 80–1
controls 78–9
effect of Margaret
Thatcher 3
meaning and
importance 77–82
parliamentary reports
79–80
Prime Minister 81–3

Prerogative powers (*cont.*)
  restoration of cabinet
      government
      committee system 88–9
      dissolution of
          Parliament 86–7
      economic policy 87–8
      international
          relations 91–2
      patronage 83–4
      public appointments
          84–6
Prime Minister
  elective dictatorship
      no basis for reform 7
      origins and effect 3–5
  prerogative powers 81–3
  restoration of cabinet
      government
      committee system 88–9
      dissolution of
          Parliament 86–7
      economic policy 87–8
      international
          relations 91–2
      patronage 83–4
      public appointments 84–6
Proportional representation
  alternative methods 55–7
  disadvantages 57–9
  failings of House of
      Commons 45–9
  second-ballot system
      59–61

Referendums
  codification 166
  preparations for reform 2
  role 21–4
Reform
  background to current
      position 1–5
  current obstacles 5–7
  methodology
      conclusions 24–5
      Constitutional
          Commission 16–24
      consultation and
          investigation 9–16
Representative government *see*
  Voting
Republicanism
  case for reform 95–6
  compromise solution 96–7
  need for constitutional
      umpire 94–5
  no automatic rights for
      monarchy 93–4
Rights 129–35
Rule of law
  basis for reform 7
  current status 5
  responsibility of
      Parliament 142–3

Scotland
  devolution of power 116–17
  enhanced Labour
      commitment 36–7

future of UK 120
history of the Union 108–10
influences on New
    Labour 29–30
legislative powers 111–13
Sovereignty
  convention 115
  entrenchment of human
      rights 129–35
  failings of House of
      Commons 42–51
Supreme Court reform 150–3

Taming the Prerogative 90
The Governance of Britain 38,
    77, 122, 165

Voting
  disadvantages of House of
      Lords 68–9
  failings of House of
      Commons 42–51
  new approaches to
      MPs 51–5

Wales
  enhanced Labour
      commitment 36–7
  future of UK 119
  history of the Union
      108–10
  legislative powers 113–15
West Lothian Question 40,
    117, 119, 155